Mission Strategy in the City

Mission Strategy in the City

Cultivation of Inter-ethnic Common Grounds

ENOCH JINSIK KIM

Foreword by Douglas McConnell

PICKWICK *Publications* · Eugene, Oregon

MISSION STRATEGY IN THE CITY
Cultivation of Inter-ethnic Common Grounds

Pickwick Publications
An Imprint of Wipf and Stock Publishers
199 W. 8th Ave., Suite 3
Eugene, OR 97401

www.wipfandstock.com

PAPERBACK ISBN: 978-1-4982-3733-8
HARDCOVER ISBN: 978-1-4982-3735-2
EBOOK ISBN: 978-1-4982-3734-5

Cataloguing-in-Publication data:

Names: Kim, Enoch Jinsik, author | McConnell Douglas, foreword.

Title: Mission strategy in the city : cultivation of inter-ethnic common grounds / Enoch Jinsik Kim ; foreword by Douglas McConnell.

Description: Eugene, OR: Pickwick Publications, 2017 | Includes bibliographical references and indexes.

Identifiers: ISBN 978-1-4982-3733-8 (paperback) | ISBN 978-1-4982-3735-2 (hardcover) | ISBN 978-1-4982-3734-5 (ebook).

Subjects: LCSH: City missions | City churches | Cities and town—Religious aspects—Christianity.

Classification: BV2653 K47 2017 (print) | BV2653 (ebook).

Manufactured in the U.S.A.   OCTOBER 30, 2017

Dedicated to G.M.F. and Frontiers workers,
and especially to my wife, Sarah Hyaeran Ko

Contents

List of Figures

List of Tables

List of Charts

Foreword

THE MISSION OF GOD is approached from many vantage points, not the least of which is the particular context. In the latter half of the twentieth century missiologists woke up to the phenomenon of urbanization. Among the many who alerted us to the challenge of the city in the mission of God was Ray Bakke from Chicago in his book The Urban Christian. Interestingly a sociologist from the University of Chicago, Louis Wirth, provided a similar awakening with his 1938 article on Urbanism as a Way of Life. The thrust of both of these contributions was to examine the impact of the city on the sociocultural experience of city dwellers.

Missiologists were primarily concerned with the anthropological insights prior to the work of the urban mission voices. Philadelphia, Boston, and Los Angeles also became centers for the study of urban mission in both writing and study in the US. The realization of urban mission was concurrently developing in cities like Bangkok, Calcutta, London, Nairobi, Sydney, and Tokyo. By the 1989 Lausanne II Conference in Manila, urban mission was a strong track for both study and strategy.

Like most new areas of study, the earliest proponents were appropriately focused on raising awareness. This varied from the alarming stories of squatters in Kibera, the rag pickers of Smokey Mountain landfill and the high-rise apartment dwellers of Hong Kong. Responses to such extreme conditions equally focused on the variety of churches, notably the megachurches of Seoul, the base ecclesial communities of Sao Paulo, and the parish work in the dumps of Juarez & Cairo.

As the field of urban mission studies expanded, new insights were added to this growing interdisciplinary field. A particularly rich area of study was the emerging field of social networks, focusing on the structure of human relationships in urban centers. A group of younger anthropologists, steeped in the structural functionalism of the early 20th century, found themselves in the growing urban centers of Africa. As the cities grew through urban migration, the tribal loyalties were challenged by the newly formed social networks through the interaction in places of work, residence, or recreation. These insights spread to the UK and other European universities as well as those in the US and beyond.

One of the most relevant fields of study was a new interpretation of Wirth's view of urbanism. Claude Fischer studied a range of locations from a small town in rural California to the center of San Francisco. The theoretical outcome was a new view of urbanism known as the subcultural theory. The relevance of this theory was sourced in the formation and interaction of smaller units of people whose relational choices were instrumental in forming new subcultures. Through the encounter of these groups either positively or negatively, the cultures of the city are further defined.

In this volume, my friend and colleague Dr. Enoch Kim provides a fresh synthesis of the contribution of social anthropology. Drawing from his experience in China, Korea, and the US, Kim explores the implications for mission strategy in the ever-expanding inter-ethnic urban encounters. For missiologists this strategic perspective offers tremendous resources for developing missional responses in the Church and through the networks formed by both proximity and social relationships. Kim provides a series of case studies to context the insights in the complexities of urban life. His command of the literature from the field of urban mission studies is a source of helpful grounding for our understanding.

This book is an important contribution to our missiological reflection as we continue to learn new things about the changing context of our urban world. As Harvie Conn captured in the title of his most critical work, we live with the tension of the "Eternal Word in Changing Worlds." Enoch Kim understands this dilemma with fresh appreciation for the mission of God.

Douglas McConnell
Professor of Leadership and Intercultural Studies
Fuller Seminary

Preface

Your City Is Bigger Than You Think!

I WROTE THIS BOOK for the following purpose: to suggest an appropriate mission strategy by identifying key issues that impact urban ethnicities through an urban socio-anthropological lens.

This book does not cover all aspects of Urbanology, but is about many ethnicities in cities. It helps the readers understand what kind of changes are taking place especially within the ethnic minorities and immigrants in cities, and summarize considerations that must take place in order to communicate the gospel to them.

This book introduces case studies that specifically deal with Chinese ethnic minorities. Yet, the underlying social perspectives are not solely limited to mission strategies reserved for Chinese or Muslim ethnic communities. Rather, this book is intended to provide a sociological understanding of how the modern urban context impacts ethnic groups residing in a diverse cosmopolitan environment. For those who need resources related to Chinese Muslims, I encourage them to use the references introduced in this book. Likewise, case studies are presented to support the theoretical position for a new effective mission strategy to ethnic minorities in an urban context.

This book is based on my sixteen years living in China with my family, conducting missionary work in urban areas. My ministry was mostly focused on evangelistic outreach to ethnic minorities who assimilated to unfamiliar urban contexts. I interacted with enclaves of ethnic minorities who had newly arrived to the city after migrating from rural areas. My experiences not only focused my attention to China, but also made me aware of the rapidly changing demographics of cities around the world, as increasingly diverse groups of people live in urban areas.

Over the years, I have grown very interested in the evangelization of urban ethnic minorities. At the early stage of my ministry in China, most literatures and introductions explained why it would be difficult for ethnic minorities to interact with mainstream society because of their historical and cultural conflicts. Those literatures also introduced some degree of cultural assimilation (within some range of government policy). Based on resources I gathered through the early stages of my mission work in China, there is evidence for both of these positions.

However, I was able to observe many different results in the modern city context that diverge from previous assumptions regarding conflict and assimilation. Interestingly enough, I have found that similar phenomena occur within Korean-American communities in Los Angeles. This community also has experienced on-going issues regarding conflict and assimilation, but at the same time, is constantly evolving and developing its own unique ethnic identity within the larger mainstream context. From these observations, I have come to realize that urban ethnicities and immigrants in many cities share similar social issues and resolutions in this respect.

Through my observations of ethnic minorities navigating conflict and assimilation, I have realized the urgent need for new mission strategies to effectively engage these urban ethnicities. An effective strategy is needed because mission outreach will certainly be greatly affected by the relationship and understanding between ethnicities.

Urban mission related literatures that I studied previously have not been fulfilling these needs. Many of them did not go beyond basic challenges—the biblical view towards urban mission or the urgency of ministry—to the need of the city. There were not too many books that dealt with questions such as, what is the state of the ethnicities within cities, what changes are they experiencing, why do they think and act in such way, or why do they have such human networks?

Meanwhile, when I studied for my PhD at Fuller Theological Seminary, I had opportunities to develop ideas for this issue with Dr. Viggo Søgaard who is an expert in media communication and mission strategy, Dr. Timothy Kiho Park, who is an expert in the Asian church, and Dr. Dudley J. Woodberry, who is an expert in Islamic studies and Muslim evangelism. Not only these, I had a chance to do research on Chinese Muslim's social changes and their network with Dr. Douglas McConnell, a professor in Urban Anthropology. The insight from Dr. McConnell and subcultural theory that I learned from him provided me a crucial lens for reading the city and its people. Through those experiences, I slowly began to see why

God was bringing ethnicities into cities. I was able to find the providence of God that connects ethnicities, which have been isolated for thousands of years, with various social networks and outside information in order to reveal the message of salvation through them.

God creates the environments in the city that enables many ethnicities to naturally encounter various information, raise children, and create new value systems. As the return of the Lord draws near, God desires the recipients and speakers of the Gospel to have more effective communication.

City makes numerous ethnicities that have been isolated and had no relationship with one another develop common ground with each other, connect, and then rely on each other more than ever. Now, the ethnicities exchange mutual support and feel the necessity of coexistence, though still uneasy. This book is written under the understanding of such phenomenon, and attempts to apply the conceptualized missional meaning and opportunities it brings into mission fields, which is the city.

Admittedly, a city has many negative aspects like secularism and ethnic conflicts. Nevertheless, the fact that city offers positive features that can contribute to effective evangelism and to urban ethnic groups can provide a place to construct a highway for the gospel to reach many ethnicities. By considering characteristics of evangelism, the gospel can spread because of human relationships. On the positive side, this means cities can bring people to escape ethnic isolation, if bridges of social interactions are built to connect networks of many kinds of people. Additionally, cities can provide opportunities to increase interaction through multiple points of contact between ethnic groups. Such networks will result in connecting ethnic groups that have received the gospel and groups that have not yet done so.

Considering that a primary characteristic of both the gospel and evangelism is being relational, cities could be filled with many opportunities to overcome obstacles of bias and mistrust against ethnic counterparts inherent in majority sentiments counterparts. Likewise, ethnic minority groups can strengthen their own ethnic identity while interacting with other ethnicities.

The author will highlight three main points: 1) Ethnic urban dwellers evolve into many more diverse ways than commonly thought; 2) Ethnic groups are actively choosing the future of their community types; 3) Modern cities create many new communication channels inter-ethnically, and also across intra-social strata within ethnicities. This is what often facilitates change. In short, this trio of social phenomena will raise the need to rethink modern urban mission strategy.

Acknowledgments

I PRAISE THE GOD who not only loves the city and its citizens, but who also awaits for them to return to Him. I thank the Son who introduced the incarnational model to the city, and I also praise the Spirit who continues to lead the city's missionaries and churches. I lift up my praises and gratitude to the Holy trinity who faithfully loved and persevered in me, a sinner but redeemed, since the beginning of writing this book to its publication.

I thank Dr. Scott Sunquist, my supervisor and dean of School of Intercultural Studies at Fuller Theological Seminary, for helping me thrive in my early scholar days. When this manuscript lost its track and wasted time he inspired me to write effectively without having academic compromise.

I express my gratitude to Dr. Sherwood G. Lingenfelter. He reviewed parts of this manuscript and gave insights as an anthropologist and an experienced writer. Dr. Bryant L. Myers has also reviewed part of this book and gave valuable comments and critiques as an expert in globalization. Dr. Evelyn A. Reisacher, as a faithful peer, reviewed the whole manuscript and shared her opinion, which breathed this book to maintain an academic standard. Dr. Judith M. Tiersma Watson also reviewed the whole manuscript, and her opinion and encouragement as an expert in the city became a wonderful soil of reshaping the chapters. The reason this book is able to sustain an academic standard was due to the experience, wisdom, generosity of these valuable peers.

In addition, I thank Fuller Theological Seminary's provost, Dr. Douglas McConnel. He was the scholar who let me have the first step into the world of inter-ethnic dynamics of the city, which introduced me to several sociologists, such as John Gulick, Philip Q. Yang, Edwin Eames, Claude S. Fischer, William G. Flanagan, and Mark Gottdiener.

ACKNOWLEDGMENTS

The publication of this book would not have been possible without the contributions of my beloved leaders of the Chinese churches. I thank Li Yuese, Li Paul, and the leaders of *Xinwangai* and Galilee Mission.

I also would like to thank my Muslim friend Ma, who introduced his family to me and currently lives as a mutton skewer seller, Li, a taxi driver and also my badminton peer, and Li's relatives. I thank Ms. Ma, a Muslim lady, who helped my family to associate with her parents who live over twenty hours away from Beijing. I would also like to mention that this book was only possible through the stories of Mr. Dong, and a Uyghur man, Mr. Hu and his wife, who are now families in the Lord, and many Muslim ladies including Mrs. Ma.

I express my gratitude towards Rev. Joseph Min, Rev. Kim Taejung, Ju Youngchan, and staffs in HOPE Missions who served me while I was serving and researching in China. Furthermore, I will not forget the grace of Dr. David Tae Woong Lee in GMF who constantly mentored and trained me, and also Professors Felipe Jin Suck Byun, Sung Geol Chun, and Andrew Ju Yun Eum.

I will not be able to forget the grace of the Frontiers leaders, Greg Livingstone, Patrick Lai, Rick Love, Tim Lewis, missionary Hyun Soo Lee, and especially my former team leader, J and Iv couple[1], for helping me perceive the Chinese Muslims with respect, and as creations of God.

I thank Roger Greenway, Viv Gregg, Harvie M. Conn, and Ray Bakke for helping me view the city through the eyes of God. Also, I must mention that this book includes the contributions from the city researchers of China: Lu Xue Yi of the Chinese Academy of Social Sciences, and Sociology professor Fei Xiao Tong from Peking University Professor of Sociology.

As mentors and academic committee members, Fuller Theological Seminary's Viggo B. Søgaard, Timothy Kiho Park, and Dudley J. Woodberry have helped establish my academic basis.

I thank Professors Timothy Par, Kwangkil Lee, and Keonsang An for encouraging and advising me throughout my writing. And I also thank my coworkers in the office, Helen Lim, David Kwon, Sang Hoon Lee, David Kong, and Jung Woo Lee for their unending cooperation and encouragement. I thank Fran Gilmore and my beloved brother in Christ, Paul Kwon for editing the manuscript despite my imperfect English, and I also sincerely thank my children, Joy Kim, Timothy Kim, and Josephine Kim. I

---

1. These are not their real name to protect their privacy.

especially would like to thank my son, Timothy Heeseung Kim, for being my personal editor who proofread this entire book for me.

I thank Pickwick's staff, especially Matthew Wimer, Jim Tedrick, Brian Palmer, and Laura Poncy for permitting the publication of this book. Thank you to my parents, Won Seop Kim and Hae Nyuh Shim, for bearing me and raising me. And finally, I express my thanks and love to my wife and companion, Hyaeran Ko, for making my life meaningful through her hope and support.

2017 Pasadena, California

Introduction

THIS BOOK IS DIVIDED into two parts. Part I provides a sociological lens to understand urbanites in the modern city and the social experiences of ethnic groups migrating there. Part II uses more of an interdisciplinary approach for conceptualizing urban mission strategy. Because Part I deals with many theories, do not skip this part if you are a student or a scholar who needs to build foundation for theories. On the other hand, focus on Part II, which focuses on practical strategy development, if you are mission organization leaders or field ministers.

Each chapter is composed of three parts; field case study, theory, and missiological reflection. Actual case part will be introduced at the beginning of each chapter to preview topics discussed therein. To close each chapter, a scenario that introduces missiological implications is given in order to demonstrate practical application in the ministry field. Overall, the body of each chapter, which introduces sociological theories, will contain mostly academic-level content. The Readers will gain an awareness of how missional opportunities can be prompted through inter-ethnic interactions conducive to city environments, and will also suggest strategies to encourage such social engagement.

Overall, Part I converges on the argument that claims the subcultural theory as an effective theory that can understand and interpret the change of an urban ethnicity. Through the five chapters, Part I will introduce five different faces of a city to the reader through a sociological lens in order to define missiological implications. The chapters will not only explain what a city is, but likewise explore the social dynamics that are present just below the surface.

A micro-level approach more so than a macro-level approach is explored, because it is a theoretical book summarizing a perspective and strategy needed for effective urban mission and urban ministry. To complement the theoretical approach, urban anthropology is used as a tool in this study as well. The detailed contents of each chapter of Part I are as follows.

Chapter one introduces what I refer to as the first face of the city. Of course, the purpose of mission is to change people, rather than a location. Therefore, the concept of an urban mission has to be approached with an understanding of urbanites and urban society. It is an exploration of society residing within the boundaries of a city. Specifically, the first face of a city is its identity as a residence of a group of people. Within that group are human experiences and personal stories residing within a locale governed by administrative districts. It means that the city is consisted with urbanite's social networks. As such, in order to understand the life of an urbanite, we will take a look at the city as a microcosm—on a micro-level rather than a macro-level.

Chapter two will introduce the third face of cities as that provides a new cultural homeland for immigrant ethnicities. The migrant experience of new urban residents will be introduced in six steps beginning with their arrival to a new land, in this case, the city, all the way to new experiences in mainstream society. Sociological understandings of early adapters who form urban ethnic enclaves and their important role in mission are also explored.

Chapter three introduces the second face of a city as the locale for ethnic conflicts and competition. This chapter will examine concepts related to ethnicity from related academic principles, to help readers realize that cities are similar to mosaics, in that their composition is eclectic and diverse. Unfortunately, a city's social mosaic can also be a source of ethnic conflict and competition when diverse groups find themselves competing for limited resources.

Chapter four introduces the fourth face of cities as places where ethnicities assimilate. Many urban ethnicities are pressured to abandon their original culture and follow common code and standard systems specific to each city of residence. This chapter will discuss the issue of how and why ethnic groups migrating to cities most often determine to evolve or to rigidly adhere to cultural traditions. Through contrasting theories of determinism and compositionalism, the argument of assimilation across urban ethnicities versus the argument of cultural continuation is compared sociologically. Within this focus, the chapter will explore how the direction of mission strategy can be influenced by the predominance of either result—assimilation or continuation.

Chapter five introduces the fifth face of cities as places where ethnicities actively choose their identity. In contrast to existing assimilation theories that say ethnic minorities will melt into a single culture unconditionally, urban enclaves of various ethnicities will take the lead in choosing their own cultural identities. In so doing, smaller subgroups among them will make many different choices rather than evolving homogeneously. Through the subcultural theory, changes among urban ethnicities will be understood as changes initiated within each subgroup. Through this, the chapter shows the importance of mission strategy, which focuses on the ethnicity unit while recognizing the diversity within those ethnicities.

Part II is about strategy composed in three chapters. Part II will pay attention to the social network of urbanites. In short, the main point is that urban ethnicity will end up with various network from the inside within the ethnicity and also from the outside, not constrained by the traditional network structure formed within the ethnicity. The meaning and opportunities of mission strategy provided by the new urban neighbors, urban friends, and changing individuals' group and network will be introduced with various charts.

Chapter six pays attention to the missional value of new neighbors that city creates for cross-ethnic missions. Especially when urbanites work together with other ethnicities in the workplace, the resulting communication is a natural interaction with the world outside of their ethnicity. This chapter observes and compares the concept of new neighbors in a changing city with the concept of traditional neighbors. The social network theory is used to explore the possibilities for divine mission through change.

Chapter seven focuses on the missional value of new friends that city creates to the urbanites in the course of cross-ethnic mission. Readers will see why friendships across familiar ethnic boundaries can create many opportunities for interactions with outsiders. The fact that friends in cities can become the bridge that crosses over ethnic boundaries traditionally blocked by outsiders is explained from a sociological perspective. Through this, mission strategy among unreached people groups and ethnic minorities in cities will be studied.

Chapter eight examines the missional values that city newly creates through transforming the groups across various ethnicities. While many groups venture into a lead role to plan the course of their own future, they have exchanges with other ethnicities. By examining social characteristics that lead some to search for autonomy and self-sufficiency while others seemingly assimilate, the chapter will explore these distinct characteristics within the same ethnic groups to determine with whom to most effectively initiate evangelistic outreach first.

PART I

Five Kinds of City Faces
toward Urban Ethnicities

1

City, Not as Just Place,
But as People and Society

IN THIS CHAPTER, WE will find many limitations of the approach to the city that solely depends on what we see from buildings and the exterior. In order to better understand the city missiologically and directly, this chapter suggests that it is important to first understand the people and society within the city. Two main areas that this chapter deals with are:

- The comparison of the two perspectives to city urbanization and urbanism; and

- Understanding the urban society through the lens of social networks

Through this chapter, readers will be more aware that the first step of urban mission strategy is to understand the people and society of the city.

A CASE:
CITY WAS MORE COMPLICATED THAN WHAT I IMAGINED

I lived in Xian, a large city in China. I had a Muslim friend named Mr. Liu, who was a taxi driver. We often played badminton together, along with his other Muslim friends. It turned out that they were also taxi drivers.

Mr. Liu was extremely interested in training messenger pigeons; he even thought of entering national competitions. On the other hand, a different taxi driver, Mr. Li, makes his living by driving taxi and doing interior design. Whenever a relative opens a new business, they donate personal funds to help facilitate their relative's new business. They live in an all-Muslim town with their wives running small shops on the streets. One of the women, the wife of Mr. Ma, was deeply in love with Korean TV dramas. Whenever she gets along with my wife, she would talk about recent shows she has watched. All three men, Mr. Ma, Liu, and Li constantly told me, "Although I live arduously without education, I must send my son to college."

As I personally engage with more people, my view of the Chinese city began to change. Prior to the change, I perceived the Chinese city as just complex streets and concrete buildings. Moreover, the image of people in the city I had was poor marketers outside of train stations. I assumed they were extreme religious conservatives who isolate themselves from the outside world. I believed that they were very different from me. Actually, these assumptions were not from personal experiences; such descriptions were products of TV or photos from mission journals I saw prior to my arrival in China.

However, as I got to know more people, I witnessed many unexpected commonalities as mine. Within the city, there lies a diverse and complex system of human relationships and groups that outsiders do not know. These features are organically connected to the enrichment and development of the individual life. There exists a hidden source of warmth, beauty, love, pride, and stories in the city.

The city was much more complicated than I thought. When we look closer into the buildings and streets of the city, we can observe numerous groups and individuals who live and dream for their own future and life. According to their needs, the dwellers help, compete, and strike deals in this complex network because people and society form a city.

VIEWS TO THE CITY

People have lived in cities since the beginning of the biblical times. Genesis shows that people built cities not long after they were created. Similarly, after the killing of his brother, Abel, Cain builds a city and names it after his son, Enoch. These two accounts can be seen as humanity's very first castle towns in the Bible.[1]

On the other hand, according to archaeologists' research, the first ancient cities are estimated to have been constructed about 5,000 years ago.

1. Gen 4:17.

These ancient cities were usually built around rivers, which raised civilizations very uniquely according to each of its locations. Some civilizations that developed from this kind of background include the Mesopotamian civilization located on the Tigris and Euphrates Rivers, the Indian civilization on the Indus River Valley, and the Chinese civilization on the Huang-He basin.[2] According to Truman A. Hartshorn, the civilization deemed the oldest, dated about 3,000–4,000 BC, is the *Eridu* civilization, created from the Tigris and Euphrates River basin. *Eridu* once was the center for religion, and also housed the infrastructure and technologies that became the economic foundation, such as creating tools and handicrafts like basket weaving. However, ancient cities like *Eridu* had disappeared as time went on, and Damascus currently holds the title of the longest maintained ancient city.[3]

Cities have developed consistently and have recently gained rapid speed; in 2008, over 50 percent of the world's population lived in cities. As cities become more embedded in our lives, more people have started questioning, "What is a city?" "What do cities mean to me?" and "Are cities good or bad?"

As part of an attempt to answer these questions, urbanologists have defined city in many ways. No-Choonhee and Kim-Iltae define city as the following:

> [A city is] where various people gather in a limited space and live under an elaborately organized social system. It is a man-made multifunctional mega complex, which is the coexistence of residence, recreation, economic activity, and various arts, also dominated by the industrial society and institutions that produce, distribute, and consume those products from the industrial society. It is also home where dynamic creation happens from art and culture.[4]

Fisher also conceptualizes the city with having four broad types of definitions: appropriate demography that maintains an appropriate size and density of the population, institutions that govern and administer the people, a center of culture that produces urban worldviews and value system, and a place for urbanites to exude their peculiar urban behaviors.[5]

2. Gottdiener and Hutchison, *The New Urban Sociology*, 21–25.
3. Hartshorn, *Interpreting the City*, 15–17.
4. Nou and Kim, *Dosihak Gaeron*, 12.
5. Fischer, *The Urban Experience*, 24–25.

City can be defined by function as well: being the center of economic activity, politics and administration, culture creation, and social communities.[6]

First, city is the center of economic activity. People migrate to cities seeking better occupations and better economic opportunities because unlike rural farming villages, cities are developed as the industrial and commercial centers that produce economic resources.

The second function of a city is to be the center of politics and administration. Weber, for example, uses Asian cities as an example to describe this characteristic of the city.[7] Western cities have centered in economic activities, whereas Asian cities had formed in a place where government offices can easily gather and administer citizens. These administrative institutions make cities the center of politics and administration, government and politically leading citizens. Cities also hold the command center in order to effectively communicate, protect, and defend the people from enemies.

The third function of a city is being the center for creating and developing culture. Cities can be the birthplace of arts, literature, and science that create the power of freedom and liberty. It is in the city where the humanism spirit and democratic spirit can prosper, where humans develop their love of exploring knowledge and justice, and where one thought meets another to create a new thought.[8]

Lastly, a city is a social community.[9] A city includes social units that have rules and personality. These social units act as catalysts with each other to create public goods and build communities that create emotions such as joy, anger, sorrow, and pleasure.

As such, there are various perspectives of seeing cities; each perspective helps acknowledge and embody different and unique colors of the city that others cannot describe. It is important that we utilize these different approaches to have a balanced perspective on the city.

---

6. Four perspectives and reference introduced here are summarized by ChoonHee Noh and Kim, *Dosihak Gaeron* 12–15.

7. Weber, *The City*; Park, "The City."

8. Robson, *Great Cities of the World*; Wagner, *The Human Use of the Earth*; Mumford, *The City in History*.

9. Banovetz, *Managing the Modern City*.

TWO KINDS OF LENSES FOR INTERPRETING THE CITY: URBANIZATION AND URBANISM

There have been many researches done by urban sociologists in America and Europe for a long time before the concept of city as a society formed by people and relationship has developed. In the early stage of urban research in America, they have developed two different approaches—Urbanization Theory research and Urbanism research—in understanding city. In this section, we will study two types of academic lens for understanding city and examine the historical background of their development. At the end, we will examine the relationship between these two lenses and how we should prioritize them for mission strategy.

Our main concern in understanding the city is sharing the Gospel. For this, we need to understand the people's lifestyles and behaviors of the city. Urban Sociology can help us understand this. Urban Sociology is literally the study of urban societies, or sociology in relation to cities. Urban Sociology explores phenomena in cities, focusing on the social aspects, through sociological knowledge and methods.

The Beginning of Urban Sociology

Urban sociology originates from Europe in the late 19th century. Several foundational scholars in European sociology and urbanology are Ferdinand Tönnies,[10] Max Weber, Emile Durkheim,[11] and Friedrich Engels.

In the 20th century, sociology developed and emerged in the United States as well. The scholars known as the Chicago School were the initial ones to acknowledge European urban sociology studies and started improving on it themselves. They were known as the Chicago school because most of them were from the Department of Sociology in University of Chicago. Some of the leading scholars from United States are George

---

10. Tèonnies and Loomis, *Community & Society (Gemeinschaft und Gesellschaft)*.
11. Durkheim, *The Division of Labor in Society*.

Simmel,[12] Robert Ezra Park, Lewis Wirth,[13] Ernest W. Burgess,[14] Roderick McKenzie,[15] William Isaac Thomas,[16] E. C. Hughes,[17] and Charles Horton Cooley.[18]

A major addition to the birth of the Chicago School was Robert Ezra Park. Park studied under Georg Simmel, who was a European sociologist and the most responsible writer in urban life.[19] Park went beyond what Weber's study of the comparison of the city's history and behaviors, and further left many achievements in research in peoples' lives and behavior in the urban setting and interaction patterns. This Chicago School's research on an urbanite's life views cities as human and societies, as opposed to just buildings and institutions, which has immensely contributed discretion in finding today's urban missions and mission strategies.

Understanding Urbanization and Urbanism

The Chicago School divided urban sociology into the city's external and internal research, which later developed into urbanization study that explores the city's function and structure from the external viewpoint, and urbanism study that studies the urbanite's life and society.[20]

Research in urbanization is the study of the externalities of a city, meaning the city's origin, history, rise and fall, characteristics based on the culture and nation, and structure and function. In order to best represent this, as it is exampled in Chart 1–1, urbanization studies frequently use graphs and charts with numbers to represent the trends in world cities.

---

12. Simmel, "The Metropolis and Mental Life."

13. Selective bibliographies of these scholars are as follows. Park and Burgess, *Introduction to the Science of Sociology, Including the Original Index to Basic Sociological Concepts*; Wirth, "Urbanism as a Way of Life"; Park et al., eds., *The City*.

14. Burgess, "The Growth of the City."

15. McKenzie, *The Metropolitan Community*.

16. Thomas and Janowitz, *On Social Organization and Social Personality: Selected Papers*.

17. Floro, Review of The Sociological Eye, by E. C. Hughes.

18. Cooley, *Human Nature and the Social Order*.

19. Simmel has taken another step from the traditional urban study, which more emphasizes on phenomenological approach rather concentrate on the cultural elements and the life of urbanites in cities.

20. Gottdiener and Hutchison, *The New Urban Sociology*, 45–46.

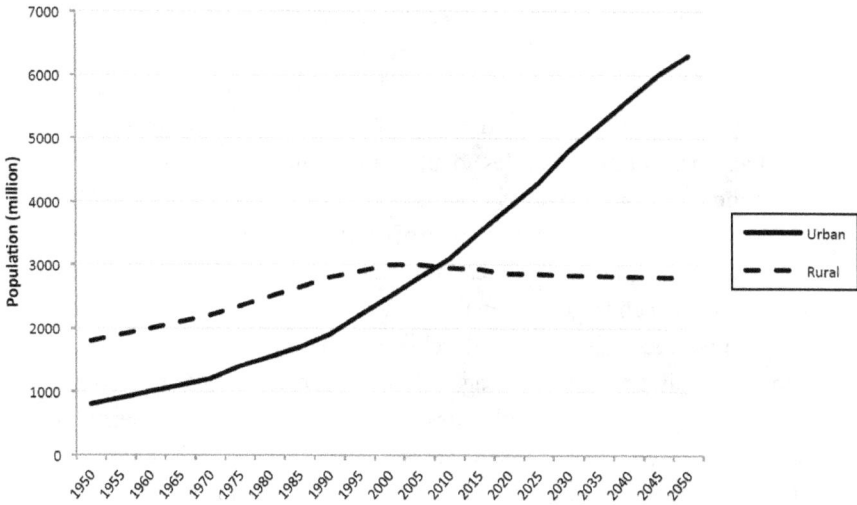

Chart 1–1: A Graph Example of Urbanization Study[21]

In simple terms, urbanization refers to the change from non-urban or rural districts into urban cities. Urbanization can refer to how a physical space changes into a city, but also refers to the social and economic changes that take place in becoming a city.[22]

Urbanization, a kind of Macro approach to the city, often highlights the external appearance and structures in growth and reduction, structure, and efficiency in its research. The research results from this can be useful in many ways: planning national policies and city plans, predicting a city's current state and its effects on the society and economy as well as predicting its future, predicting the effects of a city's facilities, culture, standards, and size on an individual's life, and studying how other cities affect peoples' lives. Because of this, physical evidence, quantifiable and numerical data, is often seen in urbanization studies. Therefore, to understand how the city environment affects the life of urbanities, studying urbanization is crucial.

The other part from the urbanization study is urbanism research. Urbanism studies the interior aspect of the city, meaning the people and society. Urbanism is considered a micro approach that studies deeper in detail. Urbanism focuses on the urbanites and their social groups: their dynamics,

21. United Nations Department of Economic and Social Affairs, "World Urbanization Perspects: The 2014 Revision, Highlights (St/Esa/Ser.A/352)," (United Nations Department of Economic and Social Affairs, Pupulation Division, 2014), 7.

22. Banovetz, *Managing the Modern City*; Palen, *The Urban World*.

emotional changes, and lifestyles. It explores the urbanite at the micro level: the city's culture, urbanites' life patterns, meanings and symbols in their thoughts, daily habits and social networks of family, friends, coworkers, and neighbors. It also studies the relationship between the urbanite and the urban setting: how urbanites adapt to and utilize the urban setting, and receive the effects and changes resulting from the urban transition. It also studies the conflicts in the city: change of dynamics and emotions, relationship between people and political and social organizations, and lifestyle differences between large and small cities.

Such research is possible by developing urban sociology and urban anthropology mainly from the Chicago School. Urban anthropology is a branch of anthropology that studies urbanites in their living, thought patterns, and relationships.[23] Ideal research subjects would include the city's uniqueness, institutions, and groups in their dynamics amongst urbanites. Some leading scholars in urban anthropology include Louis Wirth,[24] Oscar Lewis,[25] Michael Young and Peter Willmott,[26] Abner Cohen[27], and Herbert Gans.[28, 29]

Later, urban sociologists have continued to develop the research. Traditional urbanologists mentioned earlier mainly have researched on developed countries, but these recent generation scholars studied the city through the lens of globalization and localization.[30]

23. Urban anthropology is important in exceeding the limitation of seeing city as a whole in the early urban ecology.

24. Wirth "Urbanism as a Way of Life," 1, described the life of urbanites through phenomenal, relational, and psychological understandings.

25. Lewis who has researched Mexican immigrants in cities claimed that small groups in cities are able to maintain their identity.

26. Young and Willmott, *Family and Kinship in East London*.

27. Cohen, *Two-Dimensional Man*.

28. Gans, "Urbanism and Suburbanism as Ways of Life"; Gans, *The Urban Villagers*.

29. Sjoberg, *The Preindustrial City, Past and Present*; Gutkind, *Urban Anthropology*; Uzzell and Provencher, *Urban Anthropology*; Eames and Goode, *Anthropology of the City*; Basham, *Urban Anthropology*; Hannerz, *Exploring the City*; Foster and Kemper, *Anthropologists in Cities*; Aschenbrenner, *The Processes of Urbanism*; Du Toit and Safa, *Migration and Urbanization*.

30. The following sociologists have distinguished themselves in this area. Beauregard, "City of Superlatives"; Brenner, "Stereotypes, Archetypes, and Prototypes"; Davis, *Planet of Slums*; Myers, African Cities; Roy and Ong, *Worlding Cities: Asian Experiments and the Art of Being Global*; Edensor and Jayne, *Urban Theory beyond the West*; Huyssen, *Other Cities, Other Worlds*; McCann and Ward, "Relationality/Territoriality"; Peck, Theodore, and Brenner, "Neoliberal Urbanism."

Roles and Priorities of the Mission Strategy

How, then can we best understand the relationship of urbanization and urbanism studies? The urbanization theory cannot be overlooked because it is an undisputable fact that the external city environment influences greatly on the urbanite's life. In spite of this importance, Christian workers in the city often do not recognize how greatly the city's external image, buildings, administrative agencies, and traffic systems influence their ministry. They would rather highlight and put more emphasis on the urbanites' daily lives such as commuting to work and raising their children.

Urbanization and urbanism studies have a mutual interrelationship rather than opposing fields in urban sociology. It is like the relationship between a software (urbanism studies) and hardware (urbanization studies) in the same computer. In reality, people living in a city influence the external shape of the city. For example, a neighborhood where there is an ethnic middle school is located is preferred by the ethnic group, making them become long-term residents, thus maintain higher rent cost and price is maintained. Moreover, urban slum created by chain migration may cause the city to extend bus routes in the neighborhood to meet the needs of the low-cost labor population. As such, external shape of a city is affected by the life and the spread of population.

Contrastingly, the urban environment also affects the urbanite's life. For example, metropolises have easy access to a variety of restaurants, opportunities and people, because of more abundant resources available. In other words, big cities have more resources and they affect the lives and behaviors of individuals differently than small cities.

Then, which of the two, Urbanism and Urbanization, has more influence on the establishment of mission strategy? Both of them influence mission strategy because urbanites and urban environment influence each other. Not only that, depending on how we see mission strategy, we can have many different answers. However, it is still realistic to think that urbanism study has primary and direct influence on mission strategy than does urbanization study. This is because urbanite's life, values, human relationships, and research of the urban groups provide more direct resources to mission strategy. By the author's subjective examination, many missionaries until now, especially the missionaries in the third world countries, directly consider the elements from the relationships based on neighbors and individuals rather than the elements of the nation or the city as a whole. Such phenomenon requires the missionaries to study urbanism first.

Another reason to study urbanism just as it was emphasized previously, city is a society made up of people. In other words, urbanism study that deals directly with human relationship can first bring the theoretic development for the mission strategy establishment.

For this reason, this book, which deals with mission strategy, will highlight more on the urbanism study. There are many non-Biblical views and elements in urban anthropology and sociology. Therefore, it is necessary for missiologist to use both Biblical lens and secular studies selectively to screen them.[31]

A CITY IS MADE BY SOCIAL NETWORKS

Previously, we have examined that there is a perspective among the sociological approach of viewing cities as community. We have also examined the study of urbanism that understanding the city as people and society may be effective in missional approach. Let us now study how the urbanites and society are composed and how having social network theory can provide an effective tool in understanding such an urban society.

Society is a structured collection of relationships and relationships collectively form social networks. Most often, society categorizes its core relationships in the following manner: the (extended) family unit, friends, social groups, associations, and the seat of government. As we experience globalization, some individual social networks but not all, will extend even beyond national boundaries.

In the 1929 published collection, A Volume of Short Stories, Everything is Different, Frigyes Karinthy observed, "Everyone is on average approximately six steps away, by way of introduction, from any other person on Earth."[32] He believed that the modern world was figuratively shrinking due to an ever-increasing array of social networks globally. That there are six degrees of separation between us is the notion that all people are connected by social links. The growing density of these networks can make actual social distances between us smaller. The social network theory studies the dynamics and nature of this very idea.

In referring to smartphones and similar technology, the term social networks often arise. Ironically, in some cases, the term social networks are even misunderstood to refer to the technology. Actually, scholars in

31. Sunquist, *Understanding Christian Mission*, 2–3.
32. Karinthy, *Minden Másképpen Van (Ötvenkét Vasárnap)*; "Chain-Links."

sociology and anthropology have used the term for quite some time—way before technological advancements introduced the smartphone.[33] It is true that as information technology develops, such devices expand accessibility to social networks with great speed, regardless of distance. However, it is not the machine that created social networks. Rather, technology is merely enhancing what humanity had already developed socially.

Over the decades, scholars have clarified the characteristics of a social network by simply better describing and defining the concept itself. For example, J. Clyde Mitchell (University of Zambia) defines social network as "a specific set of linkages among a defined set of persons, with the additional property that the characteristics of these linkages as a whole may be used to interpret the social behavior of the persons involved.[34] Sociologists, Whitten and Wolfe define a social network as "a relevant series of linkages existing between individuals, which may form a basis for the mobilization of people for specific purposes under specific conditions."[35] Boissevain defined as "the chains of persons with whom a given person is in actual contact and their interconnections."[36] In summary, a social network is a unit defined by at least one relationship that interchanges information and emotion.[37] By the support of scholarship and commercial needs, there is seemingly a lot of theoretical research regarding social network today and this area of discipline will continue to expand.

Social Network Theory that Emerged

Like the social network guided, human society is formed around various human relationships, like family, and so on. However, this concept of society as an integrated collection of human social networks, is a familiar natural definition today, but not in the early days of research. Through many sociological research generations, the consensus was found that our society is not just made up of various groups of people, but that within

33. In sociology, this social network study has begun by John A. Barns and Elizabeth Bott. Barnes, "Class and Committees in a Norwegian Island Parish"; Spillius, *Family and Social Network.*

34. Mitchell, Institute for Social Research, *Social Networks in Urban Situations,* 2.

35. Whitten and Wolfe, "Network."

36. Boissevain, *Friends of Friends,* 24.

37. Katherine Giuffre summarized many social network scholars concepts. Giuffre, *Communities and Networks,* 7–8.

these groups people have formed various social networks across every culture and sociopolitical group.[38]

The sociological analysis of the structure and function of community began about 140 years ago and continued through with following at least three conceptual scholarships, according to Suh.[39] That notion of community now provides a basic understanding of how social networks operate.

A scholarship to this community research began in 1871 with a German sociologist and philosopher Ferdinand Tönnies.[40] He initially conceptualized the idea of a modern community. Through field studies, Tönnies arrived at a definition of community (or Gemeinschaft) as a loving organism sharing a common good, common interests, and common purposes as contrasted with society (or Gesellschaft), which he defined as a mechanical aggregate and artifact.

Robert MacIver who was a leading scholar of his generation and had similar thought, published a study on the "nature and fundamental laws" of community in 1917.[41] To MacIver, community referred to people living together in a limited territory. He categorized territories along a range of sizes, beginning with those the size of a small town or regional community all the way up to territories as big as a country.[42] MacIver further distinguished a community from the idea of an association, by saying that the latter is only a tentative, partial, and goal-oriented group (Suh, 2002). Unlike community, an association refers to a social organization that temporarily exists for the main purpose of profitably achieving members' goals. MacIver did suggest that despite these different characteristics, associations could coexist with community.

The second view of understanding community was developed with a socio-geographical view. This concept sees community as a geographical neighborhood and developed urban anthropology. This view was suggested by the Chicago school.[43] These scholars derived their theories from comparative research of urban and rural communities. In particular, research-

38. Ibid., 19–26.

39. Three concepts of community that are described here are taken from the book written by Suh. Suh, *Internet Community Wa Hangook Sahue (Internet Community and Korean Society)*, 18–21.

40. Tönnies, *Community & Society*, 7–12.

41. MacIver and Bramson, *Robert M. Maciver on Community, Society and Power*, 30–31.

42. MacIver and Page, *Society*.

43. Chicago school's Robert Ezra Park, Ernest W. Burgess, Roderick McKenzie, and Louis Wirth were major scholars for this area.

ers analyzed how traditional community elements among groups migrate from the countryside where they are either maintained or dismissed in the midst of city life. In short, scholars defined community as a geographical neighborhood. Notably, such view emerged from this period of scholarship in social networking research.[44]

Recently, there are some scholars who see community as a society that consists of social networks. They see that community is spatial and functional. They noted that all communities and associations are formed intentionally and for a purpose, through dispersion and a concentration of relationships. Therefore, community can be defined by analyzing human networks.

In particular, Canadian-American sociologist Barry Wellman's focus on networked individuals emphasized a cultural shift from group-centered networks. His analysis of networked relationships contributed to an understanding of the role of egocentrism or personal networks as a frequent structure of social networks.

Wellman's concept of social networks eventually influenced a new era of technologically advanced business applications based on his principle analysis of social networks.[45] Interestingly, the digital mobile device industry successfully applied Wellman's egocentric network concept to the structure of mobile phone user networks.

44. Giuffre, *Communities and Networks*, 27–29.
45. Wellman, *Networks in the Global Village*.

Figure 1–1: Society Is a Gathering of Relationships. Muslim Men with Friends In Xi'an City, China. (April 2010) Photo © Enoch Kim

In this perspective, it is reasonable to view city as a gathering of people, and further, it consists of social networks. This perspective allows the urban ministers to efficiently understand and approach their ministry. Viewing the city as a community and approaching it as a body of social network may allow those urban evangelists to interpret the city more effectively.

Illustrating Social Dynamics through Graph Theory

To analyze the city, more convenient and objective means are needed to figure out humans relationships, the network. Social dynamics and their interrelated connections can be complex and difficult to conceptualize. In response, researchers have used graphs to literally illustrate social networks effectively and enhance observations to document findings. As the body of social network theory developed, corresponding ways to define this concept more precisely and objectively expanded, as well. Among these, J. A. Barnes[46] used graph theory to illustrate relationships and the intensity or density of those relationships with symbols. Barnes used a system of nodes

46. Barnes, "Graph Theory and Social Networks."

(people) and lines (the relationships) to visually express the transactions, and interactions within relationships. This is Graph Theory.[47]

Graph elements can illustrate the flow of social transactions during an interaction. Chart 1–2 illustrates the direction of an interaction between points A and B. The graph displays point A influencing B, as well as illustrating the distance between them, the intensity of influence (as much as 3), and how often or how long the influence lasts.[48]

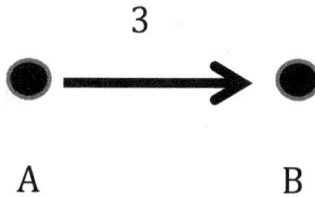

3

A   B

Chart 1–2: A Directed and Valued Graph

The graph theory has gotten much attention among sociologists since graphs offer a means to concisely and clearly illustrate research observations and support definitions of social network theories.[49]

With regards to social network dynamics in a complex urban setting, graphs provide an effective way to conceptualize the characteristics of fluid, constantly evolving relational structures.[50] These relational structures include generational social network formations, networks formed by poor urban dwellers, even newly arrived city migrants, and so on. Such relational characteristics can then be categorized along conceptual definitions of inter-ethnic versus intra-ethnic relationships as in friendships formed in the city, or ways community dwellers distinguish between members versus outsiders.[51]

47. The origin of Graph theory goes back to 1736 by Euler, *The Seven Bridges of Königsberg.*

48. The node (people) is usually referred to as the point, actor, or agent, and the line (e.g., relationship) is the arc, link, or tie. Son, *Sahoe Network Bunsuk*, 26.

49. Flanagan, *Urban Sociology*, 115.

50. Bino and Krishna, "Does Social Network Matter in Knowledge Output?"

51. The study of relationship between the phenomenon of word of mouth spreading in an organization and social network done by Travis, Virginie, and Giuseppe is a good resource. Travis, Virginie, and Giuseppe, "A Social Network Analysis of Positive and Negative Gossip in Organizational Life."

Social anthropologist Jeremy Boissevain introduced a good example. He divides the concept of relationships into two zones. Each zone represents levels of intimacy characterizing those relationships. On the one hand, the close zone consists of relationships among people in direct contact with one another. The far zone refers to indirect contacts characterized by secondary level friendships and acquaintances. Boissevain further divides the close zone into six sub-classes.[52] The close zone begins with direct contact, and the last three zones are effective, nominal, and extended areas, respectively.[53]

In modern days, Graph Theory is being used not only in human relationship but also in various places such as methodology,[54] education study,[55] medical study,[56] criminology,[57] communication,[58] and so on. Conceptualizing the urban networks and understanding urbanites will be introduced later in this book. They are developed with the support of this graphic theory.

CHAPTER PATHFINDER

This chapter aims to provide readers a perspective that the city is beyond just buildings or administrative systems, but rather a society where there are people and society. This chapter also puts more weight on the urbanism (micro) approach than the urbanization (macro) approach, and yet maintains its balance, which is important for urban mission. It also covers the fact that city is integrated with social networks and how it is meaningful for mission.

52. Boissevain, *Friends of Friends*, 47.

53. Ibid.

54. Williams and Shepherd, "Mixed Method Social Network Analysis."

55. Anderson et al., "Social Network Analysis of Children with Autism Spectrum Disorder."

56. Vecchio et al., "Cortical Brain Connectivity and B-Type Natriuretic Peptide in Patients with Congestive Heart Failure."

57. Katerndahl et al., "Differences in Social Network Structure and Support among Women in Violent Relationships."

58. Litaker, "Understanding Dual Rover Communications Using Social Network Analysis."

IMPLICATION OF URBAN MISSION

Two missiological reflections through the theories and perspectives studied so far, which can influence urban mission, will be summarized. First, we need to balance those micro and macro approaches as complementary relationship, not as counter posed. Second, for the aspect of evangelism, regardless of how much the media has developed, we should not forget that people still tend to open their hearts to those whom they trust.

Balancing the Macro and Micro View

Each city has its own unique features. We may call this city's Macro view. At the same time, there are numerous groups and individuals within the city with their own unique qualities in a micro viewpoint.

The bible also introduces such case. Jesus generalized Jerusalem as a place that kills prophets and stones God's messengers; it was a place that made Jesus shed tears of grief (Luke 13:34). However, the atmosphere changes dramatically as Jesus said about the individuals within the city. There were many networks and people like chicks that were completely different from the city's evil image. Jesus remembered every individual like hens that take care of many chicks.

The parable of the sower Jesus told also mentions the macro and micro approach simultaneously. First, individual seeds are sowed to the ground in order to bear fruit; and this is a micro concern. Jesus was interested in the soil, where the seeds fall, which represents the hearts of the people (Matthew 13:18–19). Therefore, ministry field represents people's hearts, and the different seeds may vary in speed and quality of nurturing, while harvest is based on the environment.

Urban Christian workers must understand the people of their cities. Because no matter how massive the buildings are, the people that are in it form the city and make the unique features of the city.

On the other hand, the parable of sower also shows the macro views of a city as well. In the scripture, the fields heavily influence the growth of the seeds that fall on it. Jesus identified the fields into four categories: road, stone field, thorn field, and good soil. Similarly, each individual has a different condition. Unlike the good soil, the rock field takes a long time to clear the stones first, instead of immediate sow. These stones have been here over long periods of time. For this reason, in order to have the macro approach to the city, comprehending such ecological, historical, and urbanological backgrounds are crucial. Therefore, we must not only approach from the urbanism scale, but also from the urbanization scale.

Like this, Christian workers need to have and keep balance between both macro and micro approach to the city. The macro approach enables us to know how the size and dynamics of a city influence the subcultures and individuals.

In order to maintain the balance between macro and micro view, Christian workers in the city must have certain strategies. First, they should clarify their ministry boundary, which is their field. Depending on the groups and social classes, the field environment may differ a lot. Therefore, they must know the boundary of their mission fields. Secondly, they must understand the conditions of their fields, which is the behavioral pattern of the urbanites. For example, the population, daily lives, friends and allies, families, education system, or cultural uniqueness of the people in the city are all-important matters that should be understood. Thirdly, they must know the background of the fields. Every action and behavior has cultural reasons. Within these backgrounds, there are historical, social, and emotional foundations that lie under the people's behaviors.

Fourthly, they need to prioritize their work. Should they clear the rocks or build irrigation system first? Having this integrated road map, a macro view provides an appropriate strategy to the city and its people.

The Gospel Flows Along Human Networks

The Gospel flows through relationships, because it is literally good news—information, that must be communicated through active interactions in order to advance the message.[59] So, even in a modern technological society, it is mostly through direct social interaction that the life-changing Gospel flows. Therefore, the channel (or path) of communication for the Gospel is actually a relationship between the person sending the message and the audience (person) receiving it.[60] No matter how developed modern culture is people initiate fundamental changes impacting other people.

Two years ago at a house church meeting in China, I asked members how they had been introduced to the Gospel. Surprisingly, almost of all of 100 believers at the meeting shared that they first heard the Gospel through

59. Smith, *Creating Understanding*, Proposition 1.
60. McLuhan, *Understanding Media*.

someone they knew well. At a different gathering, I asked students attending a Chinese seminary the same question. The answer was the same. Particularly in non-Western cultural zones, the Gospel flows along established relationships much of the time. In other words, the gospel flows through social networks.

In the Gospel account, the disciples were introduced to Jesus through an already familiar relationship, for the most part. In other words, Jesus utilized an interpersonal social strategy upon initially calling each individual into a journey of faith and ministry. For example, in the story of the very skeptical Nathaniel, Philip was trustworthy enough to convince his companion to meet Jesus. This also shows us the significant role of the human factor in evangelism.[61]

In Asia when someone delivers a message, the receiver often asks, "Who says so?" This is because, depending upon who the speaker is and the level of trust, authority, closeness the listener feels, and the importance attributed from the listener to the messenger will be largely be transferred with the message. The messenger in non-Western cultural zones, in particular, has a tremendous influence on the perceived authority and trustworthiness of the content of a message.

Therefore, even in the modern era with improved and cutting-edge media, the influence a personal relationship has on spreading the Gospel is still great. This is because, no matter how well developed the technology, the core of communication that is transferring people's thoughts and ideas are really the same. Therefore, as Marshall McLuhan had introduced, every media is just an extension of man.[62] Generally, in order for the gospel to be passed to individuals, both interactions through mass media and interpersonal communication have influence. Certainly, mass media can offer a hand in helping a large population of people gain an awareness and understanding of the Gospel.[63] However, a crucial time in evangelizing is when seekers enter a stage of conviction and determination. This is when a personal explanation from a trusted individual sharing a transparent testimony of faith is crucial.[64] This is the moment when microwave styled

61. John 1:40–47.

62. Ibid.

63. Rogers, *Diffusion of Innovations*, 18–20.

64. Engel conceptualized the individual's spiritual journey toward maturity along a range from no awareness of the gospel to spiritual reproduction along nine steps. Engel saw this journey as a process. Engel, *Getting Your Message Across*, chap. 4.

evangelism that offers large audiences simple and convenient sound bites may be ineffective. For earning a soul, sweat, tears, trust and testimony are consistently important factors for evangelism, even in today's world of advanced technology. Therefore, the Gospel flows not solely because of media, or a project, or a system; rather, it flows because of relationships formed through social networks. In this sense, it is strategically very important to understand whom these people in our city have relations with, and what kind of influence they live under.

2

City, a New Hometown of [Im]Migrants

IN THE EARLIER CHAPTER, we have examined the city as a place made up of people and society rather than buildings and administrative districts. In this chapter, as the second face, readers will be given a perspective of the city as a place where new migrants arrive. Many migrants finally accept the city as their new home after experiencing joy and difficulties for a long time. We will categorize the steps and examine the process of city migrants transitioning from new arrivals to being locals later though several steps. Typically, migrants go through six levels and each level has unique sociocultural characteristics of their own. Through the study, readers will understand the joy and sorrow and social issues that migrants face in each process. At the end of this chapter, we will reflect on a strategic reasoning process for an effective mission for these people.

A CASE:
DIFFICULTY, CONFLICT, AND HOPE
TO CITY MIGRANTS

In China, I enjoyed getting bread from a Taiwanese style bakery. One day, as I was standing at the counter to pay for the bread I noticed a Koran made of glass lying next to the owner of the bakery. When I asked her if she was a Muslim, she said, "Yes, I am a Muslim." From that moment, we had a conversation for about an hour. I came to know that the bakery was affiliated with Muslims and every employee was Muslim. The owner was in her early 30s and she had a college degree in English, which is very rare, for a Hui woman to be educated. The majority of Hui Chinese in Xian have lived in ethnic villages within city centers for hundreds of years. However, this woman's parents left the ethnic village fifteen years ago to live in the society where the Hans live. Moreover, unlike the Hui at the ethnic village, they sent their children to college and supported their integration within mainstream society. When I asked her if she would ever want to go back to the village, she said with determination, "I will never go back. They are too conservative and closed."

Her uncle is an Imam at the largest and most traditional Mosque in the village. Many of her relatives still live conservative lives in the village and only a few of her relatives have left the village trying to adjust to mainstream society. Even within the same ethnicity, some remain in their ethnic village while others leave to live in the main society. Those people who come to the main society with their children expand and acquire commonalities with the new community.

What kind of process would people go through when they migrate to a city and settle there? What are the missional meanings and chances in each stage of the process? International immigration has increased its numbers from one hundred fifty six million in 1990, to two hundred fourteen million in 2010.[1] Among them, most international immigrants move from developing countries to developed countries (Northern America, Europe, and Oceania).[2] Sixty percent of migrants in the world reside in developed region.[3]

They settle down in a city little by little with a variety of experiences: conflict with other ethnicities, ethnic pride, individual struggles and dreams for the mainstream society, and failures, and so on.

Based upon the researches that had been done by many scholars, this book summarizes the process that the migrants go through from settlement in city to entering into mainstream society into six-stages. This process begins with migration or immigration, staying in the city kinship based community, to ethnic segregation, slums and shantytowns or ethnic enclaves, and lastly ends with the entrance to mainstream society. Since this book highlights evangelism toward an ethnicity in the city, the process is

1. United Nations' International Migrant Stock Report, http://esa.un.org/migration/index.asp?panel=1.

2. As of 2010, 128 million out of 214 million migrated to more developed regions.

3. International Migration 2006, UNITED NATIONS, Department of Economic and Social Affairs, Population Division, http://www.un.org/esa/population/publications/2006Migration_Chart/Migration2006.pdf.

closer to the case of migrants that is consisted of one ethnicity. Now let us examine each stage in detail.

THE FIRST STAGE: MIGRATION AND IMMIGRATION

More people move today than we ever have in the past, especially though migration.[4] People today move to cities, to bigger cities, to different countries, and to more developed countries.[5]

Every word in Moangalam's definition explains the concept of migration well in detail. First, relatively permanent moving away usually means that people leave geographically, not merely emotionally or psychologically. In most cases, this moving away is long-term, and mostly never returning. Moreover, migration is when migrants collectively move together as a group, not when only one or two individuals more. It is a collective decision where the circumstantial factors and people's ideas inspire many to move.

Furthermore, migration must be preceded by decision-making on the basis of a hierarchically ordered set of values. It means that people are motivated to migrate when they are deprived of their valued possessions in their hometowns or when they believe that they could have more in the new place. Of course, this is only possible when the individuals have the systematic ability and right condition to move. Lastly, migration must accompany the changes in the interactional system. This means that the new environment and life interacting with the new environment is not merely a short trip of staying at an inn, because migration includes many structural changes concomitant with residential relocation as migrants live in the new environments.

The types of migration can be categorized into several kinds by its motivation, situation, and purpose. In his work, William Peterson categorized the causes of migration into four kinds: ecological push, migration policy, higher aspirations, and social momentum (Table2–1).[6]

The first cause of migration is the ecological push. Ecological push refers when the environment of the original place either cannot fulfill one's basic needs or contains an increase in negative elements, such as natural disasters. This kind of migration is primitive for it is natural to satisfy people's

4. Waldinger, "Crossing Borders."

5. Mangalam and Schwarzweller, "Some Theoretical Guidelines toward a Sociology of Migration," 8.

6. Petersen, "A General Typology of Migration."

most basic needs. This primitive class migration divides into two kinds depending on which route it takes. One is the wandering migration with no clear destination; this type is prone to failure for one migrates instantaneously with no information, preparation or purpose. The other is the ranging migration, which regularly moves around few different locations, which is usually seen in gatherings or nomadism. This includes people escaping from the cold winters to lowland winter camps.

The second cause for migration is the migration policy. This refers to the migration imposed by the government, or those in power. Depending on having opposition to the migrants or not, this migration policy can be categorized as two kinds: impelled migration and forced migration. Furthermore, this migration policy can be categorized as conservatism in order to protect the migrants or innovations in order to use the migrants' labor depending on the policymakers' motivations. When these two sides and two motivations are combined, it produces four migration types—displacement, slave trade, flight, and coolie trade.

Relation	Migratory Force	Class of Migration	Type of Migration	
			Conservative	Innovating
Nature and man	Ecological push	Primitive	Wandering	Flight from the land
			Ranging	
State (or equivalent) and man	Migration policy	Forced	Displacement	Slave trade
		Impelled	Flight	Coolie trade
Man and his norms	Higher aspirations	Free	Group	Pioneer
Collective behavior	Social momentum	Mass	Settlement	Urbanization

Table 2–1: General Typology of Migration[7]

The third cause for migration is higher aspirations, which refers to migrating to new areas with new dreams and aspirations. This is an individual's decision and can be considered free for its class of migration. For this migration, there are a small number of pioneers who first pave the way,

7. Petersen, "A General Typology of Migration," 266.

and are later followed by a group. A prime example of this is the people from Europe who sought for the New World or colonies.

The last cause for migration is the social momentum. This social momentum often moves many people, creating mass migration. This is more of an easy migration because migrants can easily adapt to the new area. There are already many people from the origin who well cultivated social facilities of the local, allowing the next migrants to mitigate the culture shock and adapt easily.

In contrast to the categorization by purpose and situation that I have introduced so far, migration types can also be categorized by status and occupation. This method can categorize migrants into three types: guest labors, traditional immigrants, and professional and middle-class economic immigrants.[8] These three labor forces have migrated to developed nations chronologically in different time periods.[9]

In general, the guest type laborers immigrate to the developed countries, first.[10] Most of them are low-level technicians offering physical labor force and basic technology to the developed country. They leave their families behind and support them financially.[11]

Traditional immigrants more to developed countries after the guest type laborers.[12] These immigrants arrive mostly with their friends' or families' support and work or learn the same business with the inviters. As this kind of traditional immigrants increase, ethnic communities also grow.

Following the traditional immigrants, professional and middle class economic groups immigrate to the developed countries.[13] Coming into the 1970s, the United States and European countries became willing to accept people with advanced skills as immigrants. These people are already in the professional and middle-class in their home countries and start in the similar class in the new host country as well.[14]

---

8. Gottdiener and Budd categorized three migration types based on the types of occupation. Gottdiener and Budd, *Key Concepts in Urban Studies*, 61–65.

9. Tyner, "Global Cities and Circuits of Global Labor."

10. Gottdiener and Budd, *Key Concepts in Urban Studies*, 61.

11. Amparo, Pau, and Cris, "Child-Parent Separations among Senegalese Migrants to Europe," 106.

12. Gottdiener and Budd, *Key Concepts in Urban Studies*, 61.

13. Ibid., 62–63.

14. Paul, "The Settlement Patterns of Developed World Migrants in London."

THE SECOND STAGE:
SETTLING TO FAMILIAR PLACE

At the second stage of migration, there is settlement. Urban migrants experience a big change in their initial network dynamics. In many cases, when people from rural areas and undeveloped areas move to cities, they receive help from people they know. Those who are already settled help relatives or community members from their hometowns transition to the urban landscape. As a result, enclaves of common networks develop in close proximity. In this way, communities with strong connections among members develop strong ties economically, socially, emotionally, religiously and culturally.

People continually migrate into cities. They migrate from small rural villages sometimes traveling long or short distances to cities to settle down near public transportation, such as bus stops or train stations. In an international city, it is easy to see a great number of immigrants not only from nearby areas but also hailing from abroad.[15]

An urban kinship network is important especially for first generation migrants because it provides residents with a taste of home—an emotional cultural buoy, so to speak. In such a kinship network, people maintain their original culture despite conflicts and compromises with new urban mentalities and sense of style. Even in a family, each generation has different boundaries defining their activities and relationships, despite daily functioning in a kinship network under contrasting values, desires and preferences. People with different values are apt to respond to new trends or information differently, whether with bias or preference.

In general, kinship network becomes a major source for creating chain migration.[16] People, who newly move into cities through chain migration, quickly copy life patterns of the cities where their supporters live. Additionally, there is a high possibility for this type of new migrants to join the same economic niches and to assume the same occupations as their supporters.

For instance, there is a humorous saying among Asian minorities in Los Angeles: "The job of the person who greets you at LAX [airport] on the first day of your immigration will decide your job for the rest of your life."

---

15. Following studies have researched the life of migrants that settles in various countries in diverse forms: Rebelo, "Work and Settlement Locations of Immigrants."; Schönwälder and Söhn, "Immigrant Settlement Structures in Germany"; Cathy Yang and Gary, "Immigrant Settlement and Employment Suburbanisation in the Us"; Laura and Alan, "Jewish Immigrant Settlement Patterns in Manchester and Leeds 1881."

16. Korinek, Entwisle, and Jampaklay, "Through Thick and Thin," 779.

There is some truth to this saying because many members of ethnic urban communities tend to pursue the same occupations and lifestyles as those who intervene to support them.

A migrant's new kinship network in a city can provide emotional, economic and social stability, and serve as a pathway to new social bond. However, as time goes on, and migrants become accustomed to their environments, people begin needing the information from sources outside of their kinship network. Depending on personal preferences, some individuals among certain social classes favor information from outside social influences and absorb it quickly.

Nevertheless, people are still aware of the differences between the inside and outside of their primary networks. They can experience confusion, conflict and compromise repeatedly because of this awareness.

Fortunately, these phenomena can inform Christian workers about community issues they need to address as they evangelize urban migrants. As urban migrants maintain their original culture, it is easy for them to develop strong biases against other religions. Especially when a family member accepts a new religion, conflict and resulting turmoil can arise within that group. This kind of community pressure can hinder an individual from turning to a new faith. Similar social matters hinder Muslims and Hindus from changing their religions while they remain in their communities, because the kinship network can act like a great hindrance to an individual desiring or needing change, because a traditional society generally equates change with disloyalty.

THE THIRD STAGE: SLUM AND SHANTYTOWN

Slums and shantytowns are kinds of villages in the city.[17] They are similar to ethnic ghettos or ethnic villages, (which we will study in detail later), yet different. "A slum is a concentrated, densely settled area where area

17. Studies and reports below give us understandings of slums and shantytowns in many different countries. Paul, "Creditworthiness of a Borrower and the Selection Process in Micro-Finance"; Kher, Aggarwal, and Punhani, "Vulnerability of Poor Urban Women to Climate-Linked Water Insecurities at the Household Level"; Jindrich, "The Shantytowns of Central Park West"; Gibson, "Introduction: A New Politics of the Poor Emerges from South Africa's Shantytowns"; Michael and Leonard, "Motivations for Slum Dweller Social Movement Participation in Urban Africa"; Andrew, James, and Brett, "Cities, Slums, and Energy Consumption in Less Developed Countries, 1990 to 2005"; Koster, "Mediating and Getting 'Burnt' in the Gap."

where housing is inadequate, residents are poor and community functions are lacking."[18] When we think of slums, we automatically are reminded of buildings ready to collapse. However, the integrated reason for slums having this kind of buildings is not merely because residents cannot repair them, but because of the inadequate public services, poor medical and educational care, and a general neglect by the larger society that all together makes them live in poverty.[19] On the other side, shantytowns are a form of slums that are byproducts of modernization and industrialization.[20]

Depending on the situation, the terms, slums and shantytowns, can be used interchangeably with ethnic villages, because when ethnicities first move into the city, they live in the same areas due to chain migration or in poor and cheap areas due to the economic and social unpreparedness. As a result, their ethnic villages start in slums or shantytowns.

On the other hand, there are some fundamental differences in ethnic villages and slums. People come to slums because they are poor. In other words, slums attract people for economic reasons. Therefore, in some ethnic villages, people dwell in for several generations, whereas the next generations living in shantytowns or slums are cleared to enter the mainstream society before even one generation is over. Thus, the latter is like a middle camp for those who want to enter the city's mainstream society in a short amount of time.

People in slums or shantytowns have always suffered from the lack of resources. Those who just moved in have language barrier and lack cultural understanding and information of the new city. For example, the first generation migrants have great enthusiasm for their children's education and success to enter the mainstream society and are willing to sacrifice. However, many of them pass down poverty to their children due to the insufficiency of resources and information.[21]

18. Gottdiener and Budd, *Key Concepts in Urban Studies*, 135.

19. Ibid., 136.

20. Ibid., 136–37.

21. Wilson's findings from African American enclaves tells how segregation in two institutional spheres, residence and employment, produces racialization at two class levels—among the impoverished and the middle class. George, "Racialized Life-Chance Opportunities across the Class Structure."

THE FOURTH STAGE: ETHNIC VILLAGE

A great structure and power called city provides opportunity and hope to people, but also it often neglects and damages many people as well. So, people develop coping system, learn how to protect themselves and live a life in such city environment. For this, people with commonness gather to live together or find their own lifestyle. There is a pseudo hometown in modern city that is being fueled with new migrants from rural areas or other countries continuously. One of these is the ethnic village. This ethnic village is a kind of a coping strategy that develops a cushion against external threats and serves as a mechanism as the economically and socially weak people live together.[22]

For example, Eugene B. Brody says, ethnic ghetto is a kind of ethnic village that provides cultural buffer zone to migrants as below.

> The ghetto is one type of mediating organization, although it may not always have the effect. As a geographically and socially defined unit in which the new arrival finds others of his own kind, sharing common norms and language, it can act as a buffer mechanism permitting him a pause for personal and social reorganization before making his way into the larger cosmopolitan urban environment.[23]

Ethnic villages have various social characteristics. First, ethnic village is a place of refuge where ethnicities can rest and have stability. Immigrants experience drastic emotional, economic, relational, and cultural changes. Migrants lose the support of social and environmental familiarity and all the familiar patterns and values that once sustained their lives when they leave the origin. They also become very vulnerable to diseases, poverty, threats, ambiguousness, and lack of social resources. At the same time, ethnic villages become middle ground that connect cities and the origins and also provide new nest for migrants. People from the same origin gather in a place in the city and develops ethnic village gradually. They root their own culture, traditions, language, and system in this new city once again.

Second, ethnic villages provide information and resources to the same ethnicities within the city and become a seedbed for individuals to do social activities easily. The ethnic village is not only a dwelling place but also

22. Fong and Jing regarded human ecology, dual labor market, ethnic enclave, and occupational niche as the presupposed elements for ethnic minorities to gather in one location, as they study the phenomenon of Chinese immigrants in Canada gathering in one place within a city. Fong and Jing, "Explaining Ethnic Enclave, Ethnic Entrepreneurial and Employment Niches."

23. Brody, "Migration and Adaptation," 5–13.

develops as the soil to maintain ethnic supremacy, culture, and traditions.[24] At first, the town may be small in number but as migrants continuously add on, the village becomes more diverse and stronger. Later, they develop ethnic events, religion, institutions, and ethnic politicians and businesses will gain more leadership. Private organizations, leadership, religious institutions, and governments of the hometown can also become a counter partner and make relationships with those institutions in ethnic villages.[25]

Third, ethnic village is a place that creates a unique third culture. As they become larger, ethnic villages create their own cultures. This urban ethnic village culture is neither the original culture nor the mainstream culture of the city but rather a different urban subculture. The subculture created from the city ethnicity is the third culture made from the combination of traditional culture and the mainstream culture of the city as basis. People in ethnic villages bring traditions and culture from the origin but they constantly interact with city environment through media, schools, social activities and so on. People exposed to the mainline society more likely to become leaders of change and recreation of city ethnic culture.

Fourthly, ethnic villages carry a self-governing nature. Internally, there are inside leaders recognized by everyone who are different from the central government leaders, and everyone knows the leaders in religion, business, and the technical and professional world.[26] This kind of autonomous structure has preserved them from the influences of other ethnicities and the central government for many years, and this is a necessary component for the building up of the ethnic pride and village structures.

THE FIFTH STAGE:
DIVERSIFIED GROUPS IN ETHNIC VILLAGE

Unlike the outside's notion that the inside would be the same, the inside of the ethnic village is actually a very complicated one and carries dynamics, which the outside cannot easily understand. The village has many sub sects within it. Understanding the structure of sub-groups existing within the

24. Fong and Jing, "Explaining Ethnic Enclave, Ethnic Entrepreneurial and Employment Niches," 1619.

25. Garcia found that Latino immigrant population have three distinct yet interconnected subnetworks, a traditional subnetwork, a church subnetwork, and a contract subnetwork. Saracostti, "Social Capital as a Strategy to Overcome Poverty in Latin America."

26. Warren and Troy, "Explaining Violent Intra-Ethnic Conflict."

village is also very important in missions because each sect differs in the degree of exposure to the outside and openness, which directly affects the effects of evangelism and spread to the inside.

There are various ways of categorizing groups within an ethnic village, but they can be categorized into at least three groups: the isolated or single-race group, the selective group for internal and external culture, and the actively interacting group. First, the isolated or single-race group is a community that isolates itself from external culture and lives with those who are familiar with familiar ways within the original culture. Second, the selective group refers to those that use ethnic culture as well as the culture of external mainstream society selectively. For example, when they do business or attend school, they act in a way that is done in the mainstream society and conduct their personal work according to their ethnic cultural code. Third, the actively interacting group refers to the group that has more interest in assimilating into the external mainstream society rather than their own ethnic group to follow and spend more time with those in the mainstream society.[27]

The attitude and openness of many groups within ethnic village toward external society is a very important element in mission strategy. The group that is more open toward external society has less resistance toward outsiders and is active in receiving information from outside. Examining groups within ethnic villages with such perspective, the result of research about Mexican Americans in a Dallas barrio done by Shirley Achor is a notable case for missionaries.[28]

Achor conceptualized those four groups' dynamics in Chart 2–1. Achor divided people's groups within ethnic villages by connecting the openness of each group into macro (majority) society and micro (minority) society in the diagram, though the following four groups: insulationist, accommodationists, mobilizationists and maladaptive.

Insulationist group is isolated from the external culture, has biases to outside cultures, receives poor social benefits and mainly has internal resources and culture. The people form a defense mechanism toward outside, have pride in their domestic culture and use their community (barrio) as a refuge. They travel out of town only for specific and selective purposes, and have strong endogamy and preferred religions. A significant number of families sent their children to parochial schools, for they believe that the public school has contaminating influences.

27. Mainstreamers introduced by Ulf Hannerz would fall in this category. Hannerz, *Soulside*, 38–57.

28. Achor, *Mexican Americans in a Dallas Barrio*, 116–21.

MACRO

	HIGH	LOW
HIGH	Mobilization	Insulation
LOW	Accommodation	Alienation

MICRO

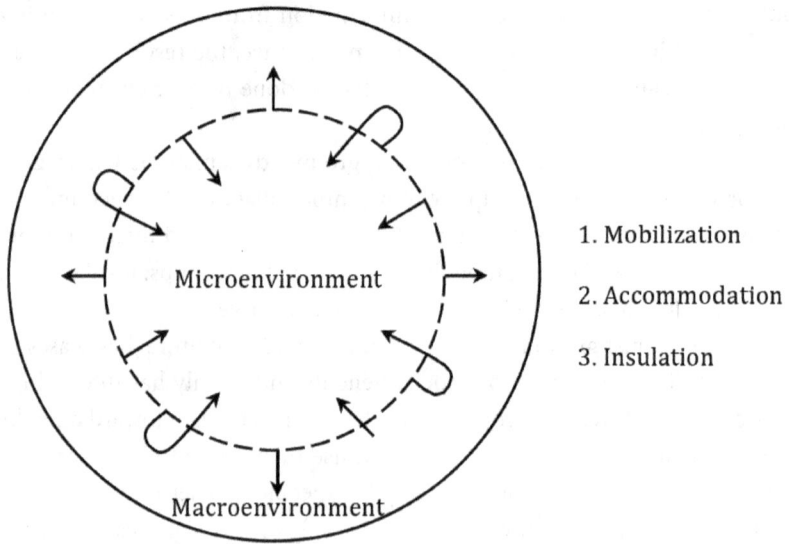

1. Mobilization

2. Accommodation

3. Insulation

Chart 2–1: Achor's Four Different Subgroups in Barrio[29]

29. Ibid., 115.

Accommodation group is a community that eagerly attempts to enter the mainstream, but have not achieved it yet. People eagerly learn Anglo in order to successfully cross over the ethnic boundaries. They encourage their children to learn English, and actively collect outside information because they believe that those are the key to upward mobility. Their extended family ties are weak, and the number of interethnic marriages and converts to Protestantism from Catholicism increase. Sometimes they have sufferings from identity crisis, being rejected from both of Mexican and Anglo society.

Mobilization group is people who move between two groups of people to mobilize the Mexican community. Their concern is the renewal of the Mexican community. They do not wish to merge with the dominant society; rather, their efforts are directed toward altering the existing systems with the aim of achieving economic, social, and political parity for the community.

Finally, alienation is a group of people who never get into the dominant culture or the minority community. Some people are so overwhelmed by the environmental stress that they become deeply alienated from both the barrio and the Anglo social worlds.

Achor's Diagram describes the life goal and direction pursued by each group. An interesting point of this diagram is that both the mobilization group and accommodation group may use the external information and resources and yet have completely different ways of use. The Mobilization group is no different than the accommodation group in terms of its openness to the outside, but it differs by having more leadership in the ethnicity and desire to use the outside resources for its own ethnicity. For this reason, the mobilization group contains much potential in mission strategy. This is because the gospel is considered as outside information in ethnic villages, and for this information to spread inside, the group that is more open to the outside can contribute as bridges. Moreover, the mobilization group has high influence to the village, which is necessary for diffusing the good news to the whole enclave. In this way, mobilization group has huge potential in mission to the whole ethnicity, because it is opened to outside information, having the leadership and sense of duty to the ethnicity.[30]

30. Aleksandra, "The Role of Different Forms of Bridging Capital for Immigrant Adaptation and Upward Mobility."

THE SIXTH STAGE:
THE LIFE OF A MAINLINE SOCIETY

Migrants in the city who adapt to an ethnic village or their descendants usually want to move into the mainstream society as they adapt to the urban culture. As they contact with the mainstream society they experience identity crisis, family conflict, anxiety from uncertain future, need for the ascent of status, and so on.[31]

City always overflows with migrants who begin new lives in a new place. The adapting process is difficult and dangerous. Some of the difficulties they face in the process of adapting include the following.[32]

First, Immigrants need to set up all their foundations of life again. Many migrants still face economic and social difficulties. Once appreciated positions and skills in their original cities have too many deficiencies to be welcomed and acknowledged in the new city. This is especially true if the particular skill or knowledge carries cultural and ethnic qualities that cannot be practiced with the original license or educational career. The migrants thus work as janitors, cooks, automobile repairmen, or other occupations that are associated with socially low statuses rather than working as lawyers, accountants, doctors, or other professions. Migrants in these low statuses, though they work without rest, live with very constructed economic activities.[33]

Second, women migrants may lead to difficulties through sudden shifts in their role. Many women are not ready to accept sudden social changes. It is not easy for them to newly create their position, and roles in this new society. Sometimes women who excel in social adaptation can get unprofessional jobs or manual labor provided by the people of the same origin. Ironically, this kind of occupation may even give women more opportunity; and ironically these women often lead the family's economy.[34]

Third, the migrant's status and role between husband and wife also undergoes changes. The husbands will naturally exert authority as it is in

31. Hiebert and Meneses categorizes the urban worldview themes: acceptance of diversity, clearly divided public/private, individualism, consumerism, time-and-future-oriented. Hiebert and Meneses, *Incarnational Ministry*, 315–20.

32. Ibid.

33. Winders, "Seeing Immigrants: Institutional Visibility and Immigrant Incorporation in New Immigrant Destinations," 58.

34. Following researches have examined the changes in the position and role of women immigrants. Truong and Gasper, "Trans-Local Livelihoods and Connections"; Oishi, "Women in Motion Globalization, State Policies, and Labor Migration in Asia"; Mahler and Pessar, "Gender Matters"; Piper and Roces, *Wife or Worker?*

their original patriarchal society, but as the women experience the city life, they desire freer positions and opportunities. The freer and carefree lives in the city may give both opportunities to advance personally, but also may ethically put the family in danger.

Fourth, child education is both one of the largest issues and most difficult issues for migrants. Many parents move to developed nations for their children's education. The migrated parents desire their children to join the mainstream society.[35] It is education that enables the migrants to join the mainstream society. As a result, most of these people are eager to educate their children expecting them to satisfy the dreams of the parents.[36] However, the reality is that their children also have limitations for success because the parents lack social, economical, and cultural support for their children's success.

Fifth, generational conflict is also a big issue in migrants.[37] We must pay attention to the occurrence of many conflicts when different generations with different worldviews live together in a home or at an institution.

The ultimate question that disturbs migrants more than the questions we have discussed until now is "Who am I?" They are confused about how much cultural appropriateness they need to acquire. They are different from the people in the mainstream society, but also are different from the people of their origins, as they have lived in a city for a long time. At the same time, they learn their own defense mechanism. In other words, they learn to put on different mask every time they visit the hometown, as they live in the mainstream society, and within the ethnic group.

CHAPTER PATHFINDER

We have studied the third identification to the city: the city as a place where migrants make a new home. There are six steps these ethnicities go through as they accept the new environment as their homes. For change of direction, we have studied that that there is no single direction. The reason why we define each step is because God gives unique missional opportunities in each of these steps. Each stage requires different strategies as well.

35. Portes and Rumbaut, Legacies.

36. Todaro, "Urbanization in Developing Nations."

37. Hiebert and Meneses, Incarnational Ministry, 285.

MISSIOLOGICAL IMPLICATION

In order to plan appropriate mission strategies, this chapter interests in understanding urban ethnicities and the challenges that they are facing. Therefore, understanding the process of adjusting the new city, as their new home for a new ethnicity's migration is quite meaningful. Therefore in this chapter, we studied the peoples' migration, settlement, slum and shantytown, isolation, interaction with neighboring ethnicities in the cities, and their entering into the mainstream society through a step-by-step process. Even now, many ethnicities around the world are migrating, settling down and creating ethnic towns. Such stages may not occur chronologically or even loyally toward one direction; in some cases, certain stages are even omitted or switched in opposite directions. City people live under God's providence while they carry their own hopes and sorrows, along with their own passions and disappointments. God wants to introduce the Gospel with understandable ways in each stage as they pass many different steps. Therefore, the church must comprehend the city ethnicities realistically and set up mission strategy.

A New and God-Given Mission Opportunity.

Numerous residents in shantytowns live in pessimism and despair rather than hope. Lack of education opportunities, poor public systems and unceasing social problems repeatedly cause failure of dreams and efforts. The Christians serving in these areas must first have the heart of sympathy God provides. They must be able to approach those facing financial and daily hardships, with the heart of Christ.

Ministry strategies for these shantytowns must have very practical approaches. Mission methods that bear successful fruit in the third world can be a good case to see. Compassion ministries, such as ministry to the poor or prostitutes, micro capital loans, and community developments may bring hope, solve practical problems, and save them from structural disorders. Since it is too vast and demanding (of professional) for one church do this alone, it is important to cooperate with other professional mission organizations.

On the other hand, migration patterns are also changing. Rather than just migrants from wars, natural disasters, or poor-paid labor, today's migrants are voluntary, and well prepared for the life in the new place. Many of them remain in similar classes in the new home, as they had in their original places. The privileged now go to work in modern business buildings and live near international schools for their kids. They exchange the world's news rapidly through modern transportation and high-tech equipment. At the same time, they are able to pass down their culture and language to their children and simultaneously enjoy the foreign information.

Such phenomenon lets us have a novel perspective to the ethnic towns and Diasporas. Significant numbers of unreached urban ethnic towns also leave from their traditional shapes and begin to interact with the outside, change, and develop. It means that the numbers of people who are open to outside information are growing; the Gospel is also information from outside. Urban ethnic towns are waiting for the modern Apostle Paul. They need someone who would share the gospel, in their lives and economic activities, and synagogues and social centers.

Be Aware of the Ethnic Segregation

Ethnic isolation affects the church and ministry largely. Long periods of ethnic conflicts or indifference can be a potential conflict among church members and can serve as a barrier for sharing the gospel to other ethnicities. Christian workers must examine what an appropriate reaction is to such ethnic conflicts. Especially, they should not see the ethnic issue too naively, but quite realistically. If not, though those ethnicities can gather together in the church for a while, it may not sustain for a long.

Overlooking ethnic segregation can also cause errors in setting mission strategies. Foreign missionaries tend to focus only on the ethnic group who are easily reachable, like the *Chosun* people in China and *Goryoyin* in Central Asia who speak Korean or English, or ethnicities that are opened to outside information. Then, the missionaries believe that the Gospel will automatically spread on to the neighbor ethnic groups. However, this assumption is easily flawed. Because there are too many obstacles for the reached ethnic groups to naturally spread the Gospel to the next. When missionaries understand the dynamics of ethnic segregation, they can have a realistic alternative and establish an effective mission strategy.

Compassion toward Urban Ethnicity's Insecurity and Agony

Moving with family to a new place and adapting the culture must be very challenging for the migrants. Many migrants settle down in the new city without enough resources and information. They suffer countless hardships: lack of economics, new status, lack of local information due to language and cultural differences, incapability of using previous skills due to different rules and regulations, family issues, ethics problems, children's education, generation conflicts, and finally struggle with unclear self-identity. All of these difficulties can be compressed into the terms called "anxiety" and "fatigue." Migrants in cities live with anxiety and fatigue. How does God want city Christian workers to view these types of urban ethnic minorities?

The story of Abram and his 318 men who set out to save Lot is quite an appropriate story in the Bible for Christian workers serving for the urban ethnic minority and migrants. Lot was a migrant and ethnic minority in Sodom City. When the entire Sodom had gotten into war with another kingdom, Lot was deprived of all his possessions and was caught captive along with his family. After hearing this, Abram risks his own safety to fight the king and saves Lot and his family along with their possessions (Genesis 14).

God wants to introduce Christians in the city to ethnic minorities and migrants who search after a city's benefits but in reality struggle from the unexpected hardships. They should also have Abram's willingness and attitude that took risks and confronted with God as an intercessor to save Lot and his family (Genesis 18:17–33) from the judgment plan to Sodom. The people need the heart of Abraham who prayed for the lives of an urban ethnic minority and migrants.

3

City, a Place of Ethnic Conflict and Competition

IN THE EARLIER TWO chapters, we have examined the city as a place made up of people and society rather than buildings and administrative districts, and as a place where many ethnicities live together with competition, conflict, harmony, and create many dynamic relationships. This chapter will examine the city in detail as a place composed of many ethnicities. Many ethnicities form cities not only to live together but also to have conflict, competition, and reconciliation within it. To understand conflict, competition, and reconciliation among ethnicities more scientifically, using sociological theories is needed. This is because to be able to work for the urban ethnicities, the ability to do objective analysis of conflict and competition between ethnicities is necessary. For this, this chapter will identify six elements that create conflicts or reconciliation within urban ethnicities. Moreover, conflict between ethnicities will be categorized into four steps from weak to strong, and will address what phenomena are going on in each step. Lastly, we will also examine characteristics of ethnic conflict in the mission field or non-Western world, comparing them to the Western world.

A CASE: URBAN ETHNICITIES LIVING IN CONFLICT AND COMPETITION

Niujie (牛街), a place located in the southeast corner of Beijing, is a village meaning "Oxen Street." The name was given as a symbol for Muslims who do not eat pork, but eat oxen and lamb as their dietary staple.[1] One day, I took a taxi to visit Niujie. When we arrived at the village, the driver who was a Han pointed at the Muslims in the village and said, "The reason why they do not eat pork is because their ancestors are related to pigs." If a Hui had heard this, it would have been very insulting. I was able to feel the hatred toward Hui even from the tone of his voice and expressions on his face. Of course, I did not believe what he said nor wanted to hear him. I did my best to think positively about the Hui ever since I have accepted God's calling in my life to love the Hui.

Such hostile feelings and biases toward other ethnic groups also exist among the Hui. While I was passing by one of the major roads in a Hui village in Lanzhou, Gansu in 1999, an argument began between a Hui and a Han. In less than three minutes, dozens of young Hui men from the village came and surrounded the Han man and threatened him with hostile attitude. They did not even try to listen to the argument and expressed hostility toward the Han man by telling him that he did wrong no matter what.

The Han and Hui have coexisted together in the same place for 1,300 years, yet the opposition remains. They were aware of each other's presence, but rarely encountered one another in daily livings, as if the other ethnicity did not exist. Therefore, the Hui are familiar strangers[2] who have lived in China for a long time, but still strangers. At the same time, hostilities and biases toward one another still remained in people's hearts that could go off anytime. Such attitudes continually develop with new features even today.[3]

Ironically, such Hui's ethnic bias, conflicts, competition, and pride provide soil for the creation of many ethnic folk tales and cultural symbols.[4] These confrontations between ethnicities are generally expressed through neglect, business competition, and criticism, but if necessary, it could also bring conflict and even slaughter between ethnicities.[5]

1. Niejie meas a place where Muslim oxen butchers live, the name was given during Qing Dynasty. Shoujie, *Niu Jie Huimin Shenghuo Tan" (Discussion of the Lifestyle of the Oxen Street Hui)*.

2. Lipman, *Familiar Strangers*.

3. Gladney, *Dislocating China Reflections on Muslims, Minorities, and Other Subaltern Subjects*.

4. Li and Luckert, *Mythology and Folklore of the Hui, a Muslim Chinese People*.

5. The Hui people have lived in China for about 1,300 years. In the early stage of their history in China, there were few ethnic conflicts and riots in the historical recorded. However, from the Ming Dynasty (1368–1644), and Qing Dynasty (1644–1912) as the Hui numbers and forces grew, the number of conflicts increased. Broomhall, *Islam in China:*

Traditionally, many Hui lived as farmers in the rural areas. Those who live in cities form their ethnic villages with business and live within their own ethnic area for the most of their lives. Therefore, even though two different ethnicities live together within the same city, the two groups have isolated themselves from each other or have lived as if the other parts do not exist. As a result, the two groups have coexisted without much conflict with very few exceptions.

Recently, China has experienced rapid urbanization. The problem is that modern cities do not allow these peoples to neglect one another or isolate. Modern cities force the two ethnicities to interact endlessly. Different ethnicities encounter one another at parks, markets, schools, etc., and as a result, exchange and cooperate, or compete creating constant conflicts.

City literally is the place where many ethnicities coexist. Therefore, city is not just a gathering of people, but also a gathering of ethnicities. Moreover, ethnicities within cities have their own unique history. They did not just appear. Therefore, they bring in their historical experiences as they understand themselves and interact with other groups.

On the other hand, ethnicities in cities are changing. Ethnicities are demanded to change by the strong power called city. They are now pressured to respond in any form as they make frequent contact with neighboring ethnicities. Children in public schools and young adults in their work places now must absorb the influence of cities and exchange with other ethnicities in the same space.

How can urban ministers who work in an environment where fast growing exchange between ethnicities takes place understand conflict and interchange between ethnicities? Furthermore, what are some sociological dynamic compositions and theories that urban ministers must know, which exist within conflicts and competitions between ethnicities? This understanding provides an important foundation for the development of a mission strategy. Urban ministers must understand the people they serve by their ethnic sentiments developed throughout long history, consideration and bias toward each other, and the positioning and dynamic relations between ethnicities that have been restructured. Now, let us take a look at the elements that affect the relationship between ethnicities.

A Neglected Problem, 64–68; Findlay, The Crescent in North-West China; Lawton, "Muslim in China." Leslie, Islam in Traditional China, 115, 19, 129–30. Lipman and Harrel, "Ethnic Violence in Modern China," 71–73; Dillon, China's Muslim Hui Community, 164.

SIX ELEMENTS THAT AFFECT
INTER-ETHNIC DYNAMICS

We hear stories and news from all around the world through mass media on a daily basis. We cannot easily forget these events. These kinds of ethnic conflicts have been with us ever since ancient societies. As a civilized society, why do we still have to face these endless conflicts? Actually, we experience the ethnic issues in many different ways, not just through physical encounters. For example, ethnic conflicts take various forms such as competing for the vested rights in choosing the official language, for more educational opportunities and its benefits, for prior occupation of the media, competition in economical and political unity, and so on.

In a modern society, these ethnic conflicts have become an important issue in mission strategy. Many years back, those ethnicities would live in the countryside or within their clustered zones; however, nowadays, cities offer more diverse professions and higher mobility. This has increased contact and cooperation, and sometimes conflicts, more than any other time period in history. These complex relationships affect urban ethnic ministry both directly and indirectly. Understanding ethnic relationships and dynamics of surrounding ethnicities is quite important when conducting mission work among the urban ethnicities. There are six elements that contribute to the conflicts and unity of ethnicities today: history of the inter-ethnicities, recent political situations, globalization impacts, urbanization impacts, social welfare, and media. Let us examine these six elements in detail.

First, conflicts may occur through the experiences formed by a long history between the ethnicities. This conflict is not formed overnight but over hundreds of years based on smaller conflicts.[6] Different religions and social hierarchies, conqueror and the conquered relationships, the strengthening of one group over the other, and other reasons cause these conflicts. Long conflicts between the Flemings and Walloons in Belgium, the central government and minorities in China and Russia, many small language religious groups in India, and the Mestizos and Natives in Peru are some of the examples of such conflicts that exist today. Conflicts and problems still exist today in numerous areas in the world, which come from long history.

Secondly, modern political problems can cause these conflicts. For example, after the Second World War, many countries have gained independence and new countries were born. In some cases, once colonialized

6. Rydgren, "The Power of the Past."

groups have developed their own independency after the withdrawal of the developed country, they have drawn borders between nations. Sometimes, conflicts within countries have divided the land into two or three independent nations. It has become easy for conflicts to arise within the country or with bordering nations, if a group has not been well prepared to interrelate with other ethnic groups, if the government has established an unfair ethnic policy, or if the government has not fully taken into consideration the ethnic opinions.

Thirdly, globalization has a big impact on inter-ethnic relationships.[7] As international interaction increase, ethnic groups are entering into new states that allow them to compare themselves to other groups more easily. Developed countries also face these new cultural challenges through the global economy. A good example of this is in Europe. Northern Europe rapidly became a multiethnic society as they attracted a large amount of foreign labors, especially from Southern Europe. Social stratification issues are not only influenced by domestic factors but also from international dynamics.

As the international market grows and barriers of labor market and capital flow are lowered, the society needs to face new ethnicities, and new stratification orders are formed among the ethnicities.[8]

Fourthly, migrants moving to the city have impact on the inter-ethnic relationship. After migration, migrants adjust their lives to the life patterns and social rules that have already been established by cities. People continue to interact with other ethnic groups in everyday life, as they commute to work, give rides to their children at school, abide by the city's rules, and so on. In this process, each group has varietal relationships with each other by forming prejudice, adjusting, pursuing profit, inter-depending, clashing, and so on.[9]

Fifthly, the social welfare system in the modern nations has amplified the interaction between ethnic groups. In the traditional society, ethnicities had limited interactions, and remained isolated and maintained their own life styles. However in the modern society, multi-ethnic states have welfare systems that go beyond of the ethnic borders. This gives a lot of social mobility to ethnicities in their social hierarchies. In some cases, by helping this system, the ethnicities in the lower class gain capital and social power as time passes. By this social elevation in the stratification, some ethnicities

7. Olzak, "Does Globalization Breed Ethnic Discontent?"

8. Bell, "Ethnicity and Social Change," 151–52.

9. Weidmann, "Geography as Motivation and Opportunity."

revive their culture and traditions. Especially countries that have welfare systems that provide greater benefits to the lower class allow more social mobility to the ethnic minorities in the low class. This allows their children to take classes with other ethnic groups and adults can achieve equality in the work place regardless of their ethnicity. As the result of it, how the government continues to develop interactions between different ethnic groups within the same country that are increasing like never before has become an important issue in the countries.

Sixthly, the advancement of the media plays a big role. In any society, media has been used to initiate and advertise the government in order for many ethnicities to comply and follow the rules and regulations set by the government in maintaining public order. Also, through media, the government encourages different groups to acknowledge one another to adjust and live together. On the other hand, there are some cases when media creates ethnic conflicts and enlarges ethnic biases through manipulations of politicians.

We have searched six representative elements that affect the relationships among the ethnicities in the city. The ethnic problems have not only existed when human rights were not a concern, such as during the times of savage dictatorial conquest or slavery. In fact, it also is the issue of the present era where the ethnic minorities that were previously clustered within their own groups are now is becoming more active in interacting with other groups due to the new environment. The ethnic issue today becomes even more challenging and difficult. This frequent interaction with different minority groups has created higher mobility within the groups.

Christian workers in cities should not forget that the ethnicities they work with incessantly interact with other ethnic groups. Missionaries who do not discern the differences that have existed and still exist among the ethnicities are prone to be blinded by the elements that can cause ineffectiveness in the ministry.

TYPES OF ETHNIC CONFLICTS

Since city is composed of ethnicities, to understand city, we must understand the conflict and competition that exist between ethnicities. It is easy to predict conflict and competition among them when two ethnicities live in the same place called city. Mission to the ethnicities without understanding the background may cause a dangerous result. Ethnic conflict is any expression of hostile intention against other ethnicities, which begins with simple sentiments that become diversified actions and social structures, which unveils the expressions.[10] We can categorize the types of ethnic conflicts into at least four kinds by categorizing them through involved ethnic parties and expressions. First is the most common type, which is the conflict between the majority group and a minority group. Generally, the group that has the greater number, the majority, becomes the dominant group, while minorities become marginal groups.

However, the dominant ethnicity is not always decided by its numerical factor, but through those that occupy a dominant position. In some rare cases, the minority ethnicity rules majority and monopolizes the resources. This phenomenon, in which the majority possesses a small part of the resources, can create a huge ethnic gulf between the rich and poor both politically and economically. On the other hand, when the large numbered majority with the higher degree of dominance seeks to possess the minority's rights and resources, the minority builds up unity within the group and dissatisfaction of the majority group due to the victim mentality.

The second conflict type is the conflict between the majority group and multi numbered minority groups. This occurs when minorities think that the majority group, which possesses national power, appoints unfair policies on other minority groups. In this case, all minorities would come against the majority as their common opponent, while keeping unity and cooperation within minority themselves. For example, even though the Uighur in China, descents of Turkish, and Hui, mainly Eastern Asians, are ethnically different, they have been voicing out similar concerns toward Han, the ethnic majority, and their government as they find commonality as ethnic minorities and as Muslims.

The third type of ethnic conflict is the case that happens in between the majority and minority that is supported by foreign forces. This is the case where minority group is supported by the foreign power opposing the majority group. A good example is the Uyghur Muslims in China, who seem to have tacit support from pan-Turkish nations and Islamic countries to fight against the Chinese government.

The fourth type of conflict happens among minorities. Ethnic minorities within the same country may create conflict. The cause of the problem arises from the relationship between minorities, rather than from the majority or government. For example, there may be some religious conflicts

10. Yang, *Ethnic Studies*, 189–90.

between the ethnic minorities. The original group may feel threatened by the new ethnic group weakening their niche, or by rapidly increased interactions as new residents infiltrate into the original group's place, causing many cultural, politico-economic problems.

In many cases, ethnic conflicts are ignited by many complex reasons. They usually do not happen over a single day, but reasons for conflict have been formed over the course of their long history.[11] Furthermore, the reasons that cause conflicts are more complex today. Modernization, urbanization, secularization, media revolution, and other factors contribute to the rapid changes of governmental policies, socio-political situations, culture, and traditions, creating many complex variables to ethnic relationships.

LEVELS OF ETHNIC CONFLICTS

Ethnic conflicts can be categorized into three different levels in its aggressiveness: nonviolent, hostile and violent.[12] Nonviolent confrontation refers to hostile expressions and actions done to other ethnicities without violence. For example, boycotting a certain item that relates to a certain ethnic group, or peacefully resisting showing opposition by marching falls in this category. Hostile expression is expressing hostile sentiments through verbal, written, or symbolic form of expressions. Wallpaper, graffiti, rumor, gossip, and all kinds of abasement are included. Violent confrontation refers to violent actions such as lynching or rioting against members of the ethnic group. Though this may not be a large-scale violence, such attacks on the ethnic group destroy their symbols, institutions, or individuals, and cause fear and damage.

For conflicts between ethnicities to be emerged to the surface level, there is a process that accumulates recognition, sentiments, and expressions against others as each ethnicity passes through different stages. This process begins with an ethnic centered view, which exists within each ethnicity. Such view naturally develops into ethnic prejudice and is further expressed as ethnic discrimination. If this advances further, it could develop racism that is systematically expressed and acted out by an organization. Now, we will step by step examine the concept and content of the ethnic centered view, which is the beginning of the ethnic conflict, to racism, which is the worst possible form of the conflict.

11. Ibid., 202.
12. Ibid.

Ethnocentric View

Ethnocentric View is a conscience but unconscious concept that argues that one's own culture and society is the more effective and advanced.[13] All ethnicities view themselves and other ethnicities through the lens that the ethnicities have formed for a long time. When the ethnocentric view works in healthy way, it can enhance an ethnicity's self-esteem and create a legacy of its unique culture. On the other hand, if they apply this view in distortive ways, it becomes ethnocentrism, a starting step of bias and discrimination to others. This causes them to consider their own cultural symbols, signs, social systems, relationship, and worldview as superior to those of other groups.

All of humankind are comfortable with their own cultural values, attitude, thoughts, and behavioral patterns, and believe that whatever is natural for them is better or even superior to other groups. Therefore, it is easy to develop prejudice and bias against other cultural zones.[14] Most people have such ethnocentric view, because it is difficult, and even almost impossible to overcome their own views and cultures.[15]

Ethnic Prejudice

Ethnocentric view can develop into ethnic prejudice against other ethnicities. Most of the time, ethnic prejudice is used as a negative term to discriminate other ethnicities.[16] Once people develop ethnic prejudice, they repeatedly view and believe other ethnicities as lazier, less hygienic, slower, less punctual, less trustworthy, less educated, and less able to promote socially. If this idea becomes universal, it creates stereotypes amongst people. As a result, the ethnicity that is viewed with ethnic prejudice continually loses the opportunity and environment to grow their power and establish social positions. Furthermore, the ethnicity becomes weak, and structurally remains as a low class throughout generations due to the stereotypical image of the ethnicity in society.[17]

13. Ferraro, *Cultural Anthropology*, 23; Ember, *Cultural Anthropology*, 15.
14. Andrew, "The Geography of Ethnocentrism."
15. Heydari et al., "Influential Factors on Ethnocentrism."
16. Wagner et al., "Prejudice and Minority Proportion."
17. Yang, *Ethnic Studies*, 116–17.

Ethnic Discrimination

The stereotypes created from ethnic prejudice can go further and become ethnic discrimination. Ethnic discrimination is defined as unequal or unfair treatment of individuals on the basis of their ethnic membership.[18] It often refers to negative actions taken by members of dominant groups toward minority groups.[19] If ethnic prejudice is considered as peoples' thoughts and attitudes, ethnic discrimination is the terminology that highlights people's systematic actions and behaviors. In an extreme case, the government implements disadvantageous policies toward a certain ethnic group.[20] The persecution of Jews under the Nazi rule with political reasons is a good example of this. Apart from these kinds of discriminations driven by government, it is easy to find a similar phenomenon when there are two or more ethnicities.

In general, ethnic discrimination is discrimination by a majority group against a minority group by creating unequal policy. However, as we take a closer look, there is also discrimination between different minority groups and even discrimination from the minority group against the majority group. Therefore, ethnic discrimination is unequal or unfair treatment and systematic action[21] among any ethnicities and by any ethnicities.

Racism

Intensified ethnic discrimination may develop as racism. Racism may even be a form of discrimination. Racism is more than personal beliefs or some action of a group, but rather it is more holistic and systematic. Racism can be expressed in the following four shapes. First, it is ideological racism, which is a belief system stating that a certain racial group is biologically, intellectually, or culturally inferior or superior to another. Second, it is attitudinal racism or racial prejudice stating that a racial group and its members are based on faulty or inadequate information. Third, it is behavioral racism, or racial discrimination, which refers to discriminatory actions, taken by individuals and groups. Fourth, it is institutional racism that refers

18. Healey, *Race, Ethnicity, Gender, and Class.*
19. Feagin and Feagin, *Racial and Ethnic Relations,* 15.
20. Lefranc, "Unequal Opportunities and Ethnic Origin."
21. Levin and Levin, *The Functions of Discrimination and Prejudice.*

to law, policies, or practices of social institutions and organizations, which favor one racial group over another.[22]

Institutional racism transforms the whole society into a discriminatory system. People become more racist in their thinking and act as they become exposed to such discriminating environment that exists throughout society. Thus, institutional dimension, combined with the other three shapes, accelerates racism. As we consider these four dimensions, racism cannot be overcome just by changing the thoughts and actions of individuals.

As of now, we have studied five developmental stages of ethnic conflict process—Ethnocentrism, ethnic stratification, ethnic prejudice, ethnic discrimination, and racism. The process does not always develop sequentially. Depending on the society, conflicts may happen in the middle of another stage, or a social situation may stimulate the process and jump from the middle to an edge state of the sequence. In order to diagnose or find resolutions of the interethnic dynamics, we must not oversimplify the problem and our way of approaching the problem. These kinds of ethnic issues arise from various problems, requiring assistance different people from different dimensions. Some problems can be resolved through individual relationships, while some need an organizational approach. Others that are quite institutional and are deeply rooted in their history and culture may need governmental policies and campaigns to be involved.

Churches also need to put an effort in resolving the ethnic stratification. For example, churches can emphasize on reconciliation and forgiveness with other ethnicities in their programs and bible studies. At the same time, church members need to be encouraged to perform activities and programs with other people groups, without compromising the effectiveness of the program.

When church only seeks individual sanctification and has no interest in ethnic issues, that means that the church believes that such individual sanctification resolves all of these ethnic problems. However, personal effort has many limitations in resolving the ethnic conflicts, unless the social structure and organization's policies change along with it. Of course, church must continue to encourage individual sanctification, as well as educating its members to love and get along with other ethnicities. At the same time, church also needs to speak up and inquire organizations and governments to change ethnic policies and law to prevent deteriorating ethnic relationships.

22. Farley, *Majority-Minority Relations.*

TYPES OF ETHNIC CONFLICT
IN NON-WESTERN WORLD

Until recently, ethnic conflict researches have been mostly based on America's ethnic minorities, especially between African Americans and White Americans. Unfortunately, their situation is quite far from the context of the ethnic issues in the non-Western world. Especially, missionaries in the non-Western world quite often experience such ethnic conflicts described above. What missionaries experience in the mission fields are quite more complex than the three expressions of ethnic conflicts: nonviolent, hostile expression, and violent. Recently, most ethnic minorities that immigrate to developed countries come by their own will. Unlike those who are in the U.S., ethnic minorities in mission fields had to migrate against their own will due to many reasons, rather than voluntary immigration. These situations may include occupation of country by strong forces, war, or by economic reasons. Here are several types of ethnic conflicts that can occur in mission fields.

For developing mission strategies in the cities in the non-Western, identifying the elements of ethnic conflicts that appear to be stronger in non-Western context is important. There are at least five common types of ethnic conflict in non-Western areas. Since many mission fields are located in non-Western world, the following can be understood as the factors of ethnic conflict in the mission field city context.

The first is the case of an ethnicity, which has been deprived of its territory or dynasty it once had. For example, Tibetans in China, Mongolians, and Uyghur once had their own territories and governing systems, which were ruled by strong dynasties or tribes.[23] Today, their territories are owned by China, but they still yearn for the restorations of their land and independence of their nations at any cost. Therefore, anger toward the majority group and minority group's desire for independence increase. This is especially true if the land has much of natural resources or has many majority group members who have moved into their traditional land, which becomes a threat to the economics and politics. In such case, the ethnic conflict and sense of deprivation intensify.[24]

Second, if a group has a richer ethnic heritage and a sophisticated cultural system, ethnic conflicts strengthen and become stronger. For instance, when group has its own language and history or has developed a

---

23. Heberer, *China and Its National Minorities*, 130.
24. Mackerras, *China's Minority Cultures*, 221.

strong social organization within the group, the group would apply to this case. Especially, if the ethnic economy is strong, systematic resistance in the case of ethnic conflicts becomes possible.

Third, a nation's systematic ethnic discriminatory policies can ignite ethnic conflicts. This becomes especially true when the ruler or government of a nation that represents a certain ethnic group explicitly persecute another group, which causes the subjugated group to collide for survival. The ethnic cleansing in Rwanda in 1994 shows a typical example. The political balance in Rwanda was maintained when Tutsi group occupied only 14 percent of representation, while the Hutus occupied 85 percent. However, in 1994 when the president was assassinated, those in power began the ethnic cleansing of the other. As the new revolutionary army acknowledged the threat, it also began the ethnic cleansing, and this caused the subjugate group to execute a counter ethnic cleansing for self-survival.[25]

Fourth, even though a once-colonialized nation is now independent, the unresolved policies passed down from the colonizing government can induce ethnic disorder. In the Rwanda example above, Belgium, the once governing country provided the original reason for ethnic conflict. When Belgium ruled Rwanda, it traditionally controlled the country through kings whose backgrounds were Tutsi, who were minorities. Such control strategy caused great dissatisfaction from the majority, and once Rwanda achieved independence, the once neglected balance of power caused tragic massacres between the Hutus and Tutsis.[26]

Fifth, rapid industrialization, urbanization, and welfare policies of non-Western countries can create ethnic conflict. As people enthusiastically pursue modernization and commercialization, every ethnicity have more interactions with other groups in schools, workplaces, and business districts in cities. The segregated groups that once had to keep autonomous governing systems now must follow the national laws and economical policies with other ethnic groups. Furthermore, their residence is not traditionally divided by ethnicities but transformed by the individuals' economic level. This means that individuals in modernized traditional countries have no choice but to have larger and deeper contact with other ethnic group members in various areas of life. As a result, the expanded contact opportunities cause many unprepared ethnicities to conflict with other groups in

25. White, "Scourge of Racism: Genocide in Rwanda."
26. Ibid.

the mission fields.[27] Meanwhile, the urbanization and industrialization led by nation can be seen as threats to ethnic minorities, because minorities feel that they can lose their identities by those new waves.[28]

Ironically modern national systems and their welfare policies can create ethnic conflicts. Due to welfare system, ethnicities that were once politically weak are now strengthened and even are able to express their opinions with big voice. Consequently, ethnicities that had no interest in mutual benefit or even simple relationships begin to have new relationships in many mission fields.

Until now, we have studied five major factors of ethnic division on non-Western countries in order to understand the dynamics of division in the mission field. The theory of ethnic change, derived mostly from developed countries, also has these factors, but the five factors can be more seriously affected as we explain the division in a non-Western context. Missionaries should refer to the theories developed in the West, but they must not overlook the unique characteristics of their own mission field.

CHAPTER PATHFINDER

The previous chapters provided a perspective of city as a place formed by people and society, and explained the people experience several steps to settle in the new city. As the third face of city, this chapter highlights the aspect that city is a society made up of ethnicities. We have learned about the types of ethnic competitions and conflicts in the city.

Understanding the conflicts and competition among ethnicities greatly influences the development of the mission strategy for the city. For this, we have examined how ethnicities can have bias and negative sentiments toward other ethnicities, and also the phenomena resulted by greater influence of these sentiments that exceed the individual level and that are applied in law and social system. Lastly, we have studied the characteristics of ethnic conflicts in a non-Western environment.

27. Weidmann, "Geography as Motivation and Opportunity."
28. Gillette, *Between Mecca and Beijing* 233.

IMPLICATION TO URBAN MISSION

The modern city is made up of various kinds of ethnicities. Moreover, these ethnicities continue to have competition, conflict, and also create a third culture through integration. With what kind of attitude should God's workers serve within urban ethnicities that grow in such complexity?

When missionaries from outside of the city share the gospel to an unreached ethnic group, which area should they be sensitive to in the relationship between ethnicities? Or, in a case of sending a missionary to another ethnicity within the same city, what considerations should the leaders have? What kind of considerations should be taken before planting a multi-ethnic church within a multi-ethnic cosmopolitan city? What can a modern church teach to the congregation about living with other ethnicities? As we close this chapter, some of the thoughts to these questions will be recapitulated.

Understanding the Ethnic Relationship

When missionaries first arrive in a new mission field, it is necessary for them to study the historic background and relationship between ethnicities there. The ethnic conflicts and competitions among them could have taken thousands of years to develop. Moreover, their sense of stratification formed between ethnicities must also be examined. Missionaries must be able to show culturally and biblically appropriate attitudes toward relational dynamics existing between ethnicities.

The Chinese church I led had a group of Muslim background believers. At first, the church happily accepted them as newcomers, but as time went by, various conflicts arose between the Muslim background believers and Han people. The Muslims had a difficult time with Han food and could not go near it even though it had been long since their conversion. This was because Han food often had pork in it. As the number of Han Christians increased, the Muslim background believers were left out from important decision-making processes in the church. Later, when I was removed from the church ministry, the new group faded away from the church. This is a sad example that shows what could happen when mainstream society members fail to care for ethnic minority groups or understand the minority culture.

Missionaries must be aware of the social stratification formed within the ethnicity they minister as well. Even members of the same ethnicity may have a difficult time getting along if different social strata exist within the Christian congregation. When I first began a student mission organization, there were students who were not willing to be in the same group though they were all from the same ethnicity.

At school, there were two different groups—a group admitted through a formal admission process, and another group admitted through the school without the permission of the Department of Education, also known as *zi kao sheng* (自考生). The two groups displayed their proficiency and people's expectations. In addition, there existed class differences and biases, and the students did not want to be with one another.

It is definitely biblical and true that there are no high or low class ethnicities or individuals in the Lord (Gal 3:28). Therefore, it may not be biblical if missionaries accept the existing social structure without critique. At the same time, missionaries must not rush to deal with biases and stratifications among the locals, because those were formed over a long history. Forced attempts can block communication channels between church and the community, and can hinder the missionary's ministry for the long-term side. Therefore, missionaries should remember not to simply agree with the ethnic biases and unequal stratification among the locals, but maintain the perspective of the third person.

However, as a long-term goal, missionaries must continue to minister to all people and share the truth by overcoming ethnic difference and stratification to treat all people equally in the Lord as brothers and sisters (John 1:12–13) (NIV). Moreover, they should encourage the local church leaders to solve this longstanding problem by creating a multi-ethnic community by their own method. If they only think about the social aspect and do not attempt to overcome the ethnic barriers, the church will fall into the trap of relativism.

Urban Church with Ethnic Conflict

Churches today interact with different ethnicities more than ever. Therefore, churches must learn to live together with different ethnicities in harmony and also to care for them. The world may endlessly burrow into ethnocentrism and racism deeper, but churches must be able to speak up and say 'stop!' to the ethnic conflict that stems from human sin and our egocentric nature.

In big cities, not only multi-ethnic but also ethnic minority churches continuously come in contact with other ethnicities. Thus, it is important to educate the church to have a biblical attitude toward other ethnicities. Even small things, such as serving those from a weak ethnicity who come to bible study to help them feel the dignity they have never experienced in the world is meaningful. Not only this, urban churches must continue to pay attention to ethnic minority churches or other ethnic churches that are weak. Urban churches may volunteer to serve weaker churches through programs and events. Furthermore, urban churches may even be involved in raising leaders of minority ethnic churches. Some denominations have many ethnic minority churches within the same city. It is also important to develop a strategy for serving dependent ethnic minority churches that are within the same denomination or neighborhood.

4

City, a Place Where Ethnicites Are Assimilated

THE PREVIOUS CHAPTERS INTRODUCED the three faces of city: society of people, a new home for migrants, and a place for ethnic conflicts and changes. The fourth face that the readers will be introduced in this chapter is that the city is a place where ethnicities choose between cultural assimilation and continuation. This study is also valuable because expecting whether ethnicities will assimilate or continue their original culture can give crucial information in setting mission strategies. To understand such issues, this chapter will cover sociological theories such as the Assimilation Theory, and the Determinism that attests change, and the Compositionalism that attests continuation.

A CASE: MISS MA

While we lived in Beijing as missionaries, from time to time my wife and I received Chinese language tutoring from Miss Ma, a Muslim student who attended the same school. As an ethnic minority, she grew up in an ethnic village where an ethnically homogenous group lived together. Moreover, she learned to have a strong sense of rivalry and defensive attitude toward Chinese majority ethnic groups, from the people in her village. She came to Beijing in her adulthood and showed hostility toward other ethnic groups and expressed much pride for her own group even while having a conversation with us. Often times, she would teach us about the food culture in a Muslim restaurant and said, "The Han Chinese are not clean, and we cannot dine with them."

As we continued our discussion, I had two conflicting images in my head. Miss Ma would express defensiveness to other minority groups and pride over her own ethnicity, and yet I also felt that in reality she admires the urban culture and the mainline society. In Beijing, she had many good friends who were Han Chinese. She was very different from a typical Hui, who has many negative sentiments toward other ethnic groups. She was virtually the only one studying in Beijing from her hometown. Moreover, she detested going back to her hometown. It was her dream to stay in a big city, like Beijing or Tianjin, and work for a company or the government. This would mean that she would have to interact with different ethnic groups daily and accept the mainline society. In retrospect, I think that she had a pride for her own ethnicity in her mind, but preferred the majority's pattern in reality.

The story of Miss Ma is not just hers, but also a story of many Chinese ethnic minorities who moved to cities. In other words, many immigrants slowly accept the urban culture without knowing, as they settle down in a city. Furthermore, such phenomena of assimilation and ethnic identity change not only happen in China, but in all local cities as well as in major international cities of the world. Today, the globalization is causing the interethnic interaction to be more active than ever. When people immigrate or migrate to cities, they bring their traditional ethnic identities with them. As they interact with many ethnic minorities in a new city, their identities may be maintained or challenged. Whether it is different Asian ethnic groups in LA, or different ethnic groups in Thailand who immigrated to Bangkok, they all may maintain or lose their own cultural inheritance that are so precious to them.

In many cases, when one moves to a more developed society than the one's original society, one will easily accept the new social system and culture. Consequently, cultural assimilation phenomenon occurs everywhere. Especially in the case of immigrants in developed countries, ethnic groups put much effort in learning new languages and social systems of the developed countries they immigrated to. Such assimilation becomes an important element in understanding the urban ethnic groups and in establishing mission strategy.

In this chapter we will examine the cultural assimilation phenomenon between the ethnicities. Additionally, we will examine the changing and continuing factors to ethnic boundaries. This research can provide important information and perspectives in formulating the mission strategy for ethnic minorities. There are already many studies done by secular scholars in this area that provide meaningful data to our study. However, we should not forget the biblical criteria in the process of the research, because the criteria provide us a guideline what data we can adapt and what we should not.

ASSIMILATION OF ETHNIC MINORITY

The interaction between two ethnicities sharing an ethnic boundary increases as time passes. If both ethnic groups have unequal forces of power have frequent interactions with each other, or one of the group forces its influences compulsorily on to the other, there will gradually be cultural assimilation.

Assimilation refers to the phenomenon, which occurs when an ethnic minority interacts with another ethnic group or the majority group, learns the ethnic majority's culture and identity and then slowly becomes one of them.[1]

Assimilation is a concept that was better developed from the study of a change phenomenon development, in which immigrants in America began making contact with the mainstream society. R. Park is an early scholar that conceptualized the assimilation process. He claimed that immigrants would contact society through the 'race relations cycle' through four stages—contact, competition, accommodation, and assimilation.[2] This assimilation is often interchanged with accommodation but it is more appropriate to understand assimilation as the outcome, which happens after accommodation.[3]

So far, many sociologists have researched assimilation in order to predict the future of an ethic group. Currently, many assimilation process researches have been studied with ethnic groups within developed nations such as the US.[4] Therefore, it is unreasonable to instantly apply the assimilation theory that has been developed in Western culture to non-western

---

1. Gordon, *Assimilation in American Life*.

2. Park, *Race and Culture*.

3. Hill and Turner, *Dictionary of Sociology*, 1; Spradley and McCurdy, *Anthropology, the Cultural Perspective*, 17–22, 179–84; Conn and Ortiz, *Urban Ministry*, 321.

4. Most of immigrants in America are considered as minorities. Since we will use many theories that have been developed in America, the terminologies in this section will use both of minority and immigrants.

culture right away.[5] Nevertheless, to understand the assimilation phenomenon of the urban ethnicities in the mission field, though situation may differ, it is valuable to study the assimilation research in developed nations.

Assimilation

As time passes, immigrants learn the city's orders and further absorb the city's culture. Immigrants to developed countries or migrants in major cities often voluntarily pay high prices to settle there. Their adoration of the new city's culture further leads desire for their children to succeed in the new culture. As a result, we can see the rapid cultural assimilation phenomenon in these places.[6] Andrew M. Greeley's Anglo Conformity Perspectives Model introduces typical assimilation phenomenon.[7]

The Assimilation phenomenon in Greeley's conceptual model is mainly about immigrants in America. As the name, Anglo-conformity perspective/Assimilation Theory model, shows, the immigrant minority is absorbed by the host group, the Anglo culture, and takes on the Anglo values and patterns as time passes.[8] Likewise, the ethnic minorities gradually lose their identity and finally accept the host culture through the assimilation process.[9]

Then what specific steps do assimilation pass in order to form the process? Generally, assimilation is expressed as a process. A process refers to a form those progresses step by step in one direction.[10]

A representative theory that studies assimilation as a process is Daniel Glaser's introduced assimilation process and identity change, which is

5. Alba and Nee, "Remaking the American Mainstream Assimilation and Contemporary Immigration."

6. The receptivity and communicational satisfaction contributes major role in South-/South-east Asian origin immigrants for their accepting the life and culture in Hong Kong. Chen and Feng, "Host Environment, Host Communication, and Satisfaction with Life."

7. Greeley, *Ethnicity in the United States*, 304.

8. Park, *The Race Relationship*; Gordon, *Assimilation in American Life*.

9. Crandall and Eshleman, "A Justification-Suppression Model of the Expression and Experience of Prejudice"; Sidanius and Pratto, *Social Dominance*.

10. Glaser, "Dynamics of Ethnic Identification"; Greeley, *Why Can't They Be Like Us? America's White Ethnic Groups*; Parham and Helms, "Relation of Racial Identity Attitudes to Self-Actualization and Affective States of Black Students."

consisted of four steps.[11] Glaser developed this model based on the process of the migrants' immigration in US.

The first step of the ethnic change is segregation. The first generation of immigrants spends the most time separating them from the outer culture. They mostly depend on and relate themselves with the people from the same origin. Although they have lived in the new place for a long time, they still maintain the worldview of their origin and ethnocentric view of their ethnic enclaves as they evaluate the new world. People who are in this segregation stage avoid contact with people from the mainstream society, insulating and segregating themselves in their own society, making a safe zone.

The second stage is the marginal stage. New immigrants slowly adjust their lives to the new world with much uncertainty. They then gradually begin the assimilation process and naturally expand their contact with the mainstream communities, which can either be pleasant or offensive. As marginal people, immigrants who go through such process become confused about their social identity.

The third stage is desegregation. Immigrants in this stage intentionally avoid parts or their whole ethnic identity and make effort to assimilate into the new culture. In general, by this point, their attitudes toward their original background become negative. They hanker after the majority culture, and they do everything to become a member of the mainstream society.

The fourth stage is the assimilation. During this stage, the immigrants are accepted by the mainstream society and it becomes hard to find their original identity in daily lives. Daniel Glaser introduces an assimilation process table with four steps: segregation, marginal, desegregating, and assimilated.[12] Glaser's model is meaningful in a way where each step shows its own uniqueness in ethnic ideology, associated preferences, emotions, and other dimensions. According to Glaser, very few people will get to this stage.

On the other hand, this four step process can be seen as an attempt to oversimplify the complicated lives of immigrants. Generally, an ethnic group must live in the newly migrated district for several generations in order to take off the original ethnic identity and put on the new identity. Thus, a person may spend his or her entire life in assimilation, but the assimilation process is too long to experience as a whole. Furthermore, we must remember that the assimilation process is not an issue for one or two persons. The process of assimilation can differ greatly depending on the

11. Glaser, "Dynamics of Ethnic Identification."
12. Reminick, *Theory of Ethnicity*, 30.

individual and location. Not only that, we must also remember that the assimilation process can have variables between individuals, in the ethnicity as a whole, and also between the host and original countries.

As we examine the assimilation process, we must not only pay attention to the direction but also the speed of the assimilation process. The speed of the assimilation process is determined by various elements. One of them is the phenomenon of migrants creating the third culture. When the number of migrants increases, they will set up their own organizations and leaders within the new city. This creates the third culture and structure between the traditional culture and new city's culture. This third culture and structure plays the role of a safety zone that diminishes the burden of having to one-sidedly absorb the new city's culture. This third culture also affects the assimilation process in a complicated way. The leadership, organization, institution, and structure of the third culture zone affect the direction and speed of assimilation.

Second, the history and emotions the ethnic group carried originally also affect the speed of assimilation process. If the ethnic group strongly carries a hostile relationship with the majority group or had been isolated and had developed its culture for a long time, the assimilation process will be very slow even in the city.

Thirdly, the city and country's policies and institutions also affect the city's ethnic minority's assimilation speed. If the newly migrated urbanites prefer the city, culture, and country structure more than their original ones, they will voluntarily participate in the assimilation process.

Likewise, we must remember to study an ethnic group over a long period of time in order to understand the assimilation process, and that there are various multi-dimensional elements that affect the speed in the process.

There are process types similar to the Glaser model. For example, Andrew Greeley produced a six-step model that considers more various elements than Glaser's.[13] Also, Helms and her associates produced a spiral form model that conceptualizes the assimilation process in steps. In contrast to Greeley and Glaser's linear process models, Helms and her associates described this cultural assimilation by progressively using the screw shape. The name of the model is the racial-ethnic identity developmental model, and Helms and her associates said immigrants pass through four

---

13. Greeley, *Why Can't They Be Like Us?*, chap. 5.

stages: pre-encounter, encounter, immersion-emersion, and international-ization for assimilation.[14]

Couple of models we have seen so far have similarities in two areas: they divide the whole process into several stages and premise that minorities will stabilize as so-called true Americans at last. This kind of model well expresses the general assimilation process. However, there are two areas that need to be reflected upon as we apply these theories in the mission field. First, we must understand how these theories are based on the conditions of the U.S. Second, the fact that even within the U.S., the speed of assimilation may differ depending on the ethnic group, while some may even relocate to the opposite direction.

Such models that express the assimilation process as one-sided will face many unforeseen accidents in reality not only on the mission field, but even in American society. It is because not all minority groups are assimilated in just one way. For example, especially Europeans, whose culture is similar to that of America, could assimilate into the American society very quickly. On the other hand, Hispanics or Asians show slow or even stagnated assimilation speed, and even revive in their ethnical identity as their numbers grow rather than be absorbed into the American culture.

Melting Pot Theory Being Challenged

For a long time, there have been many attempts in sociology to explain the ethnic minorities' transformations with the metaphor of a melting pot. The melting pot theory states that as the government spreads its national policies to all the individuals, the lives of minorities will also transform into the common worldview and life patterns that the authority leads them into.

The melting pot theory originally symbolized the American dream.[15] The main idea of the melting pot theory is that ethnic minorities will melt to form a common culture. This model looks similar to the assimilation, but there is a difference. The biggest difference is that it calls various ethnic groups and melts them to create a common culture. However, assimilation promotes only one direction to the host culture, whereas the melting pot

14. Cross, *The Negro to Black Conversion Experience*, 13–27; *Shades of Black*; Helms, *Black and White Racial Identity*; Parham and Helms, "Relation of Racial Identity Attitudes to Self-Actualization and Affective States of Black Students."

15. The term was first coined as Israel Zangwill's 1908 Broadway drama title with a love story between a Russian Jewish and Cossack.

theory argues that the host culture is not already set but will endlessly go through changes.[16]

Can the melting pot phenomenon happen in the mission field? Some areas, because of the lack of diversity or the strict uniformity in national policy, may hardly have ethnic diversity. On the other hand, there are cases where the government's power and administration are not enough to influence the ethnicities, and they naturally become widely diversified. Some mission fields force various minorities in one political order and social common code due to the lack of energy to consider every group and its situation. This becomes more like a melting pot. For example, the Chinese government provides ethnic schools in the traditional minority villages in order to give preference to them. However, parents complain about the inferior quality of education and the lack of economic support for such ethnic schools compared to those of public education systems. Furthermore, ethnic schools can cover only up to elementary school in most places, and in order to attend a university, ethnic minorities must take an exam in the common language, Mandarin. Therefore, though it may have begun with diversity, as the education goes on to high school level, diversity is not maintained or it is led toward one method. This is because in order to receive education higher than the high school level, all minorities must receive a professional education in the language of the Han culture. As a result, schools do not form the diversity of ethnic minority groups, but turn them into the general Chinese population, which is a process that forms ethnicities into citizens who are able to understand at least the minimum of the standardized policy. This can be seen as a representative example of inducing the melting pot phenomenon through a nation's powerful standardization policy.

For a while, this melting pot theory was in the spotlight as a very persuasive theory explaining the modern city.[17] However, as social studies have developed and as nations created modern governmental policies regarding ethnicities, scholars have found the issues of ethnic changing uneasy to explain with simple theories. As they live in modern nations, scholars came to understand how ethnicities are stratified, intensifying their identity, and diverse and distinct rather than unified as the melting pot theory claims. For a while after the melting pot theory was introduced, scholars became skeptical of the theory and expressed this new idea using words beyond the

16. Greeley, *Ethnicity in the United States*, 305.
17. Devos and Banaji, "American = White?"

melting pot.[18] Because in reality, though there are some factors that easily melt, there are still many unchangeable factors in the ethnic identity.

Scholars have now found that the ethnic commonness does not increase much over time and the government-driven cultural influences will also not be imposed on ethnic identities as broadly as they had believed.[19] Furthermore, the scholars have found that there are many resources and abilities for maintaining identities in each of the ethnicities.[20] Therefore, the new social atmosphere and diversity in modern states prevents ethnicities from simply melting.

WILL THEY CHANGE OR CONTINUE?

We have seen the Assimilation Theory that centers on the Melting Pot Model and noted that there are several points to be aware before understanding the urban city's ethnic group issues in one way. It is important to predict how the ethnic groups will change from a missionary's perspective.

When we take a closer look at ethnic groups in cities, groups have cultural assimilation in one situation, but also reinforced cultural identity. For example, if one's home country is in an embarrassing situation, falling behind economically, or experiencing political conflicts, one will deny the original identity and assimilate into the new culture quickly. On the contrary, if one's home country becomes very strong, receives compliments, and expects a bright future, people regain their ethnic pride and want to revive their identities. Ethnic groups also show different complexion depending on whether the new place is less developed or more developed compared to their home country. When immigrants move to a place that is superior to their home country, the motivation to keep their own culture weakens.

If so, do ethnic groups in cities really assimilate or continue? There have been two contentious arguments amongst sociologists: the argument that ethnicity is completely destroyed and absorbed or that it is continuously maintained.

Especially, in order to understand the urban interethnic dynamics in the non-Western places, it is important to carefully research how the ethnicities interact. As mentioned earlier, when two ethnicities interact, a

18. Glazer and Moynihan are representative scholars in this area. Glazer and Moynihan, *Beyond the Melting Pot*, v.

19. Hartmann and Gerteis, "Dealing with Diversity," 227.

20. Lewis, "Urbanization without Breakdown a Case Study."

cultural adaptation phenomenon easily happens. To understand this phenomenon of ethnicities' cultural adaptation in the city, we must study how the traditional community reacts from the external influences first.[21]

In urban sociology, there are two theories worth examining for this issue: Determinism, which states that urban ethnicities will change and will completely be absorbed into the common culture, and Compositionalism, which states that ethnicity remains the same without changing. Both arguments have their own persuasive evidence based on theoretical and site research of their own. Also, these conflicting phenomena are actually happening this very moment amongst our surrounding urban ethnic groups.[22]

They Will Be Changed: Determinism

There is a perspective in which the city's radical growth brings isolation to individuals and society, which destroys traditional culture, allowing people to be absorbed into the city's common culture. This perspective is called Determinism. Determinism states that this it is necessary for people, but also has functions of destroying humanity and human relationships.[23] The term 'determinism' is used in various ways in sociology. This word is mostly used in describing a phenomenon where individual freedom or characteristics are either decreased or limited due to a certain social structure. In urban sociology, determinism is used in describing a phenomenon where many groups, especially the immigrant ethnic minorities, lose their ethnic characters due to the massive structure called city.[24] Claude S. Fischer uses an urban sociological view of determinism as the following,

> Determinist theory (also called Wirthian theory or the theory of urban anomie) argues that urbanism (i.e., population concentration) directly alters people's social lives and personalities, mostly for the worse.[25]

21. Michael, "The Political Economy of Ethnic Change."

22. Many ideas of sociological approach that are summarized from the next part are derived from Fischer. Fischer, *The Urban Experience*, 28–41.

23. The Chicago School had developed this determinism. They stated that cities develop people intellectually and technically but due to individualism and yearning for freedom, cities may also increase solitude and disconnect the relationships in peoples' mentalities and lives. Sennett, *Classic Essays on the Culture of Cities*.

24. Abercrombie, Hill, and Turner, "Dictionary of Sociology," 105.

25. Fischer, *The Urban Experience*, 25.

The Determinist theory began when Robert Ezra Park first introduced its concept in his paper "The City: Suggestions for Investigation of Human Behavior in the Urban Environment."[26] Wirth also stated that urbanism produces social disorganization and personality disorders (being alone, suffering physical deterioration).[27]

Ethnic groups gradually forget traditional cultures in urban cities. In the busy lives, people prefer the future to traditions and modern technology over the ethnicity's inheritance. Also, individuals must follow the lines of public order and structure accustomed to mass production in the city. That is why in the city, individual lives become smaller, and ethnic traditions diminish even more.

We often too easily put negative connotations with cities because of pollution, complexity, impersonality, and competition. When comparing the city to the suburbs, the negative sides of the city are even more emphasized. We often feel excluded from the city especially due to its rapid development and institutions that treat people like products in bulks. This kind of negative perspective of the city also had its dominant times within the urban studies academia.

When immigrants move to a city, they often move from traditional kin and friends, and work in an anonymous society. As a result, urbanites tend to live away from the native society made with affection and love, and enter a functional society individuals are isolated and live in loneliness. Determinists describe such phenomenon as depersonalization and isolation of city life.

Determinists believe that urbanization brings the anomy phenomena, depersonalization, and isolation.[28] With this anomy effect, the determinist theory studies urbanites' psychological issues as well. Determinists believe that weakened social cohesion and loneliness create high psychological stress for urbanites.

In some cases, cultural assimilation frees individuals from the yoke of long traditions. The newly begun city life grants freedom to the tightened community centered life formed from old customs. This motivates urbanites to improve themselves and rise in status.

Determinism argues that ethnicities in city would lose their ethnic identity. Because they believe those ethnic groups and various groups lose

26. Park, "The City."

27. Wirth, "Urbanism as a Way of Life," 1.

28. Roberts reports a good example of this disorganization, disorders, and anonymity of city. Roberts, *Organizing Strangers*, 11.

their traditions and the city uses its great power to assimilate them to the common culture. As the urban ethnicities and urbanites become over-individualized, they lose the traditionally held sense of a community, thus losing their support groups. As a result, urbanites lose their power to overcome pressures from the life in the city. Moreover, they also lose the traditional relationships that can help them emotionally when they become weak and old. For example, a representative determinism scholar, Louis Wirth states that the complexity and professionalism of a city life complicates personal relationships and weakens the wide cohesion of the community. Louis Wirth's "urbanism as a way of life" is a pioneering article in this area.[29]

Determinists believe that the urban ethnic boundary is getting weak because the ethnicity's cohesiveness is deteriorating. The boundary is even weakened when it exposes to the industrial society.[30] Determinists claim that the reason for the ethnic structure collapse is because of its interaction with modern politics and the economic system, which demands transcendental ethnic allegiance and universalistic principles rather than sanguine or cultural relationships. Therefore, the thought of agreeing and defending each other for the sole reason of being the same ethnicity will no longer be sustained but become extinct as ethnicities face universal principles such as justice, humanitarianism, philanthropism, market economy, international order, and modern trends. Determinists argue that these challenges will collapse and change the traditional concept of the ethnicity.[31]

Determinism focuses on the points of individual lives and the depravity in their lives as they move to cities that grow rapidly. They believe that ethnic boundaries will weaken, and in the end, ethnicities will be absorbed into city culture by the dominant power of the city.[32]

This determinist theory provides a helpful tool in understanding anomy and the disorganization phenomena of the urban minorities; that is, if it exists. It also gives an anthropological lens to understand assimilation, dissolving interethnic and urban ethnic village dynamics.

---

29. Wirth, "Urbanism as a Way of Life," 1.

30. Similar to the concept of determinism, there is a functionalist view. Marshall, *Class, Citizenship, and Social Development*; Lipset and Rokkan, *Party Systems and Voter Alignments*; Geertz, "The Integrative Revolution."

31. Tèonnies and Loomis, *Community & Society (Gemeinschaft Und Gesellschaft)*; Weber, *Economy and Society*, 927–36.

32. Fischer also admits that Determinism also read the city correctly in some point. Fischer, *The Urban Experience*, 32.

Despite this, Determinism carries a few weaknesses as following. Firstly, it over-emphasizes the fact that an individual life becomes devastated. If the city were as negative and difficult to live as it sounds, why would people swarm into cities? Why would people migrate to cities to grab opportunities and hope? These questions are difficult to explain with the existing Determinism theory. The theory can only partially explain the ethnicity issues.

The determinist explanation of the ethnic boundary also reveals its limitation. To the European-descent immigrants who have spent several generations in the US, the fact that ethnic boundaries weaken over time is acceptable. Furthermore, to ethnicities who have stronger individualism, ethnicity can disseminate rather quickly through choices of the individual, rather than that of the group as a whole. However, to those who center on blood descent or community, those disadvantaged in ascending social status and those with apparent skin color differences, the ethnicity does not dissolve so easily. Even though they may be fluent in the common language or advance into the middle class, the society may not accept the ethnicities completely as members. Many countries excluding the US and countries in Europe lack governmental protection for ethnic minorities. In such cases, ethnic minorities must unite even more for survival.

In some ways, people in the city may experience more direct discrimination and ethnic conflicts than in the suburbs. Such experiences and environment let people in the city brings up their ethnicity even stronger, rather than diminish. A weakness of Determinism is that though it has many approaches in understanding the city, it has too many simple approaches and biased analyses that do not view the city objectively.

They Will Not Be Changed: Compositionalism

One of the main challenges for the determinist theory is the compositional theory; this theory denies the effects of the deterministic theory. It argues that the attributes of cities and rural systems define and form the characteristics of people's lives, but the systems themselves do not alter particular ways of life or personalities. This means urbanism itself has no effects.[33]

33. Gans, Lewis, Reiss, etc., are important scholars of the compositional theory. Gans, "Urbanism and Suburbanism as Ways of Life"; *The Urban Villagers*; *The Levittowners*; Lewis, "Urbanization without Breakdown a Case Study"; Reiss and Columbia, *The Analysis of Urban Phenomena*.

Compositionalists do not believe that urbanism has much effect on the ethnic boundary change.[34] This is because generally people form their networks based on groups that are part of, or related to, their work. This is called cultural differentiation. Different cultural networks are formed depending on people's activities, tasks, and preferences, and based off these networks, each individuals' lives are separated. In the city, such technical networks are not necessarily confined within the ethnic network. However, since those networks are quite functional, though the individual networks may be divided and spread into different parts, they have little effect on people's ethnic identities.[35]

The Determinism theory we mentioned tends to view the entire city as one piece, namely as a macroscopic view. However, as urban ecology develops, we realize that there are more unique societies and groups within the city. Much different kind of groups exists, including kinship, ethnicity, neighborhood, occupation, lifestyle, and similar social attributes that live according to their own unique dynamics and elements. Likewise, a city forms when different groups come together as one in harmony. This is why Compositionalists describe the city as *mosaic of social worlds*.[36]

Many urban subcultures have their own unique social dynamics. This means that to understand them with just one method is difficult. Moreover, these social worlds will not go extinct or become parts of the homogeneous groups. Nevertheless, many social worlds have ability to maintain their uniqueness. This is because their traditional culture and social frame that they have built through the urban life give them the power to remain in their identity. Furthermore, they also continue to create the capability of maintaining their resources and culture.

For example, in *Xi'an*, China, there is the Great Mosque that started in AD 741. The Great Mosque in *Xi'an* begins its history from the Tang Dynasty, or about 100 years after Muhammad died (632). Surrounding the Mosque, there are large Muslim villages that carry long histories. It is extraordinary to maintain such Muslim village in the middle of *Xi'an*, a city in the center of China's history, politics, and economy. Similarly in many cities in the world, there are numerous ethnic groups and their villages that have been maintained for long periods of time.

34. Michael, "The Political Economy of Ethnic Change."

35. Barth and Bergen, *Ethnic Groups and Boundaries*; Gellner, *Thought and Change*; Michael, "Towards a Theory of Ethnic Change"; Hanham and Hechter, "Internal Colonialism"; Hechter, "Industrialization and National Development in the British Isles."

36. Timms, *The Urban Mosaic*, chap. 1.

Figure 4–1: Grand Mosque in Xi'an, China (April 2010) Photo © Enoch Kim

The city of Los Angeles also has various areas where Asians can live along their own groups such as Japanese Town, Pilipino Town, China Town, Korea Town, etc. Furthermore, Hispanics, Armenians, and Indians, along with ethnic minorities from Africa and South America, all live with their own ethnic groups in the same neighborhood. After they settle down in the US, immigrants slowly move up to the middle class. At the same time, they move from their ethnic towns into neighborhoods where other ethnic groups live. Especially in suburban areas, we see immigrants who seek to live in the neighborhoods that fit their income level and have good schools for their children's education. However, their actual relationships are developed with those when they feel emotionally comfortable and culturally stable. Even though they interact with people from various ethnic backgrounds in their workplaces for professional occupations or simple labor, immigrants find answers within the same ethnic group for others activities such as religious activities, meeting with lawyers, or trusted business partnerships, or relationships with other parents for discussion of their children's education.

In the earlier discussion, we have learned that determinism views the city as a place where immigrants lose their ethnicity's emotional stability and abundant relationships that they had obtained from the traditional society, and where ethnic identities are faded. However, the city is more than just a Melting Pot. Instead, it is where ethnic groups unite, maintain, and improve their cultures throughout the city. Moreover, many ethnic groups travel long distances to return back and visit their hometowns during holidays, in order to confirm their relationships and repeat traditional rituals to affirm their identities and bond with their origins. Ethnic groups in the city share areas to co-inhabit financially and religiously in their own language and culture. Some ethnic groups live with their descendants in the same city for centuries, such as the Hui people in *Xi'an*, China.

The biggest reason why the urban ethnic groups' boundaries are not weakened is because unilateral inhumaneness or seclusion is not the only factor that exists in urban life, which is different from what the Determinism theory suggests. In general, when people settle in the city, their networks are weak and they have limited abilities to interact with the outsiders. However, as time passes, they form new relationships while their financial capabilities increase. Especially, new immigrants to the city share problems and create emotional bonds with those of the same ethnicity. In other words, not everyone in the city has unstable or secluded emotions. Instead, their inter-ethnic bonds in a particular city may become stronger through cooperative relationships. The Compositional Perspective that states that urban ethnic groups do not undergo much change is a view based on these very characteristics.[37]

A pioneer of this compositional theory, Herbert J. Gans, reviewed and critiqued the determinist theory by pointing out the phenomena that most immigrant Americans go back to their original patterns of life as soon as they can. He says those phenomena that Wirth observed occurred only "during a time of immigration acculturation and at the end of a serious depression, and an era of minimal choice."[38] Gans and other Compositionalists say that the residence is not a primal source of behavior variation.

---

37. As Oscar Lewis studied rural-urban migration study in the city of Mexico, he found that some migrants did not breakdown their original lifestyle as they live in the city. Lewis, "Urbanization without Breakdown," 40–41.

38. Gans, "Urbanism and Suburbanism as Ways of Life," 644–45.

They say that it is the variation of class and life cycle that adequately explain the difference of ways of life between the big city and suburbs.[39]

Compositional theory maintains that subcultures and their individuals keep their internal dynamics no matter what their city size is or how the inter-subculture relationships are.[40]

The Compositional Theory was very influential in stopping determinism, which described the city's power as limitless. In other words, it rejected the belief that every ethnic group must enter the assimilation process, and that all urbanites are emotionally unstable and cannot have abundant relationships compared to the rural people.

The Compositional Theory also confirmed that an ethnic group could establish a town even in the city to maintain its culture. Immigrant ethnic groups within the city are culturally nourished by endless interaction with their origins, hometowns, or countries. When they gain economic power, new traditions and pride also follow. Through such process, the life span of the urban ethnic communities can be maintained for a long period of time.

On the other hand, the Compositional Theory has some blind spots. Treating urban immigrants equally as those in rural hometowns and thinking that they will not change are far from reality. The first reason is that people and groups change. No matter how slow it seems, ethnic communities in the city change. Even though it may seem like the ethnic groups maintain their own cultures within themselves, they change because they still interact with a larger society called the city. Their children are able to use the common language more naturally through the public education systems, they hear neutral information of the world through media, and they meet various religious people in their workplace. All these elements may change the traditional society. The social adaptability of immigrants and desire to raise their status also change the ethnicity. Gradually, immigrants enter the middle class, and their children have stable jobs and intermarry with different ethnic groups. These are all powers that force the immigrant ethnic groups into assimilation.

---

39. Kotter and Dewey point out the problem of sociologist failure of concerning to the rural-urban continuum. Kotter, "Changes in Urban-Rural Relationship in Industrial Society," 22; Dewey, "The Rural-Urban Continuum," 82.

40. Glazer and Moynihan, *Beyond the Melting Pot*, 203.

PERSISTING AND CHANGING FACTORS OF THE ETHNIC BOUNDARY

In people's minds, like a fence, there is a conceptual boundary outlining the concept of "one's ethnicity." Inside the boundaries is what is considered one's own ethnicity, and outside the boundaries is the beginning of another's ethnicity. In general, people decide their ethnic boundaries by two factors: territorial boundaries and psychological factors. First, the geographical boundary element is formed by the ethnicity that has lived at the same location for a long time. Because certain people have lived in certain regions, the people there automatically become part of the ethnicity, and people believe that they must live in the region. Secondly, ethnic boundaries are formed through psychological factors, which are formed concepts in people's minds. The ethnic boundary is determined by whether each other is part of the same ethnicity or not, which is answered from questions, such as what traditions to live with and whom to live with.[41]

Ethnic traditions that have thousands of year's histories cannot easily be diminished by modern urbanization. This is because ethnic boundaries originally do not move in one direction, but strengthen and weaken depending on the situation. For this, it means that there exist many factors that strengthen and weaken the boundary. Ethnicities would take such influence as a choice, and as the result of it, the boundary either expands or shrinks. For this reason, the understanding of the persisting and shrinking factors that influence the ethnic boundary becomes crucially important for predicting the future of the ethnic groups.[42] Now let us take a look at how these two factors are formed in detail.[43]

Persistence Factors of Ethnic Groups

We will first look at the power that maintains ethnicity. In order for an ethnic group to unite and maintain its identity, there must be a boundary

---

41. Romanucci-Ross and De Vos, *Ethnic Identity*, 16.

42. Barth and Bergen, *Ethnic Groups and Boundaries*, 8–39; Brubaker, *Ethnicity without Groups*; Andreas, "Herder's Heritage and the Boundary-Making Approach."

43. Many parts of this persistence factor and changing factor are comes from he idea of Fischer.

on the outer edge of the group. There are four preservation factors of ethnic groups: social ties, old identities, ethnic customs and values, and size.[44]

Social ties include blood ties, friends and kin, marriage, clubs and associations, and so on. Among these, blood ties are the most fundamental elements in maintaining an ethnicity, by providing very strong connectedness. Skin colors or families are predestined elements, which individuals cannot choose, yet, this brings a strong social tie to individuals. The preference to endogamy and its social pressure bind the ethnicity to maintain its social ties exclusively within the same ethnicity. Ethnic clubs and associations bring benefits, entertainment, and emotional satisfaction within the ethnic group and work as ethnic social ties.[45]

The second tie that maintains the ethnic boundary is the old identity. Generally, old identity divides 'we' from 'others'; for example, members vote for their own ethnic candidates and may hold old animosities through traditions against other groups. This is due to the fact that the same group members have similar attitudes toward other groups. With more people gathered together, this naturally becomes a group that holds economic and political power. Moreover, an ethnic group tends to unite more when there are urban inter-ethnic conflicts against their own ethnicity. This dynamic becomes more active if they have common enemies or profit. Most likely, ethnic immigrants have made competitors or enemies in their hometowns, and are prone to continue the same hostile relationships with the same people, even in the city. The same is true for ethnic immigrants in other cities as well, internationally. In some cases, urban ethnic groups may even have worse feelings towards each other. This is because even though rural ethnic groups have stereotypes and superiority over others, they are geographically separated from one another and do not necessarily have to interact directly, thus leading to less conflict. However in the city, they must directly face each other for the actual profit, and emotional conflict therefore continues between ethnicities.[46]

Third, ethnic customs and values persist ethnic boundaries. People's value systems, cultural expressions and habits are all taught parents from their childhood both consciously and unconsciously.[47] Language and food, especially, are habituated from a young age and are difficult to change

44. Fischer, *The Urban Experience*, 146–52.

45. Leerkes, Engbersen, and Van San, "Shadow Places."

46. Fischer, *The Urban Experience*, 151–52.

47. Ibid., 147.

as adults. These characteristics give the same ethnic people emotional satisfaction when people with common customs and values are together.[48]

Lastly, the size of an ethnicity maintains its power and influent ability. When an ethnicity is large in size or high in influence, the existence itself can fully maintain its culture. The number of an ethnic minority group gradually increases until its power increases after a certain point. This is called critical mass. Critical mass, stated here, is a sociological concept rather than a specific number. When an ethnicity first settles in a new city, because they rarely have resources or information, members would have to follow the host culture in almost every part of life. However, as the number of the same ethnic minority group increases and begins to have emotional, political, and economic stability, the groups are able to overcome social pressure and begin to have their own organizations and institutions in the midst of the host culture. The more members of the same group, the better they are able to enjoy their original culture and may even use new ideas from different infrastructures or host culture to improve the original culture. Also, groups that have surpassed the critical mass carry political and economic power that can secure social advantages in many areas. Sometimes, ethnic distinctiveness and boundaries in urban cities may lead to ethnic violence, as the chance of cross-cultural contact increases. Especially groups that have surpassed the critical mass with enough power do not need to overcome their traditional ethnocentric view, which can lead to ethnic conflict with other groups.

Changing Factors in Ethnic Group

Let us now look at the factors that contribute to urban ethnic changing. Some changing factors include changes in the social control system, interethnic contact in urban junctures, new yearnings of elevating social statuses, and the concept of changing neighbors.

First of all, the social control system of the traditional society that has been reigning individuals has changed. New migrants in the city have escaped from the community that has protected but also scrutinized them for a long time. As a result, this gives them an opportunity to escape from many stereotypes their group had over other ethnic groups. Through this, they make new friends in new work places in a new language speaking country.

48. *The Urban Experience*, 146–52.

More chances of interethnic activity opportunities also change the ethnic boundary. Through cross-ethnic contacts, they face new life-styles, beliefs, or objects. As they move to a city, people face new value systems and styles that are different from the original ones. For some people, these opportunities allow them to get rid of ethnocentrism and cultural subjectivism, and allow them to see other ethnic groups more objectively. By admitting others' strengths and their own weaknesses, people even become critical of their own ethnic group and feel the need to improve. As a result, they accept other cultures and may even enjoy them. This intergroup diffusion changes the ethnic group social ties, professions, and lifestyles and causes intermarriages.

A variety of spatial and temporal urban junctions provide interethnic communication chances. Contact with other ethnic groups has not been easy back in the hometown but now that they are in the city, it is easy and natural to meet them in the neighborhood, bus stations, parks, workplace, school, marketplace, and so on.[49] Similarly in mission fields, it is common to see unreached ethnic people who have moved to cities from the countryside. In many cases, they did not have many opportunities to interrelate with other ethnic groups in the countryside. Missionaries or outsiders living among the ethnic village in the countryside not only have many limitations, but also can create hostility for these expatriates. However, new spaces in the city allow missionaries to meet unreached people groups easily and naturally.

New desires of elevating social status, new concepts of neighborhood, and fast mobility are also good changing factors. People who move to a city now have new desires they have never had back in the countryside. For example, as other urbanites do, they put tremendous effort into elevating their social status. For this, they seek resources and information not only from their own ethnic groups, but also from other ethnic groups as well. For example, organization leaders and schoolteachers naturally interact with other ethnic members for better resources.

Finally, the changing concept of neighborhood also changes ethnic boundaries. Previously, their neighbors used to be in the same ethnic group, but in a city, different ethnic groups live next door. Instead of those who live right next to them geographically, they now recognize the individuals they see every day as their neighbors, such as coworkers.

---

49. Jacob Hibel's research shows that public education decreases the difference between different ethnicities. Hibel, "Roots of Assimilation," 135.

Similarly, modern technologies in their new urban living environment, such as telephones, communication systems, or vehicles influence the urbanites to form a new concept of neighbors. As we have seen so far, there are many factors that promote changes in the ethnic boundaries of a city. These diversified and expanded contacts, newly appeared neighbors, spatial and temporal junctions that the city provides, increased interethnic activities, and loosened social controls transform urban ethnic groups into diverse shapes and forms.

CHAPTER PATHFINDER

In this chapter, we have reviewed the several actions that ethnicities may take under pressure of cultural changes. The reason to study determinism (ethnic change) and Compositionalism (continuation) is because it allows us to expect whether the ethnic boundary will shrink or expand. We also identified the persistence and changing factors of ethnic boundaries. Understandings of the power of the two directions bring great value and meaning in missional strategy. This is because evangelizing local means promoting good change, which is only possible by understanding the dynamics of changes. Thus, power must be given to the elements that promote change. On the other hand, no matter how good the missionary's intentions are, if his or her efforts stimulate the local's constant factors that do not change, it will not only be useless but may bring a reverse effect in evangelizing them. Therefore, by learning the changeable factors and their variables, local evangelism will be much more effective.

IMPLICATION TO MISSION

The Chinese Muslim student, Miss Ma who was introduced earlier in this chapter, is a typical case of an urban ethnic minority who moves back and forth both assimilation and continuation of the ethnic culture. One day, we visited her, while she was visiting her parents' house in her hometown during her break. The place was located in a small town, which took a 24-hour train ride from Beijing.

At the time, Miss Ma's parents gathered all her siblings to welcome us. Her brothers and sisters all lived in the same city and they had different occupations. Her brother was a teacher, her sister was a clerk in a small store, and her brother-in-law was a security guard at a local market. Her parents have been living in the same city for many decades. At the end of the meal, her father said, "If you live in this city, you will be very content. The environment is very good and everything is abundant. I would never want to live somewhere else." Miss Ma's siblings have grown up and got married there. On the next day, we went with Miss Ma to visit historical sites. It was amazing to see her relatives and friends everywhere we went. Miss Ma seemed to enjoy the hometown completely and have forgotten about the dream she had about working in Beijing.

What do we need to know when we see urbanites in the mission field that are positioned in between both cultural assimilation and continuation? The following is the missiological implication related to this issue.

Balance Between Determinism and Compositionalism

Proper understanding about the effect of urbanism on the ethnic groups will be crucial for setting up a proper mission strategy for the urban ethnic enclaves. Now, let us examine how these theories view urbanization and its impact on ethnic boundaries and the cultural dynamics.

We have mentioned that Determinism can only partially explain the urban ethnic boundaries. If the determinist theory is true, missionaries do not have to set different urban mission stratagem for each ethnic group, because then all ethnic groups will eventually lose their own identities and take on a single identity. Then, missionaries will only need to use the common language of the locals and only consider the universal pattern of urban life in sharing the Gospel. Furthermore, according to Determinism, we can assume that global cities in the world will unify or become similar by the global trend. If all the cities follow a similar system by expanding global companies, we can simply expect that missionaries only have to learn a few international languages in the future to evangelize the world. This optimistic view, however, is not the case. Nevertheless, generalizations and unifications are not the only phenomena that occur in mission fields. Indigenous culture continues to develop rather than fade away. Even though the influence of the English language spreads everywhere, the people who can use it as a heart language are very few.

The problem is, the mission fields do not include only unification and universalism. It is true that ethnic groups in many mission fields are learning the common language and international languages, such as English, more and more. Therefore, quite many missionaries who use English are actively working, and the cultural threshold for missionaries is diminishing due to the decrease of aboriginal culture. If all the ethnic languages vanished and we were left only with a common language, the burden of translating the Bible will decrease. However, generalizations of commonness and internationalization are not the same as the extinction of ethnicity, language, or culture. It is because ethic culture may revive anytime by their economic growth and cultural reshaping. Therefore, missionaries must return to the basics even as they see these cultural changes. Just as Jesus entered the Jewish culture and lived a divine lifestyle, missionaries should not expect the local culture to change and try to fit their own culture, but to change their own lives to fit the local culture.

The composition theory cannot fully explain the interethnic dynamics of ethnic group in mission fields either, even though it has many supporting phenomena in the city. As relations between cities and hometowns strengthen and the numbers of people from the same hometown increase in the city, they slowly become used to the life of the city and hold more power. Cities in mission fields have outgrown the number of new immigrants because of the government's protection, special treatments for ethnic minorities, easy access between the city and hometown due to improved transportation, chain migration, and improved rural education and economic system. Not only that, but there are many countries that have many negative reasons to push ethnic minorities from the countryside to cities, such as starvation, drought, war, and diseases. The ethnic groups naturally build their own towns near long-distance bus terminals or train stations and form shantytown on the hill outside of the city.[50]

This does not mean an urban ethnic identity is always preserved. Generally, people from rural areas who move to cities are relatively more courageous, and smarter, and they hold more power. The main reason they come to the city is for hope: social elevation, escape from poverty, rather human-like treatment, sanitation and abundance, education for their children, and self-improvement. Groups coming to cities start new beginnings and have no choice but to leave from the original habits and traditions, and must immerse themselves into the unfamiliar policies, people, institutions, workplaces, and schools with different values and religions. The younger generation is especially able to rather easily accept the new value systems and life patterns through media and social trends. Missionaries must carefully observe these urban immigrants and the changing of ethnic dynamics.

50. Yang, *Ethnic Studies*, 86–87.

If missionaries only have the Compositional Theory perspective, they may end up with too much respect for the local culture, and as a result, they will hardly see the change of culture. Because urban ethnic groups will try to maintain their traditional cultures, a missionary needs to be able to introduce the Gospel in a culturally appropriate way. On the other hand, the active transformation of urban ethnic groups means new opportunities for evangelism. As the Apostle Paul introduced the Gospel differently in a way that is culturally appropriate for the Jews, to those without law, and to those who were weak (1Cor 9:19–21), missionaries also must constantly ask themselves what kind of situation the audience is in, and what are the reasonable ways to understand them as they introduce the Gospel.

Avoiding Two Dreams:
Common Culture Church and Ethnic Ghetto Church

Earlier we have learned to be careful and not to lean toward either side of Determinism or Compositionalism. This lesson teaches us to avoid two extreme predictions in the urban mission and urban ministry.

First is the view that assumes that every diverse ethnic group will have the same culture or common group after time. This perspective is similar to that of ministers who believe that everyone will be able to speak English or a common language, and therefore, the church can remain as white or majority group-oriented, and this will work for all ethnic minorities. These people may think that there will come a day when mission work can be done without the difficulty of learning a new culture. A while ago, a seminarian came and told me how Jesus rarely left his village and how Apostle Paul ministered mainly to the gentiles who came to the Jewish synagogues; therefore, it is more biblical for us to freely minister to foreigners who come to America rather than stepping out into difficult areas. For a while, I was dumbfounded and lost for words. Though Jesus rarely stepped out of Israel geographically, He himself came down to a completely different culture zone as a divine being. Apostle Paul did center the Jewish synagogues in ministry, but this because it was a more effective strategy in reaching gentiles, not because it was more comfortable. Moreover, Paul did not confine himself only to the synagogues. This idea of the seminarian could be the trap of cultural laziness that our churches, which are called to do multicultural ministry, can easily fall into. Furthermore, our audience does not assimilate into the common culture as fast as this perspective suggests.

Their generation carries at least their cultural elements, and if many ethnic groups are in one church, it is inevitable that the church would become a multiethnic church.

The second extreme perspective that must be avoided is turning the church into an ethnic ghetto church. It is natural for the same ethnic groups to attend a same church. However, it is wrong for the church to be isolated from the outside of their ethnicity or to keep their serious bias and hostility toward other ethnicities. Such church cannot properly function in multicultural environment, furthermore it is not missional. Furthermore, in such a church like the ethnic ghetto, leaders have no idea how to understand the reality of the lives of their members, who continuously interact with outsiders. The church members of today live in a city that is constantly changing. Even though they may eat traditional food and wear traditional clothes, they continuously absorb the common culture of the city in their lives.

Therefore, ministers or immigrant churches for ethnic minorities must be careful not to think that their members are culturally assimilated simply into one direction. The church must help the members to their identities even in the multi-ethnic setting, help them live with others, and play the role as the salt and light to them. Missionaries must also find and present the most suitable form of the Gospel that fits the local context.

If so, what kind of knowledge do we need for the mission strategy as we consider the shrinking and expanding of the ethnic boundary? For this, we must understand the various results that urban ethnicities choose through their cultural interaction, and also we must understand what elements motivate them to make such choices. Such case issues will be explored next chapter.

5

City, a Place Where Ethnicites Actively Choose Identities

Understanding Sub-Cultural Theory

WE HAVE A TENDENCY to think that any ethnicity is made up of homogenous people. This tendency seems especially true when we observe others through a cross-cultural lens. In such instances, this presupposition is intensified. Ironically, we know that our own ethnicity is composed of thousands of different groups, but it is hard for us to imagine that the same applies to other ethnicities. Actually, every group has its own sub-groups when you look close enough. Moreover, each sub-group can react a little bit differently to external influences because each may have experienced different outcomes due to situations unique to each background.

Likewise, ethnic minorities in the city may hardly show homogenous reactions to external change; but rather, each sub-group can display different reactions, while at the same time, maintain harmony within the whole ethnicity. As an example, Muslims in China can become unified in some situations, but in other situations, they can be divided over conflicting opinions regarding issues of urbanization.

In the previous chapter, we tried to answer the question: Are urban ethnicities culturally assimilated or continuous? As we took a closer look at the question, a premise may have surfaced for some readers regarding ethnicity if we view assimilation as a process. In other words, minority groups face the question of whether to assimilate entirely into a majority culture or continue fully or partially within the cultural boundaries of a minority culture. Consequently, the premise is derived from the idea that the culture of an ethnicity is homogeneous (e.g. no diversity in social class, status, or even physical appearance). Therefore, if it is homogenous, the members of the group simply move in the same direction regarding decisions about identity, social behavior, and values.

Nevertheless, in this chapter, we will study the fifth face of city, which is the characteristic of a city as a place that helps ethnicities to actively find their identity. We will explore the ethnicity choose not just either culturally assimilation or continuation, but many choices. Moreover, we will explore the existence of subgroups and their roles within ethnicities to accommodate social change.

In this chapter, we will examine the following.

- What are the limitations of the assimilation process theory among ethnicities in urban settings?

- In the midst of change, in addition to assimilation and continuation, what other responses are triggered among ethnicities living in urban settings?

- What are the limitations of prominent sociological theories when observing the process of cultural change among non-Western urban ethnicities?

- Why is the sub-culture theory effective in explaining the changes that occur among ethnicities in urban settings?

- What are sociological points that must be applied to missional approaches among urban ethnicities that are consisted of sub-cultural units?

To answer those questions, we will take a look at the variety of ways ethnic minority groups can choose to express their identities within a majority social environment. Social autonomy as well as internal and external pressures can push a group in many directions besides assimilation or continuation, as group members choose their own ethnic cultural identity. In the final part, this chapter will display that subcultural theory is quite an appropriate research tool that can be used to describe the realities of urban life for ethnicities.

A CASE:
SIMULTANEOUS CULTURAL ASSIMILATION
AND CONTINUATION

About 20 years ago, I attended a meeting in China with coworkers of the same mission organization who came from all over the country. The main topic of discussion was the following: "Will Chinese ethnic minority groups be absorbed into the majority group in the future and lose their own identity?" This was an urgent topic for missionaries at the time. Because if ethnic minorities in China were to fully assimilate into the Han mainstream majority, our efforts to translate the Bible and Christian materials into each ethnic language would become immaterial.

All of the missionary teams spent time learning not only Chinese but also lived in local villages with local families to immerse themselves fully into the language and culture. Therefore, if minorities were to lose their cultural identities by assimilating into Han culture under Beijing's regulations, we would then strategize to instead evangelize college students from the ethnic groups. With their presence across major cities, we anticipated that the students could become effective missionaries to their own people.

As I was having this discussion, a picture came into my head. It was a Muslim village in a city in western China called Lanzhou. For several centuries, Muslims had been living in one part of the city maintaining their own lifestyle and culture. However, due to urban planning and modernization, a big road was constructed through the center of the community, dividing it into different parts. Along the road, many modern buildings and shops were built. As a result, other ethnic group members arrived and co-opted those businesses. The result was a new settlement of outsiders into a once socially and culturally isolated area of the city of Lanzhou.

Coming to terms with non-Muslim new residents living within their traditional ethnic communities was a challenge for the Hui because they had to make significant adjustments in response to many daily life issues. One significant issue, for example was in regards to dietary rites among those who lived in the area, considering the community as a Muslim neighborhood. New residents did not necessarily share the same view about food and many living among them consumed pork. This is an offensive dietary taboo for Muslims. At first, the Muslims felt awkwardly out of place. Later, that awkwardness turned into outrage. The government intervened by offering a large compensation package to assist Muslim community members to relocate to modern affordable apartments. However, locals became offended at the offer instead feeling forced to move from their familiar community. Although in reality, just as many also welcomed the new modern-styled homes. Eventually, an enormous ethnic town that had been maintained for centuries was divided, and its former residents were scattered to live in various apartment complexes populated by the majority population. Thus, their public order, identity, culture, and language, which were obviously nurtured through common meeting places such as mosques and restaurants and led by ethnic civic leaders in the community, disappeared. Consequently, the Chinese Muslims who once had an opportunity to share a community were quickly absorbed into the mainstream community. In other words, former residents were woven into the fabric of the majority culture.

However, an interesting event happened. Minority group members did not lose their identity once they individually relocated into new unfamiliar apartment complexes. Rather, they developed and perpetuated their identity in new ways.

Through improved transportation and phone service, they frequently kept in touch with relatives who lived half an hour away. They were able to maintain their strict Muslim diets, attend festivals together, speak the dialect, and express their traditions with almost no change given the new shape of their community. Members observed religious holidays such as *Kai Zhai Jie* and avoided cultural taboos, such as eating pork. Moreover, members maintained culturally significant rites of passage, such as birthdays, coming-of-age ceremonies, marriages funerals, and so on.

Of course, with more exposure to the mainstream, members also became familiar with majority patterns of behavior, as well as, modern machinery, financial protocols, the prevailing social order, and so on. Even more, information flows from Muslim children attending school because they learn the historical context of the majority, as well as civics along social expectations.

Younger generations develop more relationships with other ethnic groups through school experiences and business. Through the younger generations, new information and value systems enter the home and ethnicity. As a result, rather than moving toward any one culture, whether remaining in conservative isolation or complete rejection of ethnic ties, individual members show a variety of responses as they adapt to the majority culture. Many selectively adapt to features of both cultures, through fashion choices, language and other social trends.

Once, during a gathering of missionaries, as I was discussing the question of whether ethnic minorities should assimilate or maintain their cultural identity, I realized that the issue is too difficult to conclude in favor of either opinion. In other words, there should be a third way for minority communities to consider ethnicity and cultural identity as they become ever familiar with and become involved in the majority culture. This is a logical conclusion considering that even within a single ethnicity, there are many different groups. And since each will have different individual experiences, each will cultivate different reactions and opinions in response. This diversity in community opinion suggests that there should be more than simply two paths to define evolving ethnic identity.

Expecting the future trend of them is crucial for urban mission strategy across ethnicities. Mission leaders should never assume that ethnicity is synonymous to homogeneity, or represents a collective identity that moves in one direction simply because from surface observations, members appear so similar in so many ways to city residents. Developing a mission strategy without considering this point is dangerous and may waste great resources and time. This is because it is possible that the missionary plan and human resources invested in the plan may not be suitably dispatched, given the socio-cultural reality within a community.

So do groups necessarily have limited alternatives in terms of their response to the majority group? Is either assimilation or continuation the only alternative? Are there any other directions? Do we have to believe that any ethnicity is socially homogenous? Or is diversity inherently present within any given ethnicity because there are also sub-groups?

The answers will be clearer if we acknowledge diversity within ethnicities as groups vary in reaction to urban social experiences. Otherwise, to only recognize homogeneity is to advance stereotypes and remain entrenched in the view that either assimilation or continuation are the only cultural choices for ethnic minorities who seek to experience the same quality of life as the majority. In the next section, we will examine actual social choices facing ethnicities in general, in an urban society.

FOUR DIFFERENT RESULTS OF ETHNIC BOUNDARY CHANGES

Despite pressures to conform, ethnic groups do not automatically follow a predetermined course of assimilation. Rather, ethnic communities actively examine the social situation and proactively choose their own fate. Urban ethnic groups do not unconditionally choose or reject change. The details of their choices may vary depending on the ethnic group; moreover, ethnicities can even limit their choices to only partially assimilate.

Donald L. Horowitz categorized one type of transformation as a combination of assimilation and differentiation. He further refined each of those into more categories: amalgamation, incorporation, division, or proliferation.[1]

Chart 5–1 conceptualizes the results of changing ethnic boundaries along four outcomes. Each of those four categories can be assigned to either assimilation or differentiation.

Assimilation		Differentiation	
Amalgamation	Incorporation	Division	Proliferation
A+B→ C	A+B→ A	A → B+C	A → A+B (A+B → A+B+C)
Two or more groups unite to form a new, larger group	One group assumes the identity of another	One group divides into two or more component parts	One or more groups (often two) produce an additional group from within their ranks

Chart 5–1: Processes of Ethnic Fusion and Fission[2]

Two Types of Assimilation

Initially, ethnicity in general begins to lose its unique social definition once assimilation begins. Ethnic boundaries begin to fade under the influence of another culture's dominance. Specifically, assimilation proceeds along two subtypes: amalgamation and incorporation. Amalgamation refers to two or more ethnic groups melding together to become a larger group with a new single identity. Former small tribes and clans that eventually merge and become a larger identity group belong in this category. Even in a so-called single ethnicity, DNA can often show that the biological heritage of the

---

1. In his work, *Ethnic Identity*, the detailed summaries of these four categories are based on Horowitz's concept in "Ethnic Identity," 115–21.

2. Ibid., 116.

group is made up of many different ethnicities mixed throughout history. This is a case of amalgamation in a social/behavioral context.

The second assimilation subtype, incorporation refers to one group losing its identity to be incorporated into another. For example, ancient clans and tribes, through repeated conquests, were collectively incorporated into kingdoms and empires. Such results likely involved repeated processes of amalgamation and incorporation.

In general, amalgamation and division occur more easily when an ethnic group has no choice but to follow a strong external authority or political influence that arises. Ethnicity can be a label assigned to people during war and slavery, deportation, infrastructure, modernization, or political revolution. For example, I was once at an ethnic arts festival in Beijing in 1999. After the festival, several young men who identified with a specific ethnicity cynically told me that evidence of their traditional rituals and symbols could only be found in folk museums or remote villages in China. Ironically, at the festival, they jokingly said that what we had seen at the festival did not represent their traditional attire but was rather something called *Zhongshanfu*,[3] which is a very typical attire worn by almost every Chinese person during the 1980s and 1990s.

Ethnic groups that experience amalgamation or division do not transform into a completely different cultural entity, at least during the early stages of assimilation. Rather, layers of cultural elements form over their original identity. Therefore, although it may seem like an individual has adopted a new culture, the original culture is still present at deeper layers of one's worldview. In other words, amalgamized cultures are similar to different shirts, sweaters and jackets a person might wear simultaneously. Initially, a person might put on a t-shirt and without taking it off, put on a button-down shirt, and later a sweater and so on. Therefore, although identity is layered and amalgamized with new layers of culture, each layer is distinct including the original culture at the core. That is why stabilizing their ethnic identity during assimilation requires a long period of time. Sometimes, it takes even several generations, as the younger members too develop their own identity.

3. *Zhongshanfu* is a very typical garment for Chinese males.

Two Types of Differentiation

Contrast to assimilation, the differentiation type in ethnic boundary change is a phenomenon of separation—specifically, when a group divides but the newest group retains all aspects of its culture. In this instance, an ethnic minority group will break off from the main group, to produce another group without changing its fundamental identity to mimic another ethnic group. This is differentiation. Actually, differentiation can be further divided into two sub-groups: division and proliferation. Division refers to an ethnic group dividing itself from the original group and developing into different ethnic groups. Ethnic divisions in Azerbaijan represent a good example of such a phenomenon. Azeris not only live in Azerbaijan, their own country, but also live in what is currently northern Iran. These two groups were originally one group, but as part of the community lost access to the other. There are about forty million Azerbaijani in northwest Iran and they speak Arabic, which is used by Iranians, as opposed to the Latin-based language, used by the Azerbaijani.[4]

This phenomenon of language division can also be found among Koreans who migrated north of the Korean peninsula into Manchuria and Russia during the Japanese occupation from 1910–1930. Actually, this phenomenon occurred over a long period of time, during when Koreans migrating to new Asian countries lost fluency in the Korean language. Like all modern languages, the Korean language is dynamic and changes as new words enter the lexicon. Of course, those who live outside of South Korea where the language is dominant and ever evolving will not share the same level of language fluency if they are not similarly immersed in the language. This distinction in fluency naturally introduces other cultural differentiations, too.[5]

Proliferation refers to a small portion of the larger group changing and transforming within an ethnic group. Asian immigrants in the US are a good example of this. These immigrants speak their mother tongue but develop a third culture by merging American culture with their homeland culture, thus forming a new identity.

Incorporation and proliferation occur much more often when people hope to gain economic or social benefits. The country into which voluntary immigrants relocate is the place where this group envisions attaining

---

4. Wikipedia Azerbaijan (Iran), http://en.wikipedia.org/wiki/Azerbaijan_(Iran).

5. Koreans in China, Wikipedia, http://en.wikipedia.org/wiki/Koreans_in_China; Koreans in Russia, http://en.wikipedia.org/wiki/Koryo-saram.

economic and social benefits if they adhere to all the cultural markers pointing to success in that new society. They have the option to choose a new situation and culture, rather than being forced to relocate due to urgent external socio-political forces (i.e., genocide, war, a destabilized government unable to control rampant violence and so on). Consequently, voluntary ethnic migrants/immigrants tend to be partially if not fully absorbed by the dominant society that accepts their new legal status. In return, the new residents will mostly move in-step with the culture of that society.

It is interesting how once incorporation and proliferation happen, the ethnic group that loses its original identity very easily and willingly does not think of regaining it. This is due to the perceived benefits from voluntarily adopting a new culture. For example, voluntary immigrants transitioning from underdeveloped to developed countries prefer the new culture. As a result, they want to adapt to the culture and learn new habits as quickly as possible. They want their children to do so, as well.

Based on several years of observation of voluntary immigrants in Los Angeles, I have witnessed that newly arrived Korean and Chinese residents prioritize both learning English and learning American culture. They also expect the same for their children. In relatively many cases, parents do not grieve their children's vanishing language fluency of their mother tongue (i.e., Cantonese, Mandarin or Korean). Moreover, there is no problem when children show a preference to speak English at home. This is because these changes in the family fall in accord with the purpose of the voluntary immigration of the parents.

The ethnic boundaries changing are continually happening in urban areas across non-Western regions as well. Many ethnicities from different towns settling in similar urban environments will experience similar processes as their ethnic boundaries alter through the crucible of cultural adaptation.

Unfortunately, the experience of this process will propel individuals and communities into chaotic instability if valuable relationships and traditions are sacrificed in a drive to join mainstream societies. Ironically, missionaries serving in a cross-cultural environment will likewise experience a similarly jolting cultural transition. Therefore, they must carefully consider the manner of conveying the biblical message with regard to the unique social context of people who are now experiencing the same ethnic boundary shifts.

As the world shrinks through globalization, many more ethnic groups will experience the pressures of ethnic boundary shifts, without exception.

In such a time as this, church and mission organizations need to strategically, with supporting missiological research, introduce the unchanging biblical message to those who find themselves trapped in the midst of chaotic identity crises.

CULTURAL PLURALISMS AND ETHNOGENESISM: WHO ACTIVELY SELECTS IDENTITY

Urban ethnicities proactively choose their futures in the face of outside influences and the pressure to assimilate. The decision to change, a passive reaction to change, or even choosing to retain one's original culture are all versions of active decision-making. This is because passivity and retention can reduce shock but nevertheless is a decision an individual makes as the best alternative for themselves and the ethnic group. Ethnicities in every country faced with the pressure to make cultural changes continually count and control the social areas of their lives and how fast to make those changes.

In this section, we will first examine the phenomenon of finding, developing and losing one's ethnic identity through cultural pluralism and ethnogenism—theories developed in America. Yet, it is difficult to apply theories formed in developed countries to ethnic minorities, particularly to those living in non-Western contexts. Yet, even though we might be able to directly apply social theories derived in developed countries, these two contexts—developed versus non-Western—still have commonalities in many areas. For one, migrants who are suddenly ethnic minorities live in contact with mainstream society with the express purpose to cultivate a better future. The models of cultural pluralism and ethnogenesis of here will remain as our stepping-stones to the introduction to the cultural-ethnic identity typological model discussed in the next section.

Cultural Pluralism Perspective

In the case of ethnic minorities, especially immigrants in developed countries, many would rather quickly abandon their culture of origin to absorb the host culture. For example, immigrants to the UK or America might easily accept the need to learn English, and embrace basic unobjectionable social values necessary for survival in those countries. As new residents adjust to important customs and synchronize parts of their lives with the host culture, aspects of the host country's social systems and daily life culture naturally become familiar. Despite this, we cannot conclude that core worldviews or ethnic internal dynamics have changed. Rather, new residents become increasingly comfortable living in the host culture over time. With increasing comfort in the host culture, migrants/immigrants don't change their original cultural structure much.[6]

An entire city's public culture does not necessarily change. Instead, immigrants change part of their own subculture as they socially approach the public culture.[7] This does not mean that they disregard their own cultures, as the once utopian metaphor melting pot or problematic idea of Anglo conformity would suggest. Rather, immigrants choose for themselves what aspects of culture to maintain and what to let go as well as when to accomplish this in order to minimize the shock.

However, cultural pluralism never overlaps an immigrant's culture with the host culture. That is to say, although ethnic minorities may learn the common language used by the majority group, it is difficult to say that there has been complete cultural assimilation minimal language ability is solely to support daily survival.

This phenomenon is even clearer when we closely observe an immigrant family. For example, teenagers in an immigrant Korean home who are attending high school in America may find it difficult to share common hobbies and interests with their parents. This is because the home creates a quasi-shelter from the dominant culture: whereas, students are fully immersed in the dominant culture.[8] The statistical outcomes of the survey further support the notion that second-generation immigrants who are able to infiltrate mainstream society do clearly experience an ethnic/cultural boundary shift.

Ethnogenesism

For a balanced and realistic portrayal of the assimilation process among ethnic minorities, the ethnogenesis perspective is a valuable model. This model seeks to explain the coexistence of changed and unchanged culture within

---

6. Yang, *Ethnic Studies*, 86–87.

7. Greeley, *Ethnicity in the United States*, 306.

8. Kim, "Unpublished Survey in Anc Onnuri Church Highschool Survey." According to Kim's survey, Korean American share very few cultural elements between themselves and their children in a genuine intimate conversation.

the same ethnic identity.[9] For instance, in order to adapt to a new city, newly categorized ethnic minorities strive to learn local mores and develop strategic network relationships to quickly facilitate an entire group's (e.g., family's) financial, social, emotional, spiritual, mental and physical well being. In spite of it, an ethnic group's traditional values, such as those habituated from a young age (e.g., food and family relationships), do not easily change over time. Therefore, an immigrant's culture tends to form a coexistent state, which is a mixture of the host culture and the traditional culture.

Generally, as ethnic groups interact with the host culture, they enlarge the common ground between them. Obvious differences between the host and ethnic cultures can be minimized, as time goes by. Ultimately, both groups will form a new culture that will share hybrid features cultivated from both cultural systems. Of course, the new culture will also be distinct from both original cultures. Consequently, if every ethnic minority holds onto traditions and transferred culture simultaneously, a result could be that the host culture then becomes a diverse form with various partially transferred ethnic cultures.

Therefore, we can say that ethnogenesis is a theory to explain the gradual willingness on the part of the immigrant to become part of the host culture. This ethnogenesis theory simultaneously describes the phenomena of cultural assimilation, the melting pot phenomenon as the voluntary willingness to mute one's ethnic culture in order to assume the identity of the host culture, and the influence of pluralism to maintain one's traditional cultures while coexisting with the host culture. The ethnogenesis theory also shows how an ethnic minority will tend to react to the host culture over a long period of time to produce a unique ethnic culture from the previous one. Chart 5–2 is a schematic diagram of the ethnogenesis model.

9. Greeley studied ethnic immigrants in America and found that ethnic minorities selectively adapt to the host culture and have a different pattern of combining cultural factors in every situation. Greeley, *Ethnicity in the United States*, 290–315.

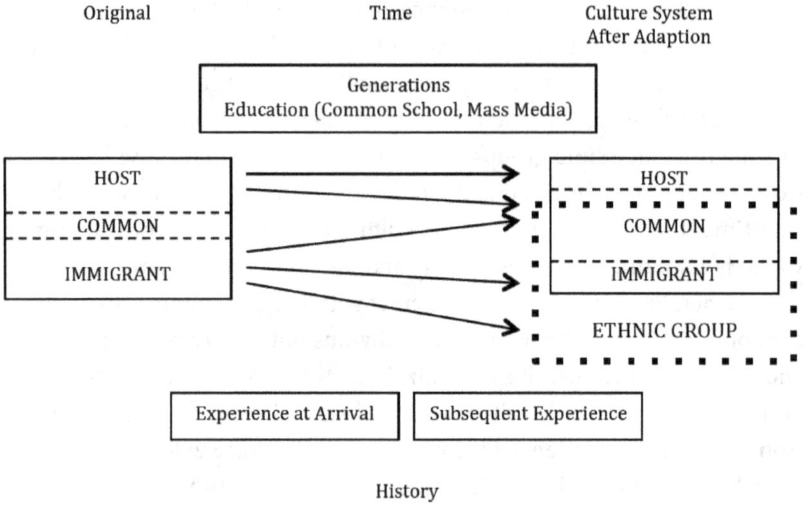

Original   Time   Culture System
After Adaption

Generations
Education (Common School, Mass Media)

HOST	⟶	HOST
COMMON	⟶	COMMON
IMMIGRANT	⟶	IMMIGRANT
	⟶	ETHNIC GROUP

Experience at Arrival   Subsequent Experience

History

Chart 5–2: Ethnogenesis Perspective[10]

In modern cities among many ethnicities, unique cultures merge with others, and create new uncompromising cultural identities. That is why Yang can describe cultural identity more precisely from the ethnogenesis perspective and more effectively than sociologists using the earlier cultural pluralism model.[11]

An example of this can be seen among Chinese and Russian ethnic Koreans. These individuals are Chinese and Russian, but have a Korean ethnic background. A mass migration of Koreans occurred seventy years ago to these Asian countries. Over time, these Russians and Chinese ethnic minorities identified with their countries of birth. Many of them no longer speak Korean; however, they did not just become localized unilaterally. A part of their Korean cultural heritage can still be found in the way they prepare food, speak Korean at varying degrees of fluency, and form social networks.

Meanwhile, since 1980, Korea has established diplomatic relations with Russia and China. Ethnic Koreans in China and in Russia stood at the frontline in countless business and personal exchanges. This is because the social behavioral influences instilled by Russia and China on the one hand, along with the added dimension of Korean ethnicity has given birth to a new modern Korean language, social trends and networks, and a new food lexicon.

10. Ibid., 309.

11. Yang, *Ethnic Studies*, 78.

However, ethnic Koreans do not unilaterally follow one culture or another.[12] Even now a third culture is rising, which is not Korean, Chinese, or Russian. In other words, ethnic Korean culture in Uzbekistan and China are being created.

In spite of the clarity in explanation, it seems difficult to equally apply ethnogenesis theory to all ethnic minorities coming to America. For example, European immigrants experienced a culturally different adaptation process from that of African, Asian, Middle Eastern, or Melanesian immigrants. Comparatively, Europeans come from a culture and background similar to those of Americans and are prone to quickly form relationships with other Caucasians in the host culture, whereas Asian minorities are slow in accepting the new culture and the language barriers are comparatively higher, which slows down the whole assimilation process.

In other words, even though ethnogenesis theory explains the general phenomenon of ethnic minorities' assimilation process in America relatively well, the actual acculturation of each ethnic group may have varied widely. Therefore, the theory actually has difficulty in illustrating the direction or the speed of the assimilation of each group.

THE INTERACTIVE ACCULTURATION MODEL

The Interactive Acculturation Model can help us understand the formation of cultural identity among newly categorized urban ethnicities more effectively than can cultural pluralism or ethnogenesis. This model is shown through cultural ethnic identity matrix.[13] This matrix was developed to fill weaknesses in the progressive model. It enables us to see the multi-directional paths of a minority's cultural changes through a cultural identity matrix. This cultural identity matrix is a two-dimensional typological model to show how much influence individuals or groups receive from either the original culture or the new culture defined by the host culture (Chart 5-3).

As pointed out earlier, we have been using process-type models to represent ethnic assimilation. Each of these theories presupposes that a newly categorized ethnic minority will eventually assimilate into mainstream society and become part of a homogeneous group. However in reality, cultural assimilation of ethnic minority groups moves in many

12. Kim, *Joongang Asia Ui Hangook Moonhua.*

13. Bourhis et al., "Towards an Interactive Acculturation Model: A Social Psychological Approach."

different directions rather than just one. Ethnic minorities may assimilate, but they may also reinforce their ethnic identity in other cases. Moreover, sometimes a third culture may develop from the melding of both the host and migrant/immigrant cultures. Likewise, depending on the context, the directions and speed of assimilation may vary greatly. Notably, the speed and direction of assimilation becomes more complicated if the relationship between the ethnic minority and host culture holds a dark history, or differs greatly from one another. Such is the limitation of the process-type model.

On the other hand, the Interactive Acculturation Model shown below includes host community identity as the vertical axis and ethnic/immigrant identity as the horizontal axis. Chart 5–3 is a matrix of four scenarios defining the ethnicity being observed. Each has varying social dynamics that influence outcomes.

Dimension 1:
Do you find it acceptable that immigrants maintain their cultural identity?

		YES	YES
Dimension 2: Do you accept that immigrants adopt the cultural identity of the host community?	YES	INTEGRATION	ASSIMILATION
	NO	SEGREGATION	EXCLUSION INDIVIDUALISM

Chart 5–3: The Interactive Acculturation Model[14]

The first identity group in the matrix is labeled integration, a profile that is strong in both ethnic and cultural identities. People who fall under this group comfortably identify with two cultures. The second group is labeled segregation. Members of this group do not identify strongly with the host culture but rather, with their ethnicity. People in this group interpret

14. Ibid., 380.

themselves and the environment that they are in based on their original culture even though they might long to join the mainstream. They often rely on their own biases when criticizing the host culture and its people. Likewise, they spend relatively large amounts of time within their own cultural zone, refusing to change. The third group is labeled assimilation and retains a strong cultural identity but weak ethnic identity. People in this group choose to avoid attaching to an ethnic identity, but rather seek the mainstream and prefer to emulate the values, patterns, and styles of the host culture. The last group is labeled exclusion or individualism and retains neither ethnic nor cultural identities. People in this marginal identity group cannot fit into any of the cultural zones.[15]

Compared to the process model, this Interactive Acculturation Model allows us to have a more diversified cultural snapshot of urban ethnicity by addressing prominent social influences. In other words, rather than assuming a one-directional assimilation by an ethnic group, which the process model insinuates, this model suggests how the starting point for social identity formation may differ, retrogress, or even stagnate in one position depending on the social context.

Generally, new immigrants begin their cultural assimilation from the segregation stage. Then they move on to the upper of the two boxes, as a small number of first generation immigrants move toward integration stage. Most people remain somewhere engulfed in the assimilation process.

On the other hand, the ease with which people accept outside cultures is related to the structure of their original culture. In some cases, every member of an ethnic group may assimilate at a similar rate and speed. However, there are also groups that have members who progress at various rates of speed. For example, every member of a group-oriented society makes changes at a similar speed and direction; whereas, members of a group with strong individualism show a larger gap between each other.

Despite the same ethnic background, different sub-groups within an ethnicity can move in different directions at different speeds as individual identity changes. Although they are all of the same ethnicity, it is important to understand how the process of changing ethnic identity is different. This naturally leads us to the subcultural theory, which we will explore in the next section.

15. Ibid., 381.

SUBCULTURAL THEORY

In an earlier chapter, we dealt with facts and theories to reveal convincing evidence regarding the process of how change and maintenance of urban ethnic identities exist, but are exaggerated in some areas. We have also explored some supporting theories. The several points of those theories can be summarized as follows:

Up until now, understanding cultural change had been built on the premise that ethnicities are homogeneous. The approaches reviewed so far take for granted that an ethnicity is a homogeneous group. In reality, ethnicities within cities are made up of many different groups.[16] If examined under a microscope, we can see that within an ethnic group there can exist various small groups, even though they are identified as belonging to the same ethnicity. Social status, income level, education level, time of migration/immigration, religion, generational values, and so many other identities can create social divisions within a group. Furthermore, in the background, these groups are connected to even more groups that are different but can provide access to an endless share of massive amounts of information and relational interactions. As such, various small groups can band together to form an ethnic identity that develops as a new hybrid or integrated city identity. Because of this, in order to accurately understand ethnicities in city, we need to see various urban small groups through a microscopic view, and recognize that each of them can be an independent group with different dynamics.

Defining a city as an integrated body is possible through the subcultural theory. The subcultural theory sees that cities consist of many subcultures and those subcultures are not only a part of a larger culture, but also work independently, interdependently, or cooperatively with other subcultures. Claude S. Fischer was the scholar who developed and introduced this theoretical concept. He defines urban life as building up plural communities and diversity through cultural groups.[17] Subculture is a group made up of individuals that have similar value, attitude, behavior, lifestyle, and etc. within the whole society.[18] Today, there is a tendency of referring a subculture group as a group that does drugs, skinheads, or others that are

---

16. Moore, Garcia, and Chicano Pinto Research Project, *Homeboys*, 157–60.

17. Fischer, *To Dwell among Friends* 194.

18. Abercrombie, Hill, and Turner, "Dictionary of Sociology," 384.

opposing the existing society.[19] "Between the late 1970s and the late 1990s, 'subculture' was the predominant sociological concept used to characterize the relationship among music, culture, and identity."[20] In spite of those tendencies, I will define city subculture as diversified groups consisting of city people, not just to marginality or groups united by specific dress.

Subculturalism is a more integrative approach to defining city dwellers and gives us a head start in understanding urbanites. Subculturalism sees a city as a mosaic of vibrate subcultural groups. In other words, a city can be described as a place where many groups define their cultural colors actively, and at the same time create harmony with the city. These characteristics can be summarized along four points.

First, the enormous organization and cultural influence of a city can positively or negatively impact various groups. When subcultural groups are influenced by the city, each group responds differently according to what meshes with their group characteristics. So, groups can decide whether to assimilate or whether to simply not change at all. Moreover, their choices may alternately strengthen the group's original characteristics, leave them to remain indifferent, partially changed, or visit them with vast changes, which could even include the extinction of their original ethnic identity.

Therefore, a city can endlessly influence the formation of subcultural groups, because a city is a society made up of people. Thus, people must endlessly interact together in order for them to maintain society. As a result, massive information comes and goes as people continually join and leave different groups. Consequently, new subcultural groups are continuously created based on the needs of the people. A city formed by live subcultural groups that responds actively to them is called "a mosaic of little worlds."[21] On the other hand, each piece of the actual mosaic is not stagnant, but rather vibrant. It changes, transforms, and influences other pieces in a way that forms a relational network over which residents respond to one another in the city. That is why urbanism produces a "mosaic of little worlds"

19. Following are the works that studied youth culture with such concept to develop the concept of subculture. Martin, "Subculture, Style, Chavs and Consumer Capitalism"; Bennett, "Subcultures or Neo-Tribes? Rethinking the Relationship between Youth, Style and Musical Taste"; Blackman, "Youth Subcultural Theory"; Snyder, "The City and the Subculture Career: Professional Street Skateboarding in La"; Huq, *Beyond Subculture*.

20. Williams, "Authentic Identities," 174.

21. Timms, *The Urban Mosaic*, chap. 1.

that touches, but does not interpenetrate. Therefore, subcultures do have inter-subcultural relationships.[22]

Second, Subculturalism shows that cultural groups in the city are connected with common codes. In a city, people from different social backgrounds often do touch (that is to say interact), through common codes such as functional language, and business systems. This is an urban characteristic that is hard to find in a rural area.

In the countryside, though different ethnic groups live in neighboring villages, interaction hardly happens. On the other hand, in a city, though urban dwellers may live and work among the same ethnicity for a vast majority of time, they must inevitably interact with outside ethnic groups in specific circumstances such as business. Such interactions are also possible through use of a city's mass transportation system, but also mostly because the city provides several common codes.[23] To increase profitability and reach outside of a limited consumer base, those who can speak the common language do not have to limit business to their own ethnic group. For example, in public institutions such as hospitals, schools, markets, or even public transportation, many different ethnic groups use a common language to communicate. Urban ethnicities that have exceeded many social structures and can understand local nomenclature are able to compete socially. Yet, because of this interaction, even ethnic conflict may occasionally happen.

Therefore, groups in the city affect one another by responding and influencing each other. In other words, an entire city does not move toward the common culture, nor does it stay stagnant. On the contrary, some ethnic subgroups may become more conservative, some prefer the common code and get absorbed into the city's middle class stream, or some will create a third culture. In this way, ethnic subgroups divide into even smaller independent groups that nevertheless actively socialize. Thus, they may have traditional ethnic boundaries on the fringes of their social domain, but their urban ethnic boundary exists on the inside as an extremely complicated form.

The third point is that Subculturalism explains urbanites' emotional dynamics quite realistically. As explained in an earlier chapter, determinism characterizes the life of citizens as filled with anomie and depersonalized. However, reality holds that in actual daily life there are multiple alternative

22. Fischer, *The Urban Experience*, 33, 39.
23. Ibid., 202–5.

ways to cope with new relationships and emotions. So, urbanites do not have to exclusively experience psychological isolation through anomie or the phenomenon of depersonalization, as unban sociologists first thought. Because, once an individual experiences anomie and depersonalization, citizens and cities also develop systems within an urban society to create social structures that can provide emotional nutrition so as to recover emotional vitality.

Figure 5–1: Urbanites Cultivate Ways to Fill Their New Sentimental Needs through Weak and Varietal Ties. A Small Restaurant In China, (June, 2009) Xi'an City, China. Photo © Enoch Kim

The physical concentration of urban populations because of apartment living and other housing in close quarters can function to nurture distinctive subcultures, encouraging new ones to emerge and old ones to be strengthened. Ironically, deviance, social turmoil, intergroup conflicts and the splintering of moral codes are not necessarily the results of alienation, nor anomie in vacuum absent social norms, but rather the growth of many diverse and divergent subcultures, each with its own moral order.[24]

24. Ibid., 273.

Fourthly, Subculturalism can explain that the ethnic boundary does not move toward only one outcome as between weakness and strength but is fluid and changing, depending on the situation. The persistent (or prevailing) as well as changing factors that we identified earlier continuously strengthen and weaken ethnic boundaries. These elements do not literally move an external ethnic boundary. Rather, the elements influence people's lives and human relationships. By categorizing factors that weaken and strengthen ethnic boundaries, Subculturalism explains how ethnicity does not move only in one direction.

As such, subcultural theory has overcome the limitations of perspective to urban ethnicity as homogeneous, by highlighting the importance of different groups within any ethnicity and their proactive leadership. Consequently, this new understanding has enabled us to better see elements that influence how an ethnic boundary can change. In other words, to understand changes along an ethnic boundary, we must understand factors influencing change occurring across ethnicities and within their different subgroups. In this regard, the subcultural theory assists in identifying relationships and sentiments specific to an urban setting.

Within a city, individuals do not just experience anomie or depersonalization, or isolate themselves within their original ethnic sentiments and relationships. Rather, experiences can represent a spectrum of changes depending on the evolving circumstances of each sub-group. Therefore, through Subculturalism observers can identify how ethnicities are able to function proactively within a new environment and system.

In this way, subcultural theory unifies many parts of theories already introduced in this chapter, including determinism and Compositionalism, and also covers cultural pluralism, ethnogenesis, and the cultural-ethnic identity typological model.[25] This is an integrated microscopic approach uniting positive sides of urban anthropology, which a bipolar moralistic view could not explain.[26]

At this point, after this examination of the pros and cons of earlier theories, I conclude that the subcultural theory best uncovers an urban ethnic group's condition and transformation. Therefore, in subsequent chapters, observations and analyses taken to understand the social context of ethnicities residing in an urban context will be reviewed using the subcultural theory. As we begin an exploration of the social network theory, the

25. Ibid., 39.

26. Gulick, *The Humanity of Cities*; Eames and Goode, *Anthropology of the City*.

subcultural theory will provide the foundation on which to understand urban dynamics and interpersonal relationships. These steps will help frame relevant social issues as we explore methods to create mission strategies.

CHAPTER PATHFINDER

Earlier in this chapter, we reviewed a case taken from a Hui village experience showing how cultural assimilation and continuation can occur simultaneously. In addition, we have examined different response of urban ethnicity to the demand of cultural change throughout this chapter. Moreover, we have examined how theories for understanding their cultural situation have developed. First, to overcome theoretical limitations of determinism and Compositionalism introduced in chapter 4, we have categorized the assimilation in four: amalgamation, incorporation, division, and proliferation.

Next, through cultural pluralism and ethnogenesis we came to know how urban ethnicities actively search for their cultural identities rather than abandoning their own culture unilaterally. In other words, urban ethnicities continue to make new choices and struggle to find appropriate clothes for them.

Lastly, we came to know that Subculturalism has advantage that can overcome limitations of many existing theories. In other words, we came to understand that the urban ethnicity can choose varietal kinds of cultural cloths, does not move together, but is varied within themselves by many small groups taking their own way.

IMPLICATIONS FOR MISSION

Since we become aware of the complex dynamics that exist in cities, it is better to say that we cannot answer simply the earlier question of whether ethnic minorities, like the Hui, would eventually assimilate to the majority culture. This is because the simple answer to such a complex question undermines our ability to truly evaluate relationships. And in terms of missions, simple answers undermine the relational potential of ministry. It is worth the time taken by urban workers to use subcultural theory to analyze relationships and cultural boundaries of local ethnicities.

Actually, many of the theories in urban sociology that we have reviewed in this chapter were mainly developed in the West, based on western communities. However in reality, Third World countries receive the most assistance from missionaries. Missionaries therefore often end up serving different functions under very different social dynamics. Therefore, it is more important than ever to consider the unique characteristics of a given urban ethnicities where missionaries serve and create strategies for those communities. To conclude this chapter, let me summarize two points of implication for urban Christian workers serving in Third World countries.

Understanding of the Dynamics in Non-Western Culture

Non-Western urban ethnicities do experience some degree of change culturally. However, the direction of these changes can vary from assimilation, isolation, and hybridization, to even the creation of a new third culture. There are several elements that caused the complexity.

First, this is because, in many cases, non-Western societies are often high grid, high group societies.[27] Such societies are more group-oriented, leaving little room for individuals to make their own decisions. As a result, the wheels of cultural change turn much more slowly than in western individualistic open societies. This kind of society generally has a very tight social structure and often has strong religious and cultural traditions. Ethnic communities in these locations tend to have strong boundaries defining elements of that culture. Their members are united by a great self-esteem for their culture. When such people face change as in the necessity to assimilate to another group for a variety of social reasons, they will hold onto their segregation stage for a very long time. Therefore, even if migrant/immigrant ethnicities do spend a longer time in a non-Western city, that group will experience a higher ratio of people who stay within their traditional ethnic enclave.

Second, non-Western urban ethnic groups who migrate to the city generally keep closer relationships with their families and relatives back home than migrants to western countries. Unlike immigrants living in developed countries who traveled far from their homeland, migrants in non-Western cities in many cases are only a four-or five-hour bus ride from their homes. As a result, urban migrants to non-Western regions remain comparatively immersed in their ethnic identity and thus changes pressured by external forces do not happen easily.

27. Bell and Douglas, "Natural Symbols," 35.

Third, migration to the non-Western cities has more complex reasons and purposes than those migrating to post-industrially advanced developed countries. Usually in developed countries, people migrate for social elevation or for economic reasons. People from non-Western countries migrate not only for the same reasons, but also to survive, to avoid ethnic conflicts, human trafficking, incarceration or the squalor of refugee camps. In the case of those that migrate for survival, such as prisoners or refugees, they are forced to live in the midst of other ethnic groups. So naturally, they may not share positive sentiments toward the majority society. Consequently, it is also difficult for the majority to accept these people. As a result, in such cases, assimilation is unlikely to happen and that group of people will tend to hold onto their ethnocentric identities longer.

Fourth, whether correctly perceived or not, newly categorized ethnic minorities in non-Western areas have a relatively higher awareness of the vulnerability of their ethnic identity to extinction. Consequently, ethnic minorities encountered in non-Western areas often face the fear of their identity being absorbed by the majority society for the following reasons: the fact that they may have been forced to immigrate, share a similar appearance as ethnicities around them, and because other ethnicities have been living closely among them for a long time and know them very well. Under these circumstances, the social status quo may be enough that others can absorb valued identities. Had they accepted the assimilation process, it would be selectively limited to economic and educational dimensions, not the traditional ancestral ritual formalities, religions, commercial supremacy, or cultural symbols, which make up a culture's core. For these reasons, urban ethnic groups in non-Western urban areas face many more complex issues in the assimilation process compared to immigrants in developed countries.

Subcultural Theory in the City of Non-Western World

In Non-Western countries, when missionaries try to understand local ethnicities and their process of cultural assimilation, they should proceed with caution as they apply these skewed observations to their ministries.

First, inter-ethnic dynamics and ethnic experiences in non-Western countries may pose more barriers to an ethnicity's assimilation than those in America. In extreme cases, a central government might not do anything about the issue. Furthermore, there is no guarantee that the final stage of a minority's assimilation process will result in accepting the host culture.

When minorities adapt to the host culture, it is highly likely that the process will be interrupted by very complex inter-ethnic dynamics so that not all social processes will move in one direction. In some cases, because of resistance to the host culture, the status of being a minority will actually strengthen identity. For example, according to research, about half of young, educated urban Muslims in China prefer to adhere to religious conservative practices.[28] In some cases, ethnicities are comparatively open to outside cultures. Yet, at the same time, they may subjectively screen outside influences to develop ethnic culture with emotional stability. Arabization of Hui in China is a good example of a group adopting and developing within Islamic culture to likewise fit into modern society.[29] Sometimes, ethnic culture revives after a decline. Singapore is a good example. Through communization and revival of China in the 1950s, a sense of dignity and pride among Chinese living in Singapore was restored and thus their power and culture were revived again. Or some groups may even experience division due to pressures from outside influences. Among non-Western societies such a complex social phenomenon once again demonstrates that assimilation does not always move in one direction.

Second, in non-Western, the global modernization trend may create different types of ethnic issues. In some cases, a government campaigns and encourages modernization. In other cases, a government may not care about modernization but ethnic groups may take the initiative to follow a global trend. In the case of the former, ethnic minorities may be confused with the host culture and modernization. The ethnic minorities may interpret those of public facilities, industrialization, and western broadcasts as part of the host culture, but not as modernization. Therefore, they do not criticize modernization or westernization, but criticize their host culture in order to protect their ethnic traditions. For example, Muslims in China seem to interpret modernization campaigns as Han culture, China's major group, rather than Westernization, and this leads some of them to return to the Muslim culture as a defense mechanism.

Third, minorities in mission fields who mostly have strong cultural roots may have less of a desire to absorb the host culture compared to minorities in the West. In non-Western societies, there are cases when a people had their own territory but became a minority group under the domination of a stronger ethnicity. In this case, unique history, culture, and

28. Kim, "Receptor-Oriented Communication for Hui Muslims in China," 99–100.

29. Gillette, *Between Mecca and Beijing*, 233.

language of the ethnicity still remain but it is not easy for them to assimilate to the majority government policy.

Examples from China involve both Tibet and Uighur, which had at one time carved out a large territory in what is now the northwestern part of the country. The Uighur were able to maintain their own language and political frameworks. These ethnicities were very slow to assimilate to China's political policies compared with many other ethnic minorities in southeast or southwest China.[30]

Fourth, assimilation in non-Western countries does not always move from minority to majority. A good example would be England's commonwealth territories such as India. During the Victorian Age, England had amassed many colonies by the early twentieth century. Of course, there were many more people living in British colonies than in England.[31] India is a good example of colonization. In spite of the relative small size of England, there are many more British cultural influences in India but not much of England has been influenced by the Indian culture.

In the same way, in non-Western countries, ethnic minorities may not always assimilate to the prevailing majority culture for political, economic, or historical reasons. Even if they do, assimilation does not only happen in one direction. Thus, the direction of assimilation outside of the West is not determined by the number of people, but by people's preference at the time and political, economic influences.

As such, non-Western cities have more complicated features regarding ethnic culture compared to Western cities. Understanding urban ethnicities living in non-Western cities is mission strategically meaningful for two reasons: many missionaries are working in the non-Western world, and non-Western churches need to understand the special circumstances that they are in. In this sense and as conclusion of this chapter, we need to pay attention to the subcultural theory once again to better understand non-Western urban ethnicities. The attempt to understand urban ethnicities through sub-groups is the first step in understanding them practically.

30. Mackerras, *China's Minority Cultures*, 218–19.

31. In 1921, England possessed territories that had over a quarter of the world's population, which are about 458,000,000 people.

PART II

Strategy in Urban Ethnicities

6

Urban Neighbors

New Communication Channels that Unlock the Gospel (I)

WE WILL NOW EXAMINE the new channels of gospel based upon the theories in Part I. As the first, we will study the concept of urban neighbors in this chapter. The city is the place where traditional ethnic groups must eventually emerge from cultural isolation to interact with nearby residents. Globally, urban neighborhoods in modern metropolitan areas increasingly reflect a mash-up of cultural diversity. It is becoming all too rare for specific cultural groups to stake out exclusive proprietary ethnic boundaries in most any urban environment. Therefore, ethnic enclaves may find it difficult to completely isolate themselves given that coworkers, neighbors, and others more often than not represent a variety of cultural experiences. In this regard, it is crucial for urban Christian workers to understand the implications of cultural diversity on relationships among city dwellers. Most important to this discussion is the reality that the gospel flows through relationships.

In this chapter, we will explore the concept of "old neighbor/new neighbor" under the social network theory. The concept of "old neighbor" refers to traditional ethnic communities where neighbors share the same ethnic/cultural identity and experiences.

An important question for Christians is the following: "What is the impact of new urban neighbors on migrant homogenous ethnic enclaves?" Part of the answer may be found in the role of new networks and common meeting spaces to enhance social interactions that bridge diverse ethnic groups. This chapter will introduce a basic overview of social networks and how these communication channels can be useful in sharing the gospel with non-Christian urban ethnic group members. Likewise, the concept of new neighbor will be discussed to explore how this concept plays an important role in social networking to introduce new messages, which can include the gospel message.

A CASE:
SIMILAR RECEPTIVITY TO THE GOSPEL, DIFFERENT RESULTS

What follows are stories of three individuals who during their late adolescent years each moved to an urban area from a Chinese rural Muslim village. The three are members of a Chinese ethnic minority group that follows the Islamic faith. In each of these stories, the role of old neighbors and new neighbors in their social networks had significant influence on their exposure to and genuine interest in the Christian message of salvation. However, at some point they each responded differently to the message because of individual social considerations. So what caused different responses to the Gospel message among these three individuals sharing a similar cultural background? The three Chinese Muslims are Wang, an owner of a small noodle restaurant, Miss Ahu, a college lecturer, and her fiancé, Mr. Hoo. We will follow their stories.

The First Story: Wang and His Respected Uncle

Wang is a married TWENTY-THREE-year-old father of one child, who migrated to the city as an adolescent from a poor subsistence-farming village for economic reasons. Since that time, Wang's only social contact in an unfamiliar city has been his uncle, who hired his nephew to work in the family's small restaurant serving noodles. Wang aspires to open a new noodle restaurant like his uncle someday. For his part, the uncle left the family village many years ago to pursue a better standard of living in the city and has been assisting migrants from his village settle into city life, ever since.

The uncle is a generous and capable man who finds employment opportunities and suggests places to live for those who move to the city from their mutual hometown village. His ethnic group typically has difficulty mixing with the mainstream as they represent a minor ethnic group and speak a different language than what is spoken in the city. So most of the migrants from the village tend to live close to each other in the city, where they share a strong religious tradition, and run small shops to generate income. Wang's uncle is well respected and very influential in the area, having developed important social contacts after many years in the city.[1]

I tried to introduce Jesus to Wang, after building a relationship with him over a long period of time. Step-by-step, he sincerely opened his heart to Christ. However, one day, suddenly and very unexpectedly, he expressed that he unequivocally rejected the Gospel message because he shared faith in Islam with his people. Yet, as I heard the details behind his sudden unwavering profession of faith in Islam, I found that his unexpected declaration to me was motivated by fear of his uncle.

Wang respected his uncle a lot, but at the same time, he was afraid of his uncle. This fear was motivated by the uncle's great influence and power over Wang's finances, reputation, resources and even perceived future opportunities. Because his neighbors equally supported and relied on his uncle, the fear was if he somehow offended his uncle, Wang's relationship with the whole community, including his income and even his future aspirations would be threatened. This was the real reason why he rejected the message of salvation through Jesus Christ.

The Second Story:
Miss Ahu and Her New Circle of Friends

Miss Ahu is a Muslim Chinese woman raised in a small border town in China. As a young adult, she moved to a bigger city to attend college.[2] Upon graduating, she remained in the big city and found employment as a lecturer at her alma mater. While she was employed at the college, she lived with just a few friends but no relatives. One day, she found a side job teaching Chinese as a second language to a foreign couple.

At first, she regarded them strictly as foreigners, with foreign ideas that she did not particularly accept. Yet, as time went on, Miss Ahu developed a somewhat friendly relationship with the foreign couple after spending time conversing with them during the lessons. Eventually, she began

1. Wang is one of the many examples of Muslim migrants who have moved to a city that the author has observed in China.

2. Miss Ahu and Mr. Hoo in here are not their real names to protect their privacy.

to understand them and respected their opinions. Three years later, while interacting with the couple at their home, Miss Ahu took a step of faith and accepted the message of salvation through Christ.

Other Christians in her social circles were excited to hear the news, but they also worried about one particular issue. Miss Ahu was engaged to a young man named Hoo (not his real name to protect his privacy). He was a devout Muslim. The general fear was of his response—what he might do when he discovered his fiancée had converted to Christianity. The question was would he react negatively to her new Christian faith? Would he even go so far as to call the police to apprehend any, perhaps all foreigners who participated even slightly in his future wife's conversion and have them deported?

The Third Story: Hoo and His Fiancée

At the time of Miss Ahu's step of faith, Hoo was working in South East Asia teaching Chinese to language learners. A few days after Miss Ahu's conversion to Christ, Hoo returned to the city to meet her. All of her Christian friends, including all local missionaries, prayed fervently seeking God's help in this potentially explosive situation.

No one knew just how Hoo would react upon discovering his fiancée's new faith. However, something amazing happened. We had expected he might attack us for his fiancée's betrayal of Islam, but instead, Hoo made an astonishing declaration himself. He confessed to her, "I came to believe in Jesus in South East Asia."

Hoo shared that there were many committed Christians at the school where he worked. They truly cared for him and treated him respectfully with the love of Christ. In a city where he had no friends or relatives, he met new neighbors who eventually shared the Good News with him. Still, after he received Jesus, he was confused by many questions. Even his new Christian neighbors could not answer his perplexing questions. However, another amazing thing happened. He encountered Jesus in a dream and asked Jesus directly to answer all of his questions. Beginning the next morning, he had no more questions. Then upon returning to China, he shared with his fiancée Ahu what had happened. He discovered that Miss Ahu, whom he had expected to be a Muslim, now likewise providentially knew Jesus. Just as Hoo, she too heard the Good News from new neighbors in the city.

A Common Thread

As I observed these individuals and their experiences, I discovered similarities across the stories of Wang from the small noodle restaurant, Miss Ahu, a college lecturer, and her fiancé Hoo, a language teacher working abroad. As Chinese Muslims, they are members of an ethnic minority. They were all born and raised in small Muslim villages and grew up in the Islamic faith. During late adolescence, each had moved away from their villages to a large city for a variety of reasons, but in general to improve their outlook for the future. Upon extended exposure to the Gospel message, all three became genuinely interested. Yet, the outcomes were different. What caused the different reactions to the Gospel in these cases? I have found that the Gospel became relatable to non-Christian urban residents when the main conduit of the message was a believer with a genuine reputation within social networks as a trustworthy and reliable neighbor. Though only two out of the three Chinese Muslims accepted Christ as Savior, a clear fact was that they each listened to the message—the Good News of Jesus when shared by new neighbors—neighbors who are not members of the Chinese Muslim ethnic community's social network.

Neighbors are crucial components of evangelism strategy. Many unreached peoples in the city come to the Lord because of a new neighbor's patient commitment to build sincere relationships across social networks. Wang, Ahu and Hoo heard the Gospel from new neighbors with whom they had built a trustworthy relationship after meeting frequently.

Neighbors are one of the representative social networks, because they function as channels for sharing thoughts and emotions. In other words, these social channels help us to share information. By venturing beyond familiar social networks to gain needed information, people may extend social networks because of trustworthy interactions with new neighbors. Therefore as urbanites feel comfortable enough to venture beyond familiar social circles across urban networks, they will share information to correspond with unique patterns of need.

The modern urbanite, especially ethnic minorities, not only have familiar social networks built on cultural traditions, but also gain "new neighbors" from social networks originating beyond proprietary circles. In most cases, newly arrived ethnic minorities in the city live among familiar neighbors—neighbors who share their language and ethnic traditions. But, as time goes on, some migrants will come in contact with people who are not members of the migrant ethnic community. And this contact will enable them to acquire a diverse group of neighbors.

On the one hand, the migrant can maintain familiar relationships among those who share cultural traditions and an ethnic identity. These familiar relationships can be found among the old neighbors. On the other hand, relationships formed with people outside of the ethnic community will increase as migrants build contacts through a variety of social activities.

To set up strategies to share and spread the Gospel among non-Christian urban ethnic groups, this chapter will introduce an overview of basic theories that have defined social networks. Subsequently, we will then compare how social network systems between old neighbors (e.g., migrant neighbors who share cultural traditions and ethnic identity) and new neighbors (e.g., urban dwellers with different cultural ties) function differently. From this standpoint, we will take a look at the kinds of missional opportunities social networks can create.

THE OLD NEIGHBOR'S NETWORK

After migration, ethnic groups in the city will likely develop at least two kinds of neighbors. One of them is the old neighbor who populates the familiar ethnic neighborhood, while the new neighbor resides outside ethnic cultural enclaves, perhaps even outside of town. Given the formidable influence old neighbors have across relationships, the social network theory is invaluable when exploring key characteristics within urban social circles to determine appropriate missiological strategies. This section examines characteristics of old neighbor social characteristics through the lens of social network.

Migrant ethnic groups newly settled in the city can get valuable information regarding housing and other necessary basic living needs from old neighbors. Consequently, old neighbors play a key role in helping members of the community settle down and feel secure in new often-challenging surroundings. The wise counsel of old neighbors is very important when considering appropriate mission strategies to develop for urban ethnic communities. In the absence of understanding the role the old neighbor plays across communication channels in a specific community, accessing local communication channels or creating the most influential ways to share the Gospel among a non-Christian social group would be difficult for the missionary at the very least. The old neighbor is usually the repository of trusted information; therefore, an outsider who understands how the old neighbor can influence the validity of a message is extremely important.

Three Kinds of Networks

The friends of migrants who have not resided for a long time in a city, but instead live in an isolated ethnic community are equally categorized as old neighbors because each shares traditional social values held by a specific ethnic group. There are three kinds of networks where old neighbors socialize: residential territory networks, ethnic networks, and occupational networks. The term residential territory network, as you might imagine, refers to networks among people who live in close proximity. An ethnic network refers to people who share a common cultural origin. And finally, an occupational network refers to people who connect through economic activities.[3]

Residential Territory Network

Prior to migration, new urban dwellers formed social networks of friends and family back home. Consequently, in the city, migrants tend to duplicate a similar network. Such duplication can create an egocentric social network of urban neighbors who could approximate relationships enjoyed with old friends back home.

Neighbors who live in close proximity make up the first component of an urbanite's network. In a new environment, gathering needed information and navigating across the social landscape can often be complicated due to differences in language, culture and social systems. Since many first generation unskilled migrants are not always financially stable, they seek to settle near people they know and understand. They may settle in shantytowns or city slums or in ethnic communities where they might find people nearby who also hail from the same villages or same ethnic groups. As a result, these migrants naturally position themselves to become neighbors in a welcoming community in a new environment. In these areas, the residents' patterns of activity or proximity to neighbors enable them to interact frequently and maintain contact.

Upon closer inspection, we find complicated dynamics in urban societies. Urban areas form segmentations by age, ethnicity, origin, and occupations. Individuals repeatedly experience harmony and disharmony as they exchange mutual benefits or conflict. That is, whether the locale is a small village or neighborhood, there are various sub-networks in it.

---

3. The overall structure of this section and the idea of three kinds of networks are come from Eames and Goode, *Anthropology of the City*, chap. 5.

Figure 6–1: Chinese Muslims Who Move from Rural Areas Live in an Ethnic Enclave of a City. (June 2011) *Donxiang* Enclave in *Linxia* City, *Gansu* Province, China.
Photo © Enoch Kim

Ethnic Network

The second component within a community of newly arrived migrants is a network of relationships among group members. Many people migrate from rural areas to cities, from small cities to bigger cities, or from urban areas in smaller countries to vast international metropolitan areas to start a new life. As part of the migration process mentioned earlier, people continuously beckon for relatives and neighbors from neighborhoods of origin to follow a similar path of migration to cities. In this way, ethnic groups will try to maintain cultural traditions and kinship ties by transplanting them to urban locales. This is their ethnic network.

Together, homogenous groups can naturally share their information through familiar languages and activities. Likewise, important but limited information from the mainstream community can be selectively distributed by those who are capable of communicating outside of their communities with the mainstream.

Figure 6–2: Members of the Same Ethnic Groups Often Seek to Live in Close Proximity after Migrating to an Unfamiliar Environment. (June 2005) *Donxiang* Enclave In *Linxia* City, *Gansu* Province, China. Photo © Enoch Kim

Every ethnic group must meet two conditions in order to evolve as a cohesive city dwelling group: cultural dynamics and structural formations. The term cultural dynamics refers to familiar tastes and expressions transplanted with migrants from their hometown. The by-products of such cultural dynamics include marriage preferences, values, morality and religion, which each strongly function as social control mechanisms. People work as the same ethnicity when they are equipped with such structures and dynamics.

SOCIAL ELEMENTS

Members of an ethnic group will refer to ethnic traditions and style as behavioral landmarks, no matter how often individual tastes may change. For instance, it is sometimes easiest to distinguish ethnicity by dress and other cosmetic aspects of individual appearance. Consequently, these dynamics will direct social behavior through a new social landscape within the boundaries of established ethnic cultural patterns.

In order for members of the same ethnic group to recognize each other around the city, an appropriate social structure must exist. That is, groups form a social identity and cohesiveness around identifying symbols from a common heritage. Symbols, in particular, accelerate structural formations, as in the case of distinct shared common physical features including skin color, hair, the shape of eyes, diction and accents, style sense, eating habits, music, and so on.

Beyond these cultural and structural factors, there are other factors that contribute to an ethnic group's identity formation in a new residential environment. For instance, if strong religious views or strict boundaries around social status are obvious and shared by all, the possibility of forming an ethnic subgroup is very strong. People from the same social status or class often have similar educational and economic levels, styles, tastes and thoughts. Therefore, it is easier for them to share emotionally stable relationships.

The size of related ethnic groups residing in a city also influences the development of social bonds. If the number of ethnic members is too little, cohesion can be lost. Conversely, when an ethnic group exceeds a certain size, observers would assert that it has passed a critical mass. The process of members identifying themselves with the same ethnicity is possible, when they have a chance to live and work in an environment with more than minimum numbers. However, once the group passes critical mass, that ethnic group becomes capable of producing a new culture on its own by establishing group pride through familiar and new traditions.

Additionally, when a city is able to accept its diversity, then ethnic traditions can settle into the general urban lifestyle. On the other hand, if a city intolerantly prioritizes a uniform culture and proceeds to politically or religiously persecute ethnic minorities based on their traditions, the ethnic culture submerges into an underground culture or otherwise collapses.

An economic network comprised of the same ethnic members is very crucial in the formation of ethnic unity. Urban ethnic groups often form their own ethnic structures and economic niches. Sometimes ethnic group members share the same types of occupations. This can be because people introduce occupations to members of their own ethnic group to form a support system that works together. So, it suddenly seems natural that specific ethnic groups gravitate to the same businesses. Outside limitations might then be introduced by the mainstream to intentionally deter opportunities afforded to a suddenly prosperous ethnic group.

Political activity is another cohesive factor. When members of the same ethnic group form a political alliance to promote the group's well being, their political demands protect their relationships and add credibility to the group. The relationships and this new credibility are sometimes used in political campaigns adding cohesion to the group.

Many ethnic groups strive in the political arena for legislation that could benefit their ethnic community and help them hold influential positions. However, as various dynamics in cities change, not only between ethnic groups, but also among of ethnic members, many different groups can newly form, separate or unify with others as they gain a foothold.

CULTURAL EXPRESSIONS

A group that recognizes itself as belonging to the same ethnicity, culture, systematical and social milieu continually reconfirms themselves as one unified group by sharing their unique cultural expressions. Unique cultural expressions can be conveyed with the same language, same foods and traditions, and the same institutional mechanisms.[4]

Language and symbols serve as very vital components in this regard. The youngest learn to communicate at an early age, from family members and extended family, internalizing their ethnic identity and language. Ethnic dance, music, religion, folklore, and mythology are all representations of cultural symbols, as well. Likewise, religious rituals and practices are important channels that express ethnic identity. These shared worldview and religious practices help an ethnic community bond together. These bonding moments are celebrated around holidays and life passages to shape an ethnic community's collective identity. The most vibrant cultural expression is through dress and other cosmetic aspects of individual appearance.

Another cultural expression is food and tradition. Food culture is represented by dietary patterns: food items typically consumed and those that are avoided (e.g., taboo foods). Moreover, this cultural expression is a powerful link maintaining connections between a family and its ethnic group. Food preparation and eating choices are informed by the group and introduced into the family often by parents. These eating patterns do not

---

4. Eames subcategorized this cultural substance into symbols, food traditions, and institutions. Eames and Goode, *Anthropology of the City*, 186–96.

change easily among members upon growing into adulthood. Sometimes adults do crave these comforting foods reminiscent of an earlier satisfying period in time, despite new social activities, health concerns or the social influence of other ethnic group.

An ethnic community often hosts one or more ethnic restaurants showcasing cultural foods, which are just as often discovered by the main-stream population. If the population of one ethnic group in a city increases, the number of ethnic restaurants and supporting grocery markets tends to also increase in that locale to meet demand.

Sometimes, creative members of an ethnic group bridge eating cultures in their new locale by combining indigenous, traditional recipes with local offerings to create a fusion of tastes. By the way, this is one example of how a community begins to create a third or new sub-culture in a new city environment.

Finally, urban ethnic groups can express their cultural traditions through institutional mechanisms. An institutional mechanism is an event during which people gather to engage in a shared experience. Ethnic sports and festival celebrations are examples of institutional mechanisms that accelerate unity among ethnic group members. Likewise, regional gatherings, media events, religious activities, commerce, and similar social activities are collective institutional mechanisms through which communication and information flow. As the population of an ethnic community increases and the social environment becomes more familiar, the speed of assimilating into the mainstream slows down. Instead, the power to maintain or improve one's own culture strengthens.[5]

Occupational Network

An economic network (or occupational network) is the third component serving as an important social structure formed by new urbanites. Finding a way to improve one's own economic circumstances and that of the family is often the central factor motivating groups living in poor rural communities to migrate to urban areas where perceived opportunities exist.

When migrants journey to a city to live, they necessarily join economic networks. This can be employed in a small store with one or two workers, or self-employed as an entrepreneur, for example. Others may find work in a factory with thousands of workers.

5. Hiebert and Meneses, *Incarnational Ministry*, 285.

Because the same ethnic members may populate similar job roles, the mainstream may associate certain jobs with certain ethnic groups. These jobs could be blue-collar positions such as rickshaw drivers, scavengers or rag pickers. Consequently, a few ethnic groups may dominate such a niche.[6] Unfortunately, as competition tightens for certain limited opportunities, conflict can arise between ethnic groups as they struggle for market share in a particular niche.

Unlike traditional rural societies with limited development, an economically vibrant urban environment can offer more opportunities to migrants in many more situations by comparison. In a traditional society, an individual's status is ascribed. Yet, in a city, social elevation is conceivably available by effort and ability. Money and competition are the generative power for status elevation. Skills and education can be an individual's competitive strength. In other words, competitive power can be derived from education and skills when seeking good employment options, upward mobility, strong wages and social status.

Figure 6–3: Community Members of the Same Ethnic Group Helping to Start a Small Business. (2004) *Xian*, China. Photo © Enoch Kim

An initial generation of city migrants tends to have a strong desire to achieve upward social mobility, as the hope to improve individual and family status are strong—since that was the motivation for the initial move.

6. Kim, "Receptor-Oriented Communication for Hui Muslims in China," 64.

Therefore, many may initially value educational resources as a mechanism to join mainstream society in the near future, at the very least, in order to learn the new language.

Concentration of Networks and Leadership

The result of mission for any community should be heavily influenced by the kinds of systems and leadership around which the community is organized. In some cases, it could prove difficult for individuals to freely hear the Gospel because community systems and/or leadership oppose Christianity. Or, even if individuals do accept the Gospel message, it may be impossible for the message to spread easily throughout the array of community social networks because of these same obstacles. Therefore, in order to work effectively, missionary teams should analyze if not be aware of the influence old neighbors have on communication through the community system compared to that of leadership.

We can start by examining relationships within the three networks: residential territory networks, ethnic networks, and occupational networks. We must explore the ways people are influenced, which in reality means exploring how network communication channels within the old neighbor network system and from leadership operate within specific social networks. Then we can ask, "How are members of a local array of networks being influenced to make decisions? Who is setting the social trends in the community?

The Concentration of Three Networks

Old neighbors congregate and interact within ethnic, occupational, and residential territory networks with everyone else in the community. The structure of these three networks in a migrant's new urban community can feel quite similar to social networks found back home. This is because, in many cases, new migrants to a city settle in an area where they can make the most out of whatever limited resources they bring with them. These resources can include knowledge about a new environment, fluency with language, as well as whatever material resources they possess. As a result, a migrant may tend to build social relationships in the new environment with people who share familiar cultural expressions. In other words, new neighbors initially live with old neighbors as the new migrant learns to navigate a new setting and social circumstances.

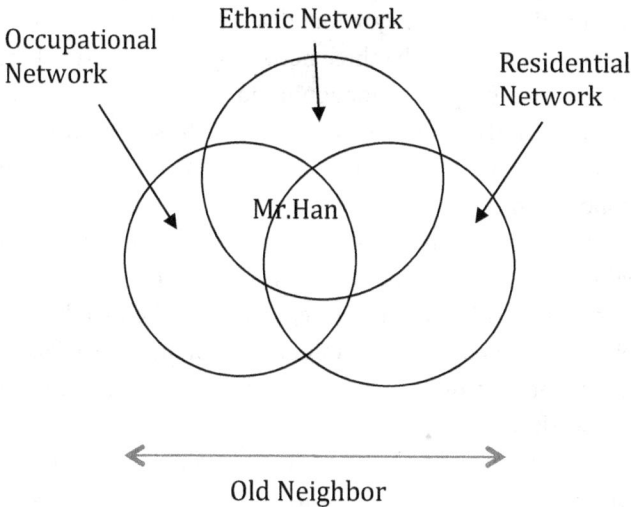

Chart 6–1: Dispersing the Secondary Networks[7]

My personal friend Mr. Han who used to enjoy playing badminton falls under this case. Mr. Han in *Xi'an* city is a Chinese Muslim who drives a taxi. His wife opens a small stall every day and sells goods near the entrance of an ethnic migrant town. They have been living with their extended family as they work to gain a foothold in their new environment. Chart 6–1 is a conceptual diagram illustrating the three networks of old neighbors. It shows how three networks overlap within an old neighbor's network, as was the case with Mr. Han.

The process of settling into an unfamiliar city environment also includes stepping into the three networks mentioned earlier: urban ethnic, residential territory, and occupational networks. In many cases, urban migrants start their new urban experience behind ethnic boundaries. Therefore, in a new social environment the three networks will easily overlap other networks as shared language and cultural perspectives will lead migrants to find initial economic opportunities among familiar neighbors.[8] In

7. Developed diagram from Kim, "Receptor-Oriented Communication for Hui Muslims in China," 67.

8. Qingfang, "Race/Ethnicity, Gender and Job Earnings across Metropolitan Areas in the United States: A Multilevel Analysis."

other words, people will tend to involve themselves in any social, economic and even religious activity in a familiar community.[9] Therefore, the concept of neighbor to them refers to those who are relatable people within each zone where the three networks are found, as indicated in Chart 6–1.

When two or more of the three networks overlap, network members are for all practical purposes functioning in one network. They often do social, economic, and even religious activities in the same community. That is why the range of neighbors in the Chart 6–1 is quite narrower than the new neighbor's concept in Chart 6–3.

When residents live and work within these overlapping networks, each individual can potentially experience layers of social insulation afforded by multiple relationships. For instance, that all of the members of a new urban neighborhood network who migrated from the same villages (ethnic network) gravitate to working as taxi drivers in the same company (occupational network) is a good case of this. Because of this social overlapping, network members can get to know each other in depth. In this case, overlapping urban ethnic networks can work as an effective protection system. For example, if a taxi driver, such as Mr. Han in Chart 6–1 cannot work because his taxi is broken, neighbors might help his family financially, and with encouragement, emotionally. The ethnic leader of their urban village might introduce him to people who sell new taxis at very low prices.

On the other hand, navigating through multiple relationships can create tensions as a natural outcome of social interactions and conflicts. For instance, conflict can arise from a familiar social flaw: within a close-knit community rumors spread quickly. So, let's say the following scenario occurs. A taxi driver's relationship with a network leader is wrought with friction, until finally the problem snowballs into a public conflict. Of course, the family of the driver could be hurt by negative rumors spread by neighbors regarding the network leader's poor opinion of the taxi driver. Yet, these rumors within the close-knit community could also complicate the family's ability to live and work peacefully within their ethnic network.

Community living among old neighbors is familiar and is hardly expected to change. In this setting, the community may have a hard time accepting new behaviors or ideas. Interestingly, an urban migrant's urban ethnic network may share similar aspects with those of a former rural

9. Fong et al., "The Logic of Ethnic Business Distribution in Multiethnic Cities"; Ndofor and Priem, "Immigrant Entrepreneurs, the Ethnic Enclave Strategy, and Venture Performance," 790.

community in a number of ways. Take for instance urban networks within the mainstream. Members may know network peers only superficially within the context of business relationships, for instance. However, villagers in rural areas frequently communicate with members from different networks and can be privy to personal information due to kinship affiliations and smaller networks with less people.

Ironically, an urban ethnic neighborhood's network may take similar shape to previous ones found back home in rural areas. This is because an urban ethnic neighborhood can be a more concentrated network than the much broader mainstream networks in a large city. Of course, shared cultural, structural, and situational components facilitate the exchange of information among members, unlike the complex highly diversified mainstream networks with fewer shared components between members. Actually, it is through a social network that members of an ethnic group inherit the group's social norms.

If an individual's behavior or value system veers away from the group's established social norms, at the very least, negative rumors about the offending person can also spread over the entire community. This would count as a form of punishment for the offender, as that society attempts to maintain itself in its own social boundaries through methods such as gossip, shame, guilt, reciprocity, mediation, or legal consequences, including punishment.[10]

In terms of evangelization and the Gospel, members of a tight-knit urban ethnic community may find it difficult to receive the Gospel, and even harder to put the message into practice because of various internal and external social pressures from their networks. Very often, when an urban migrant is exposed to the Gospel, the same social dynamics inside the ethnic network are at work limiting interaction with outside influences. In other words, the migrant's egocentric networks have a strong influence on individual behavior relative to the amount of social freedom allowed by influencers inside the networks.

Concentration of Network Leaderships

Leadership among old neighbors can wield considerable political power and responsibility. Originally, each network of the three may have their own leadership in place. However, in case of old neighbors, overlapping authority often falls on very few leaders.

10. Shaw, *Transculturation*, chap. 7.

Chart 6–2 is a conceptual diagram of a few leaders assuming leadership responsibilities across three overlapping. In this case, leaders who are old neighbors can have significant influence over members.

In this case, the leader could exercise an enormous amount of influence over an individual (also referred to as an ego) by using the three network forces.

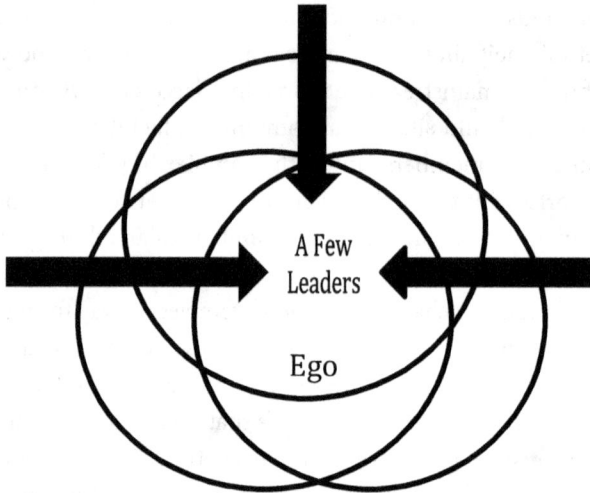

Chart 6–2: Concentrated Leadership among the Old Neighbors

Wang's story shared earlier in the chapter shows how the three social networks—ethnic, residential, and occupational—can typically overlap. Wang's uncle (the owner of a small noodle restaurant) is of the same ethnicity as Wang. He is also an influential leader in his residential neighborhood. Wang's case is a good example of a person whose three networks overlap and who is greatly influenced by an old neighbor.

In this case, Wang's uncle has strong social influence in the community. Though Wang may enjoy the social, cultural, financial, and emotional stability provided by his uncle, his uncle might also control Wang's freedom to pursue life goals and social relationships. If any individual in their community, including Wang, refuses the uncle's directions or behaves contrary to his personal social values, the offender could suffer consequences.[11]

---

11. As such, Eames and Goode said that when three networks converge into one, the network becomes something great and dominant to the individual. Eames and Goode, *Anthropology of the City*, 214

As such, few strong leaders heavily influence people living in a closed community. For instance, if a community member does not accept information that conforms to the uncle's values, that individual could likely suffer some retribution, whether mild or otherwise. In the case of the Gospel, any initial new believer from that community who accepts the Gospel message could easily be subject to social and/or economic threats.

This is because the idea that an individual accepts a new religion outside of Wang's approval can bring not only a shift in worldview but also threaten relationships and the many supportive foundations that maintain a stable existence under his life values within the social fabric of the network.

This social dynamic also applies to a person in an urban ethnic migrant village who is interested in the Gospel. Though the person is open to the Gospel, which is very new to the village, peer pressure to be socially accepted, and other practical issues present many hurdles that can easily complicate the start of a new way of life.

THE NEW NEIGHBOR'S NETWORK

When people from the countryside or small towns migrate to a big city or metropolis, they experience significant changes in their social networks. The many relationships they must cultivate greatly influence every corner of their lives, from economic survival and family development, to emotional stability and even spiritual fulfillment. The networks developed through interactions in the city provide a different array of relationships than those fostered in the countryside. The characteristics of the urbanites' modern network are complex and dynamic.

Urban social networks are dramatically evolving daily, and urban ethnic minorities are too. This is especially evident when ethnic minorities migrate into cities, because that is where they often have many new encounters but also make numerous separations. Members of networks formed by specific groups share experiences across ethnic, residential, and occupational networks: although, this too may change. As time passes, minorities gradually but increasingly come in contact with outside networks. As a result, migrants will simultaneously form social networks comprised of old neighbors from their ethnic village and new neighbors outside of the village.

Urban Neighbors

What is a neighbor? How do researchers define this concept? The concept of neighbor is very common to us though it may be difficult for us to think hard about what a neighbor is exactly. How do we become neighbors? Often, we think of neighbors as the people living in homes or apartments next to us. However, as society modernizes and technology removes distance as an obstacle to interactions, what is a neighbor, really?

In terms of new residents in a new urban setting, neighbors or the people living next door may suddenly no longer fit our concept of neighbor. This is because a neighbor is seen as a relationship, sometimes defined as a friend. Yet, the person who we interact with online might more closely fit the notion of neighbor.

The concept of neighbor has a huge influence on evangelism. If we consider the fact that people usually hear about the Gospel through those they know well, neighbors should play a very important part in strategies to evangelize modern urban dwellers.

So, again, what is a neighbor? What are the sociological conditions one must meet to become a neighbor, beyond proximity? According to researchers, at least three conditions need to be met to define a person as a neighbor in a sociological sense: identity, interaction, and linkage.[12] In traditional societies, people have initiated and maintained neighborly relationships with many people who satisfied these three conditions. As an example, in a village, there are a group of friends and relatives (identity) who farm together cooperatively and distribute (linkage) their products. Consequently, opportunities for interaction are quite abundant.

On the other hand, communities in the city may not have abundant opportunities for interaction that form naturally. For example, urbanites are prone to exclude the people living next door from personal activities, access to family or from individual interests—even community events.

Consequently, urbanites tend to have less interaction with residents living just next door. Although, at the same time, compared to what is generally available in the countryside, urbanites can have many more newly developed local gathering places available for networking opportunities.[13]

12. Warren and Warren, *The Neighborhood Organizer's Handbook*, 94–112.

13. Todd and Paul, "Implications of Public School Choices for Residential Location Decisions," 307.

As society continues to modernize, a traditional concept of neighbor should be altered from what was once defined in a different era.[14] Specifically, the concept can no longer simply refer to people living next door. Urban neighbors are different from the familiar faces traveling back and forth across a fence in the countryside or small town. The anonymous nature of the city means that conceivably an apartment dweller may never get a knock at their door from the person living in the next apartment for an entire year or ever. In the city context, "neighbor" may not simply be the person next door, but rather the individuals we encounter most often.[15]

They can be the people who take the same transportation daily, co-workers at the next desk working all day from 9 A.M. onward, or baseball club members meeting every weekend on the field. City neighbors are more prone to comprise a circle of meaningful relationships organized around occupations or special interests.[16] This may or may not include those who are geographically close in proximity.

Although neighbors may be close in proximity, they may not be close socially. Yet, new networks can be formed through business or affinity groups.[17] As a result, urbanites can be more selective of friends and diversify their social networks.[18]

Traditionally, geography plays an important part in the formation of networks, because people who live too far apart find it hard to meet regularly.[19] Modern technology, however, is changing this as people link up with one another by means of phones and computers. Networks restore a personal face to impersonal city life, offering opportunities to establish intimate relationships with other like-minded people.[20]

Having more opportunities to choose friends with similar interests socially and in business is how networks grow—through friends and interest groups. In particular, bigger cities tend to have more well-developed urban-styled neighbor networks. This is because bigger cities can easily host more people who share similar interests and even provide many opportunities to

14. Musterd et al., "Adaptive Behaviour in Urban Space."

15. Michaelson, *Man and His Urban Enviornment*, 190.

16. Claerbaut, *Urban Ministry*, 75–76.

17. Fischer, *The Urban Experience*, 140–41.

18. Ibid., 135.

19. Farrell, "Immigrant Suburbanisation and the Shifting Geographic Structure of Metropolitan Segregation in the United States," 825.

20. Hiebert and Meneses, *Incarnational Ministry*, 278.

meet and interact.[21] Though network densities around residential neighbor-hoods have decreased, urbanites have more trans-local neighbors.

Dispersion of the Three Networks

Again, the conceptual old neighbor's three networks tend to often overlap. However, nowadays, with the influence of urbanization and moderniza-tion, relationships experienced by migrants and ethnic minorities within these three networks can cover wide geographic locations. Today, urban minorities can choose from many different occupations rather than having to solely rely upon kinship ties, such as Uncle Wang in an earlier example.

Added to the migrant's aspirations for economic and social survival are new needs and desires for faster social elevation. These aspirations can include access to both higher education and new media with its abundant information resources and encourage ethnic individuals to build new networks and meaningful relationships, inside and outside of their ethnic social circles. Consequently, their social networks can grow and diversify rapidly, but show less overlap. It is therefore conceivable that their newly acquired social networks will barely share common boundaries.[22]

Both the residential network and occupational network are the social circles that have shown the biggest changes in character. This is because the concept of neighbor refers to more than people living in a shared geo-graphical location but include those with similar concerns and interests. For example, regardless of ethnic background, people will meet together to share similar hobbies, or serve together as PTA members, or be active together in an Internet community, and so on.[23] Individuals come together to form a group around similar interests and needs to exchange informa-tion for mutual benefit. When such relationships develop, individuals will participate in many social activities and share common emotions. These proximity groups are a kind of neighbor. Yet, unlike the old neighbor, these are new neighbors found outside of the circles of relationships found in the ethnic community. These individuals are neighbors in a city environment regardless of the distance between residential addresses.

21. Fischer, *The Urban Experience*, 141.

22. Eames and Goode, *Anthropology of the City*, 214.

23. Kim, "'Us' or 'Me'? Modernization and Social Networks among China's Urban Hui," 89–96.

Today the concept of residential network has evolved from the traditional concept of a cluster of people living in close proximity to include those who share a common ground, pursue the same interests, and interact frequently. Urbanites employing faster transportation and communication resources have the technological tools to find like-minded urban dwellers in order to share similar interests. This is a characteristic of typical modern urbanites for which distance is no longer an obstacle.

Members of occupational networks have also become very diversified—extended by the development of personal mobility and ability. Previously, people searched for jobs through acquaintances, but urban ethnic minorities now have more diverse job opportunities. These opportunities are accessible through information obtained from their educational and social activities. Once individuals surpass the boundaries of their ethnicity or culture, they can pursue a broader spectrum of economic activities.

Chart 6–3 is a conceptual diagram illustrating each dispersed network belonging to an urban ethnic minority. In this case, Mr. Li is the ego in the egocentric social network, which shows how distinct and dispersed the occupational network is from the proximity network of new neighbors.

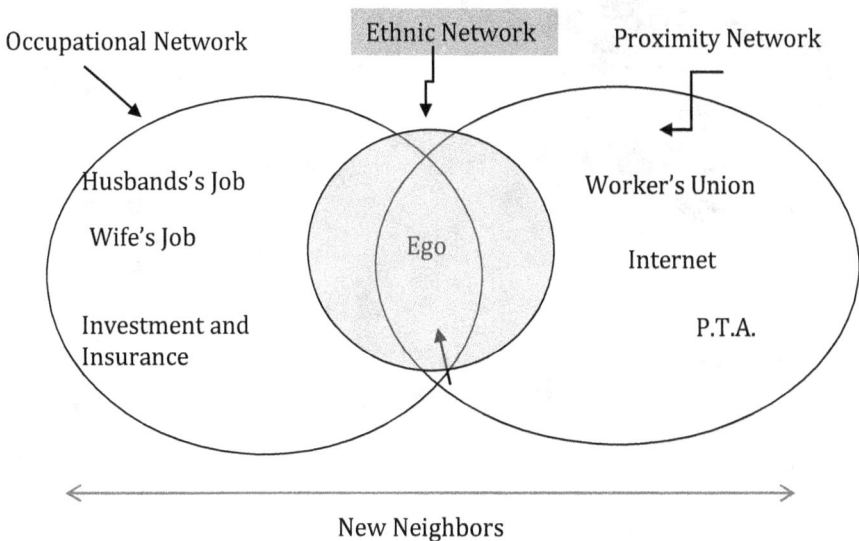

Occupational Network   Ethnic Network   Proximity Network

Husbands's Job   Worker's Union

Wife's Job   Ego   Internet

Investment and Insurance   P.T.A.

New Neighbors

Chart 6–3: Dispersing the Three Networks and the New Neighbors[24]

24. Developed diagram from Kim, "Receptor-Oriented Communication for Hui Muslims in China," 68.

As is apparent from his occupational network, Mr. Li does not bind himself to just one income source. Rather, Mr. Li generates income from a full-time job in his wife's small shop. Additionally, they earn some secondary income from stock investments and life insurance. In order to pursue these different economic opportunities Mr. Li had to network with diverse people. Therefore, within his networks, members may be different kinds of people. For example, he had to acquaint himself with white-collar workers to buy investment stocks and salespeople to buy insurance. However, he may also have to interact regularly with local small business entrepreneurs on behalf of his wife. In other words, Mr. Li has to anticipate diversifying his network relationships so as to discover and maintain a variety of social and economic activities.

Figure 6–4: Chinese Muslims Moonlighting as Private Taxi Business Owners. (2011) Gansu Province, China. Photo © Enoch Kim

Mr. Li interacts with several social networks when he engages in social activity. These groups can be defined as proximity groups. Among Mr. Li's several social engagements include activities with a workers' union, an Internet club, his children's school, and many more interactions within different proximity groups.

Of course, ethnic group membership cannot change because of its ascribed nature. On the other hand, proximity groups and occupational networks extend the ethnic member's interactions beyond the original ethnic network. Chart 6–3 shows the overlapping of three networks and illustrates the significant changed network component related to neighbors compared to the traditional network structures in Chart 6–1.

As illustrated before, old neighbors show a very narrow dispersion, but significant overlap across their social networks. This means their interactions outside of the community are limited as many of the same people may appear again in different networks. On the other hand, Mr. Li's social networks hardly overlap because of the wide dispersion of relationships he has cultivated. This means that he knows many different people. Specifically, we can see that members of ethnic networks, proximity networks, and occupational networks can all be counted as neighbors. Yet, each actual network member may not be the same. This new diversity in an urban dweller's network represents interaction with new neighbors and exposure to many more new ideas, than those traditionally held by their group of origin.

In summary, as urban ethnic minorities reside longer in cities they have a chance to build new relationships with neighbors who are from outside of their ethnic circles. The ethnic social pressure they receive to conform to group norms will decrease, as individual freedom and responsibilities increase beyond their community. Through relationships with new neighbors, urban ethnic minorities can develop a variety of social activities and general interactions with outsiders. Most importantly, at least one of those interactions can be an encounter with the Gospel.

Dispersion of Network Leadership

New Neighbors live and work within many diversified networks. As a result, they experience dispersed control from many networks rather than dominant control by any specific network. Part of the reason is that new neighbors are mostly members of non-overlapping networks. Therefore, members of the different networks may not know each other because each separate network is so diversified. Therefore, it becomes difficult for different network members to get to know each other. Because of this, the ego may act very differently and appear as different personas within different networks. At the same time, the ego may interact with members to share a variety of information in each of the networks. This allows the people to access more abundant information than members of more concentrated networks, which only the ego can contact. The dispersed scenario allows members to enjoy more freedom in decision-making. In addition, the pressure to allow control over one's life by a specific network is lessened when social networks are widely dispersed.

Chart 6–4 is a conceptual diagram showing how leadership across dispersed networks impacts individuals in a new neighbor environment. This type of leadership arrangement distributes decision-making power among many leaders, giving the individual or ego (i.e., egocentric network) little if any collective power. However, the ego in this case can enjoy relatively more freedom in his or her decision-making. This is because the ego only has to discuss a limited amount of information with each influential leader and only in their limited area. Therefore, the ego in reality can make decisions independently. This shows a different feature compared to old leadership style, which shows how power is concentrated to few influencing all members greatly.

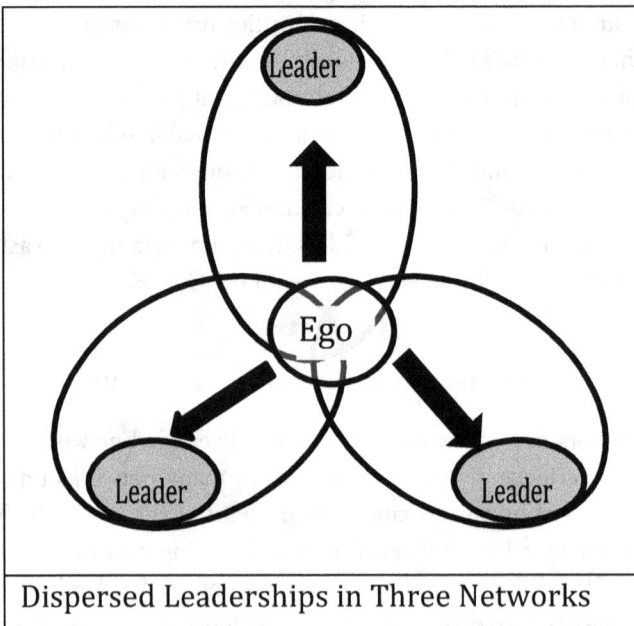

Chart 6–4: A Network of Dispersed Community Leadership

However, expecting an environment where community protects individuals or where rich human relationships can be enjoyed by the new neighbors is not easy. These modern individuals do not have a big brother to protect and to mentor them. Consequently, they are responsible for solving many problems by themselves. For example, when the people in dispersed networks face crises, they would go to the insurance company instead of an uncle. Rather than spending time with friends and neighbors in the village after dinner, they may need to further develop job skills and watch TV alone or later when they have some free time.

NEW MEETING SPACES:
URBAN JUNCTURES AS UNITS OF INTEGRATION

Any ethnic group that has maintained and developed its culture and customs over a long period of time has likely distinguished its own culture and practices from every other ethnic culture. For example, all members of a group can identify some foods as "ours" and some as "theirs." Ethnic groups also have developed ways of expressing a distinct lifestyle beyond food, such as concepts of space and location, usability of time, preference of occupation, entertainment, and relationship dynamics.

The problem is that it becomes difficult for ordinary people to interact and build relationships with others because of the unique systems of each culture. As a result, people tend to associate with people and events that feel comfortable and familiar. When religious beliefs or personal philosophies are added, developing relationships beyond familiar social circles becomes even more difficult. This ethnic disconnection can make mission strategy difficult to plan for, because if the group sharing the Gospel and the group that needs to receive the Gospel are active in separate areas, evangelism becomes unnatural. Thus, fewer opportunities will arise. Of course, few natural opportunities to share the Gospel will occur in a traditional non-Christian village society.

However, cities can provide a variety of venues for meetings—whether casual or formal—to feel natural and authentic. Such venues help people feel comfortably connected to the social environment despite differences in social class or ethnicity. And, such a sense of comfort encourages and promotes individuals to naturally mingle. These city locations are termed "urban junctures (or units of integration)."[25] Diversified junctures in a city offer groups a place to live and interact together outside of the negative pressures from conservative and/or biased people.

25. Eames and Goode, *Anthropology of the City*, 216, 15–54.

These junctures are important spots for strategic mission, because it is necessary for urban ethnic minorities to come to such places in order for them to interact with other ethnic members. At the village, people usually do not feel naturally comfortable interacting with outsiders including other ethnic groups, and sometimes can even become hostile to them. However, once individuals come to a so-called neutral zone outside of their ethnic village, they are forced to meet or naturally interact with different groups for business and other social activities. Depending on the situation, some places are perceived as neutral zones because of the diversity among residents who live and work together. This has strategic value for missions among ethnic minorities, particularly when outside evangelists or mission workers find it difficult to approach members of communities with the utmost respect and ease.

These neutral zones or urban junctures can be classified into four categories: the situational urban juncture, temporal place, structural formation, and virtual-modern space. The first type of urban juncture is the situational urban juncture, which refers to a city's neutral facilities and services that are available to anyone. Neutral facilities include public areas, eating and drinking establishments or fast-food restaurants (such as McDonald's), parks and marketplaces, service institutions (e.g., schools), hospitals, government agencies, and transportation hubs.[26] Typically, a city offers public facilities and services for use by residents regardless of ethnic or cultural differences.

Consequently, different ethnicities can take the bus and spend time at the park. Mostly anyone who is sick goes to the hospital. Those with children can send them to school. These areas are perceived as places where individuals can come to naturally function and interact among diverse ethnic groups. Characteristically, most urban junctures have been constructed over time as urban areas modernize.

The second urban juncture is the temporal place. The temporal place refers to celebrations and events participants engage in for a limited time. A representative example is a sporting event. During international sporting events, citizens of the same country but from different ethnicities can unite to cheer the "home team." Besides sports, there are some celebrations such as national holidays in which any ethnic group can participate, because the government or third party institutions sponsor these. All ethnic groups would have an opportunity to comfortably attend, and avoid cultural conflicts.

---

26. Sander estimated the effects of residental location and dducational attainment at age sixteen. Sander, "Educational Attainment and Residential Location."

On the other hand, celebrations and festivals attached to specific ethnic or religious affiliations may limit universal participation by a specific culture. Yet, despite these differences, and difficulty in identifying with a specific group associated with a celebration, such events can have universal elements, which people may enjoy regardless of the celebration's origins.

The third kind of urban juncture is the structural formation. This refers to physical structures used by the community for elections, political campaigns, and sporting clubs, in recreation or leisure. Each person can join different groups or be involved in political activities for different purposes. The benefits of sporting or other leisure events are opportunities for people to identify with a common interest while avoiding ethnic or cultural differences.

There is one more type of juncture—the fourth kind of urban juncture, which is becoming more prominent as technology advances. That is the virtual-modern space juncture. People gather in virtual and modern spaces to purchase videos, or surf the web at Internet cafes, and to enjoy gathering places where different people gather to engage in similar interests in the wake of technology. Today, the world is smaller because technology has bridged time and space. It is in this new space where people gather despite social or cultural affiliations. This is because it is not always clearly obvious whether ethnic tradition prohibits access to these locations. So, whether a Muslim living in China may eat at a "pagan" Western restaurant (e.g., KFC—Kentucky Fried Chicken—Restaurant) often requires that person to define pagan. People enjoy foreign media programs across ethnic boundaries. For example, Hollywood, Korean, or Hong Kong movies have wide appeal across different ethnicities.

Figure 6–5: KFC Motorcycle Delivery Man (April 2010) Xi'an City, China.
Photo © Enoch Kim

Individuals do enjoy similar entertainment, food, fashion or activities based on interest across space and time. In this modern virtual space, people can get together and interact with one another freely to build common bridges.

The virtual and modern space where people meet regardless of ethnic affiliations is rooting itself deeply in our lives and altering our concept of space and distance. Sales figures from leading corporations show that millions of people are buying smartphones, computers and other technological devices. So, the virtual and modern space is expanding as more people gain access. The interactions in virtual-modern space junctures are similar to what occurs in physical spaces but outside the limitations of space and time constraints. Therefore, technology assists even more people across cultural and ethnic boundaries to share similar interests than was possible before the digital age. Information can be accessed anonymously while protecting privacy, offering an easy method to freely contact people and groups in a society that is very cautious of how others view them.

If one's mission target is a conservative group that does not have much contact outside of its community, an urban juncture can become very important mission strategically. Because, urban junctures are the places where anyone can naturally interact with other neighbors, especially with people from outside of their ethnic group, meetings can become more organic between individuals. Some interaction can be very casual, and lead to actual meetings such as in a park. Other interactions can be critical, as in the case of consulting with a medical doctor. Or a juncture can be a place where different ethnic groups can meet naturally and interact over a long period of time, such as a high school. In this way, an urban juncture can be the place where those who held biases for others and/or were isolated have a meeting space to share information and ideas and even spirit.

IMPLICATION TO MISSION STRATEGY

Earlier in this chapter, we looked at the case of Wang, who was able to work for his uncle at a noodle shop. We also met Miss Ahu, who taught at a university, and her fiancé Mr. Hoo. They each were Muslims who migrated to a city from a rural area when they were teenagers. Each later heard the Gospel from people outside of their communities of origin and became interested in the message. Yet, Wang had a difficult time accepting the Gospel. We have analyzed the reason from sociological analysis.

As the earlier overview of sociological research in this chapter should suggest, the diversity of content and information an urbanite is exposed to and the level of freedom the person feels to develop personal opinions about such information can be heavily influenced by the social network to which that individual belongs. Urbanization provides the opportunity for individuals from traditional ethnic communities to a society that is not only interact with old neighbors, but also with new neighbors who will share new and unfamiliar ideas.

By all observations, Wang's decision to reject the Gospel message was due to what he perceived as pressure from the community—the heavy social influence from his neighbors. Social considerations he perceived would impact his future aspirations and standard of living, if he did not listen to and follow directions from the old neighbors in his community. Therefore, Wang's situation represents the sociological reality of a strong social system of overlapping networks that can disturb individual decision-making. On the contrary, Miss Ahu and Mr. Hu had developed a diversified network, which allowed them to interact with new neighbors from many different places. Consequently, they felt a freedom to make their own faith decision based on the facts of the information received.

It is true that urbanization may have many negative consequences for residents. Yet, it is important for us to consider the positive impact city life can have on mission outreach, at the very least. A city offers urban junctures where diverse residents can be exposed to the Gospel through natural comfortable encounters. Then, how should we apply the social dimensions of old and new neighbors as well as urban junctures to mission outreach? What strategies should we consider if we are to share the Gospel in a culturally diverse urban environment?

Two Different Approaches

Since the social circles and socio-cultural experiences of these two categories of neighbors are quite different, a mission strategy seeking to interact with both types of neighbors has to consider the best approach to each group in order to coordinate the best outcomes.

A mission strategy for the old neighbors in an urban ethnic neighborhood, where mainly old neighbor networks exist could be similar to a strategy for outreach to a traditional, homogeneous, and rural society. In this case, just as missionaries would live together with the people in the village to learn their language and culture to gain their trust, they may use this same model, to live in and learn an urban ethnic minority community. Another effective mission strategy for this context can be serving a neighborhood's poor through community development projects intended to help improve quality of life. Such a strategy can be very appropriate depending upon specific circumstances.

A big brother, like Wang's uncle, who holds tremendous power, can solve all kinds of problems that the village needs to solve. Setting up a mission strategy to this old neighbor network, without asking for this big brother's help—the one who could open or lock the door to the Gospel message to the whole community—could limit the whole plan to failure, potentially.

Now let us consider how we might approach a people in the ethnic community that is already connecting to networks beyond familiar social circles Urbanites continually cultivate networks as they engage in social activities. For example, when they chose an occupation, meeting new neighbors and positioning the self for some personal benefit related to interests are main motivations. When urbanites choose their occupations and neighbors, not by traditional criteria, but universally, personal considerations addressing wants and needs take priority in decision making. As a result of exposure to pan-ethnic neighbors, various ethnic groups begin to mix geographically, socially, mentally and even biologically. They spread into various areas and live with various people.

The mainstream also may have a fully developed infrastructure that avails residents to various opportunities. Consequently, as ethnic minorities enjoy local school systems and find employment, for instance, mainstream members will find themselves in contact with ethnic members more often. Furthermore, minorities may even attend a church where a majority is dominant. In these instances, missionaries and local church leaders must consider what God is doing through such outreach opportunities.

Like the temple of Jerusalem in which the Court of Gentiles provided an opportunity for non-Jews to pray to Almighty God, we may need to save some space (in terms of our concern and time) for minority visitors. Evangelism to the new neighbor is an approach undertaken when relationships naturally develop beyond familiar social circles. In order to realize successful mission outreach to the new neighbor, the church must see the need, have awareness for the opportunity, and prepare well. Finding the commonality between majority and minority can be a good Gospel channel. Certainly, the objective of this book is to find ways to reach the unreached ethnic minority.

Today, unreached migrant social circles are not solely limited to specific geographical regions, but now extend to networks inhabited by outsiders. As churches in global cities grow increasingly diverse with migrant populations, leadership should put in place strategies to reach out to the various communities where their own ethnic church members reside. If one church cannot accommodate various ethnic groups, it should consider cooperating with mission organizations that work closely with specific subcultures. Otherwise, a church could consider ministry among specific interest or occupation groups as a way to reach out to a minority group. The fact that they provide privacy for well-known faces is a good example of a ministry understanding the social context of a particular social network.

Using Urban Junctures Effectively

The strategic value of urban juncture is crucial in planning ways to reach new neighbors. Traditionally, missionaries migrate to culturally diverse ethnic communities for ministry. However, soon thereafter, a substantial cultural gulf often creates a complicated period of time during which missionaries must adapt to a new cultural environment. Consequently, many subsequent opportunities to meet with locals become awkward and even difficult to encounter under natural circumstances; such interaction just do not easily happen.

In reality, the city can provide a variety of natural meeting locales, or "urban junctures" where Christians can more successfully interact with unreached ethnic groups. Such locales can provide non-threatening settings in which to minister to members of an ethnic group, because of a sense of familiarity derived from such an urban juncture. Strategically considering appropriate urban junctures should suggest where and how missionaries and their organizations could set mission outreach starting points. In this sense, mission organizations should encourage local missionaries as much as they can to use a strategic lens and research ways to effectively work in urban junctures. The optimal result would be teams of missionaries with the proper abilities assigned to productive projects in the most strategic junctures.

In order to effectively deploy missionaries, at least two issues should be considered. First, with regard to integrated urban demographics, missionaries can improve outreach strategy by analyzing social context from a missiological perspective and field-centered viewpoint. Therefore, in all respects it is important to study the kinds of urban junctures present in any given city in order to determine the best manner in which to interact with unique urban populations.

Of course, in order for field-centered strategies to be effective, all members of a missionary's support team—especially the base leaders must respect and trust field experts and their analyses. Unfortunately, it is as if mission organizations send missionary candidates to locations based on random preference, rather than to specific fields where they are needed.

Urban ethnic minorities encounter a variety of neighbors and are even interacting with other ethnic group members though they might often feel awkward. For the missionary, this is a new God-given opportunity to bridge cultural gulfs, because there are places in an urban environment where people do share common socio-cultural experiences and can feel comfortable enough to be receptive to new information. It is well advised that organizations look at the sociological reality of relationships as social networks in order to use outreach opportunities to create a mission system that can flexibly share the message of the Gospel in ways that resonate with every unique community.

7

Urban Friends

New Communication Channels
that Unlock the Gospel (II)

FOLLOWING THE NEW NEIGHBORS examined in the earlier chapter, chapter seven will study the second new channel of the gospel that cities provide. The second channel is a friend within a city, which is a new social network. Upon analyzing network characteristics of friends within cities that fall under the second network, we will recognize the endless opportunities for making friends provided by city. We will examine the reason why we should see cities as a gold vein in the mission strategic perspective, and how Christians are to prepare for this.

A CASE STORY:
A NEW THINKING FROM NEW FRIENDS—
MR. DONG'S STORY

Mr. Dong was born and raised in Pinglang in Gansu Province of China, which is known for its large population of the Hui Muslims.[1] Most Muslims in his hometown live in a barren farmland as farmers. His father and older brother work as truck drivers. While he grew up in his village, he rarely interacted with other people groups. However, while he attended high school,

---

1. Mr. Dong is a brother in Christ with a Muslim background, who used to attend the fellowship meeting in China. Assumed names were used for Mr. Dong and Professor Ding, but the story is founded on fact.

he had several good friends who were non-Hui because there were many non-Hui in his class.

Later, he entered college even though his family was not able to support him financially. For this, he moved to a big city called Lanzhou, which takes a day by bus from his hometown. The college he attended had many ethnic minorities including the Han, the majority.

There was a professor named Ding at his school whom Mr. Dong respected. Although the professor was not Hui, Han still respected him a lot. Mr. Dong often visited the professors' house and office for fellowship and counseling. One day, the professor introduced the Gospel to him and after several days of struggle, Dong received Jesus Christ as his Savior. Later, Dong told me that the main reason he had decided to receive Jesus was because he trusted the professor's character and moral influence. From that point on, Mr. Dong regularly attended a Christian gathering that the professor was leading. He was amazed at how he could meet many school friends at the gathering. At the gathering, there were a lot of Tibetans, former Muslims from Uyghur and Hui. At the gathering, Mr. Dong's faith grew very fast as he participated in the fellowship with his friends.

After a long summer vacation at his parents' place, Dr. Dong no longer wanted to participate student prayer meetings. It was because he was distressed from lying to his parents to keep his Christian faith. Setting the differences of faith aside, he thought returning back to the former religion was the right thing to do for the relationship with his father and brother. Professor Ding, I, and leaders of the gathering (a Uygur sister, and Hui and Han brothers) sincerely helped Mr. Dong overcome the issue. Graciously, Mr. Dong came back to the Lord and his faith grew strong until his graduation. Many years after his graduation, I heard that he went back to his hometown as a middle school teacher.

Like Mr. Dong, many ethnic minority young adults in China make new friends who are from other ethnic groups in schools, work places, and through social activities. From their own experiences, they begin to realize that there are many other people groups that are different from what they were told by their parents as they grew up. In just two years, Dong had made many friends from different backgrounds who had a variety of beliefs and religions. As the young adults become more active in social activities, they experience a greater gap between their friends and family in their thoughts. And because they are caught in between two different worlds, they feel alienated.

In this chapter, we will study, from an urban anthropological perspective, the urbanites whose primary network consists of relatives and family, along with a social life that comprises their secondary network. We will take a look at who are the friends of urbanites among those secondary networks and where they are located. Then, by analyzing the differences of the information between friends and kin, we will identify the role of a friend in terms of sharing the Gospel for urban ethnicities. Finally, missionaries will be challenged by the need of well-designed friendship evangelism strategies.

THE TWO DIMENSIONS OF URBAN NETWORKS

Anthropologists view social relationships in predetermined categories, starting from birth and evolving throughout an individual's lifetime.[2] Social networks can be classified into effective segments and extended segments based on closeness and intimacy, which are called "egocentric."[3, 4] In particular, this division is useful in revealing the dynamics in relationships among urban people. What is important here is that networks shared by urbanites can be classified into primary versus secondary networks, or ascribed networks depending on levels of intimacy and social distance.

The Primary Network

The primary network is not the sum of relationships built by individual effort. Rather, relationships in this network class are innate and are naturally developed. Family and kinship are the most representative example of a primary network.[5] This means that blood relationships form the basis of community in the primary network.[6]

Fischer defines primary groups as "social networks typically involving intimate relationships," which are fully identified, and are ends within

2. Morgan, *Systems of Consanguinity and Affinity of the Human Family.*

3. Wellman, "Physical Place and Cyberplace"; Wellman and Gulia, "Net Surfers Don't Ride Alone."

4. McCarty, "Structure in Personal Networks"; Wasserman and Faust, Social Network Analysis.

5. Bohannan, *Social Anthropology*, 55.

6. Eames limits the primary unit to direct bloodlines such as family, kin, and domestic unit Eames and Goode, *Anthropology of the City*, chap. 4.

ethnic groups, friends, and kin.[7] The networks are primary units of generally predestined, unconditional relationships.

Besides this biological relationship, situational relationships can be regarded as primary networks, too, depending on circumstances and the nature of the relationships. For example, in relationships established through adoption, auxiliary family members (e.g., godparents) can be regarded as kinship. This is likewise true of adult friends of parents whom children will sometimes call aunts and uncles.[8]

Furthermore, there are some hometown relationships that survive through time. There are many people from the same background and hometown who migrate to the city but maintain close relationships and give each other support. These kinds of relationships may fall somewhere between kinship and friendship. In Korea, there is a saying, "neighbor-cousin," which means that neighbors can be regarded even more closely than far-off relatives. Therefore, non-kinsmen in urban areas can be amalgamated into one's network through the process of putative or fictive kinship.[9]

Urban ethnographers have shown that kinship has a more crucial role during early stages of migration. This is evident when households and kinship networks in urban environments build social niches. Migrants often join such social niches early after settling into unfamiliar urban environments.

As they face modernization, since Chairman Mao's era, families of ethnic minorities in China have experienced great changes over time, which have introduced new social challenges.[10] These challenges represent many changes affecting urban Hui kinship dynamics. For example, the family unit and filial piety traditions are not unfamiliar to the Hui, a Muslim ethnic group. In 2006, to address Hui kinship dynamics including filial piety,

---

7. Fischer, *The Urban Experience*, 143.

8. Bohannan expresses this socially approved substitutes for the biological relationship as "quasi-kinship"; Bohannan, *Social Anthropology*, 55.

9. Following is the list of good resources for the recent urban kinship network and dynamics. Harris and Skyles, "Kinship Care for African American Children"; Gallo and Scrinzi, "Outsourcing Elderly Care to Migrant Workers"; Chaonan, "A Household-Based Convoy and the Reciprocity of Support Exchange between Adult Children and Noncoresiding Parents"; Tess and Ramón, "The Mediating Effects of Family on Sport in International Development Contexts."

10. Wen, "*Ershishijijiushiniandaizhongguominzurenkoudebiandong Jianping* (20 世纪 90年代中国各民族人口的变动 简评)," 105–6.

the question Enoch J. Kim posed in a field survey[11] was the following: Who is the person you respect enough to seek counsel from regarding important issues? Based on responses, the answer was clear, parents.[12]

The next survey question asked the following: Who is the person you would least likely share a shameful experience with? This question was also designed to understand who the real community leader is. Again, the answer was clear. Parents, again.[13] Therefore the data clearly shows that parents and filial piety is strongly alive in the primary network among the Hui. Since most of the respondents were in their twenties and thirties, they may not regard themselves as fully independent persons from their parents.

The Secondary Network

An individual's social network extends farther than a kinship-based network. A network beyond the original network, which includes friends, coworkers or acquaintances encountered on the streets, is called a "secondary network." A secondary network can expand its relational networking quite far, because a person's acquaintances also share various networks.

Compared to the primary network, the secondary network is an even wider circle of extended relationships. The self (ego) expands its relationship beyond the circle of kinship and natural relationships.

In a traditional society, all members similarly stay in a kinship network, so egocentric relationships do not become that varied. However, the modern ethnic urban dweller does individually build various and complicated networks.[14]

As city size grows, the chance of a community being limited by original personal ties drops rapidly. To fill this relational vacancy, urbanites seek

11. Kim, "Receptor-Oriented Communication for Hui Muslims in China," 61.

12. Among respondents, 57 percent answered that they respect their parents; 29 percent would not seek advice from anyone; and, finally, 12 percent would go to a friend. Amazingly, only 1 percent would go to a religious leader. Ibid.

13. Among respondents, 77 percent answered, parents; 12 percent, ranked school and company friends and coworkers; neighbors ranked among 4 percent or respondents; and both religious leaders and teachers were equally ranked by 2 percent of the respondents. Ibid.

14. Eames states that urban social networks have more choices of contact Eames and Goode, *Anthropology of the City*, 157.

and join social clubs or formal associations. Generally, people naturally create various second networks in modern city.[15]

The earlier stage of ethnic minority or migrants' secondary network is quite similar to the original one. At first, many of individual traditional networks are limited to the inside of the ethnic network or community. They have spent time within other secondary networks, and few of them connect with outside of their ethnic boundary.

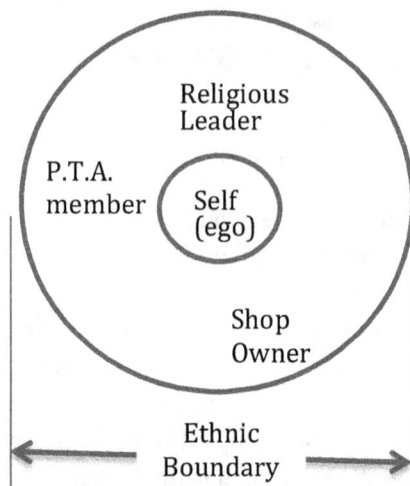

Chart 7–1: The Traditional Secondary Networks[16]

For a better understanding of the urbanites' secondary network, a conceptual diagram is introduced. Chart 7–1 shows a case of the secondary network of an ethnic minority who arrived in the city not long ago. In this model, the secondary networks of the individual are connected only within his or her ethnic boundary. It is quite similar to the network in the traditional village. For example, there are shoemakers inside and outside their community, but the traditional minorities usually go to those of the same ethnic group. This shoemaker may work near the ethnic village or may locate himself at the entrance of the ethnic village; however, regardless

15. There is a different way of second-network development through the modernization process of China, which involves political context and urbanization led by the government. Whyte and Parish, *Urban Life in Contemporary China*, 353–56.

16. Developed diagram from Kim, "Receptor-Oriented Communication for Hui Muslims in China," 65.

of location, people habitually go to the familiar shoemaker who has the same ethnicity as their own.

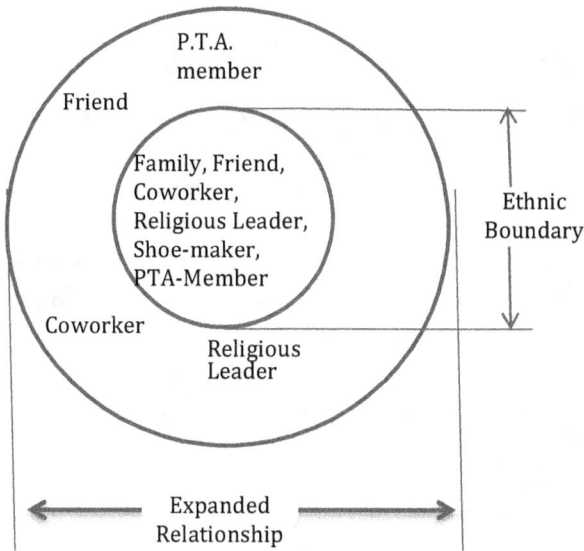

Chart 7–2: Expanded Secondary Networks[17]

As time goes on, after the ethnic minorities settle in the new city, similar to what new neighbor did, this secondary network structure also changes. Depends on how you see, this friend and neighbor can all be the same part of the secondary network. Chart 7-2 shows a new secondary network that expands beyond the ethnic boundary. A careful observation is need for the phenomena that their connections and communication channels are beyond the limitation of the community. The city life and its social activities have allowed the urban minorities to expand their abilities, mobility, and social relationships. It enables them to reach multi-ethnic and cross-ethnic networks.[18] Some individuals can now enjoy new fashions, have friendships with people in different religion, and work or study beyond their community.[19] As a result, people's network changes may seem like an expansion of ego or self. Such an expansion means that the new

17. Developed diagram from ibid., 66.

18. Edling and Rydgren, "Neighborhood and Friendship Composition in Adolescence," 1.

19. Kim, "'Us' or 'Me'? Modernization and Social Networks among China's Urban Hui," 93.

minorities in city can be more active in social activities and have more freedom to act and choose among other ethnic groups.

FRIEND THAT IS CULTURAL

To understand the concept of a secondary network, we cannot omit the meaning of friendship. This is crucial. In contrast to relationships formed within the primary unit, individuals form friendships by choice, though many friendship-forming zones are often limited to neighbor and kinship boundaries. Modern society offers greater mobility and a wide array of social activities to urban dwellers. These opportunities do provide more chances for urbanites to make new friends.

The concept of a friend varies in different culture. Furthermore, even in the same ethnic group, depending on the location, whether a city or countryside, the dynamics in making, maintaining, and recognizing a person as a friend is different.[20]

To understand the correlation between cultural zones and the concept of friendship, the Grid-Group theory developed by Mary Douglas is useful.[21] Grid-Group theory tries to understand characteristics of culture by categorizing them into high vs. low grid societies and high vs. low group societies. Additionally, Mary Douglas categorizes cultural zones into four areas (see Chart 7–3).[22]

20. Fischer, *The Urban Experience*, 155–58.

21. Douglas, Cultural Bias.

22. Lingenfelter, *Transforming Culture*.

High
Grid

Low
Group
← → High
Group

Low
Grid

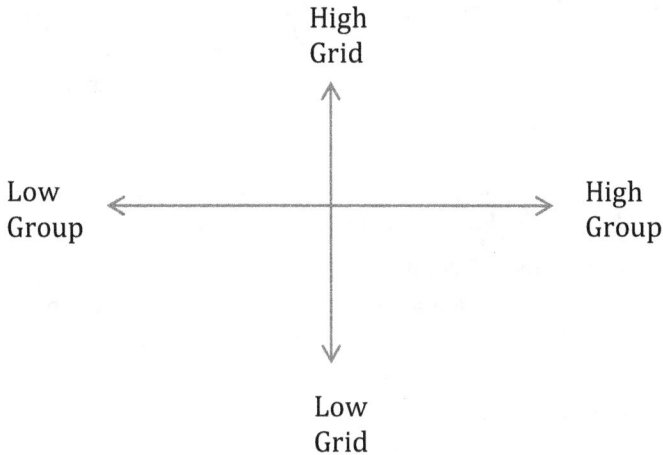

Chart 7–3: Grid-Group Four-Quadrant Map

Among these, the high grid society has greater density in its structure. Consequently, the distinction between higher and lower class becomes clear. Becoming a friend in this society is not easy because many conditions need to be satisfied, since the sub-groups in this society have strong boundaries. The layers between higher and lower classes are very dense and complex. Therefore, becoming a friend in a high grid and high group society—the hierarchical society, is even more difficult.

In this social category, friendships develop gradually after considerable effort to build trust and long relationships through similar tastes and abilities, within comparable age ranges, gender roles and social status. The majority of non-Western societies are high group, and some of them are even high grid. Because of this cultural distinction, having a friend is not so easy in this society, but naturally once a person becomes a friend, compared to other cultural zones, that friendship can be stronger and longer lasting.

On the other hand, in Western societies and low group societies, making friends is not so difficult. Sometimes, Asians feel embarrassed when Westerners refer to them as a friend after only a brief meeting. There is a less layered distinction among the notions of casual to serious friendships. Among Westerners, the word "friend" can be used equally to refer to casual acquaintances as well as life-long relationships. The distinction is revealed through action. However, in Asian cultures titles reflect a much more specific relationship to the speaker. Therefore, a "friend" is a social role that means the conditions of friendship have been met. As an example, an American English speaker can call a stranger "friend" in the absence of knowing that person's name in order to show casual politeness. However, among high group and high grid societies, "friend" is an actual social role and is used accordingly.

There is a strong bond in relationships among friends in a shame-based culture.[23] The bond naturally builds peer pressure, and people can feel shame or honor from peer values. "My family, rather than me; we, rather than family; and my country, rather than we, come first." This saying used to stimulate heroism among many Asian men throughout history. In this regard, as one might expect, Asians often feel shame when choosing personal and domestic priorities over society's higher status, bigger issues.

In a group-based society, friendships develop in ways to share practical benefits, not to simply provide emotional satisfaction.[24] As in the case of chain migration, people move to cities and settle there through the help of friends. Or beneficial information can be conveyed through friends just as social elevation can be easier when accomplished through friends.[25]

In China, friends become an important social fixture from the time of early adolescence, as they share new and outside information among circles of friends—different from primary networks—up through the late teens years. Many Chinese people answered my question of when they made their most significant and lasting friendships, with the answer that it was during their high school years. During that time, adolescent friends share information useful in their social circles, but not so in the family.[26] By leaving parents, people learn secondary values from friends, school seniors, or teachers. They receive non-traditional values especially from school or the workplace. If one grew up in a traditional ethnic family but goes to a school or a company in an urban area, the individual may find himself or herself immersed in both distinct value systems.

23. Muller, *Honor and Shame*, 6, 9, 10.

24. Garcia did phenomenological study in how secondary network of Latino immigrants in the United States become a capital conveying network. Saracostti, "Social Capital as a Strategy to Overcome Poverty in Latin America."

25. Musterd and Deurloo, "Unstable Immigrant Concentrations in Amsterdam."

26. Wang, Lao, and Zhou have found the social network of urban workers from rural area in China has great influence in the individual income. Wang, Lao, and Zhou, "The Impact Mechanism of Social Networks on Chinese Rural-Urban Migrant Workers' Behaviour and Wages."

CITY'S VEIN OF GOLD IN THE TRIPLE
INFORMATION CHANNELS

Mission to ethnic minority, especially unreached people group is like finding a vein of gold.[27] In order to find gold, miners do not dig the ground right away, but need to find the vein first. After much effort, Miners find a vein of gold. Once they find it, they can just follow this path and find even more. The same principle can be applied in finding special people in the city. Though it is difficult to find specific groups among several thousands of subcultural groups of the city, once the missionary finds a couple members, we can follow the track and continually find other members who are connected, like a vein of gold.

Missionaries who work for the unreached urbanites should take this principle into consideration. Missionaries who are called to work for the ethnic minorities or unreached people group need to identify where they are and understand how they live. This means the missionaries need to understand their secondary network dynamics.

For this, let us now look at channels of communication and its connection with the urban ethnic minorities and immigrants. Urban ethnic minorities carry at least three kinds of information channels that they interact with for their living and work. Roger S. Greenway summarized the types of information channels that urban ethnicities have.[28] Chart 7–4 is a conceptual diagram that shows how one ethnic minority individual interacts with a neighbor through these three channels. This diagram shows effectively how a person (P)'s secondary network connects as the person relates within and outside of their ethnic zone.[29] The vertical lines represent different ethnic groups and horizontal lines represent different social classes. P is a member of ethnic group Y and social status X, which allow P to interact with related people within the group Y and X. This P can freely share information within Y ethnic people who have the same language and culture. At the same time this P shares information with other colleagues, who are partners of the same class, and friends for a long time. Modernized cities, however, allow this urban ethnic minority to have one more channel—social group Z, which intersects with the others. The Z group

---

27. Greenway uses the metaphor of a vein of gold to explain an urbanite's network. Greenway and Monsma, *Cities*, 117.

28. Ibid., 124.

29. Ibid.

stands for social group. Urbanites have many social activities that are not economic, and they share a lot of information while they participate in these activities as well. For example, town women's club, bicycle club, or religious activities are good example of the group Z.

Y (Social Groups)

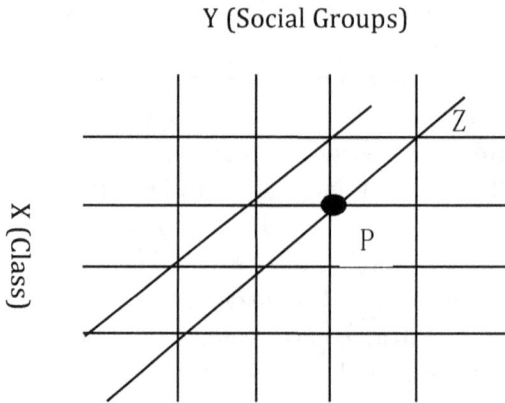

Chart 7–4: Greenway's People Groups within a City[30]

Urbanites can enjoy more diversified social activities through these diversified informational channels. Through enforced mobility and new networks, individuals can expand their relationships beyond ethnic borders. This is not easy, given traditional ethnic biases, geographical isolation, and so on. Therefore, these expanded networks enable urbanites to join many different network groups, to share their ideas, and to create new behavioral patterns. Information is not barricaded in a specific group but rather spreads quickly through the diversified personal networks. For example, the early morning soccer club members interact with much information while they get together, and as the game finishes, they disassemble with newly gained information from the club to the next groups that the individuals are part of. Such information spread to the other groups then proliferate to even more diverse subcultural groups, continually. Within these different interconnected networks, individuals can express different preferences and value systems regardless of shared ethnicities. As a result, different individuals in shared ethnic groups can develop unique responses to new outside influences such as the gospel message.

30. Ibid.

This kind of social atmosphere helps people make their own decisions with more confidence. The mobility from the increased and diversified social activities also help individuals not to thoughtlessly follow the values or preferences set by one subcultural group but selectively receive values and preferences from various groups that they are part of. Consequently, urbanites have more freedom to make decision with their own value and preferred methods than to follow the group's overall value systems. People in the traditional societies show similar response to the Gospel as well. However, urban ethnic minority members can express their own idea on Christianity shaped by the different information, both negative and positive, they received from rumors, television, neighbors, the lifestyle of Christians at the workplace, or the Gospel.

IMPLICATION TO MISSION STRATEGY

The secondary network provides new ideas and information based upon the trustworthy. To those who now have more freedom to choose and decide on their own, the Gospel could be included within the new information. In the closing of this chapter, we will see the implications of these transformations to the ministry and how we are to prepare for the constantly changing mission environment.

Approach for the Primary Network

The more a community is involved in daily life on a traditional level, the more it influences individuals along primary networks. When a person from such a traditional network has new faith in Christ, he or she may experience serious conflicts with their community network members, usually with primary networks. In general, traditional churches requiring a lot of time for fellowship may be perceived as working against the primary group, if one of their members comes to accept the Christian faith. Because those types of fellowship easily push the new converts to be a church-centered rather than family-centered.

Highly intellectual (academic) based college Bible study groups also may be perceived as working against the primary group. Because knowledge-centered change often causes conflicts contrast to the life changing centered.

Having trust from this primary network is crucial in urban mission. This is because in many cases, these urban ethnic groups are still deeply rooted in their own tradition, which is their primary culture. No matter how long they have lived in a city or have such many friends in other people groups, many of them still live with their own people group and spend more time within their primary culture. Sometimes, this ethnic village may revive rather than shrink. If the number grows beyond critical mass, or have some incidents that raise the ethnic self-esteem, the people in the ethnic village may unite and strengthen their power based on the cultural identity. Therefore, for success in urban mission setting up a method for mission work within the primary network is needed more to address this case.

For mission to this primary network, we need at least two different efforts. First, we need to disciple new believers to be respected not just within the Christian community, but also within their primary network. In other words, rather than just providing a lot of knowledge, we must be encouraging them to be the salt and light wherever they are. Once they believe in Jesus, they must be recognized by their family as a changed person who is more faithful and responsible, before sharing about Jesus through words. Rather than having a lot of Bible study, we need to help them learn how to receive the wisdom and power from the Holy Spirit by learning to walk with the Spirit. This is the life that their family truly admires and wants to follow whether they are Hindus or Muslims.[31] To transform into a genuinely better being, to be a wiser being is closer to the fundamental and biblical transformation rather than knowledge-centered change or excessive time expenditure in church fellowship, while being set apart from the family.

Second, the Gospel should be contextualized, so that it includes familiar traditional and natural elements that can be accepted at face value, not as foreign symbols of social class derived from a majority group.

If the Gospel has an image of a majority or a foreign flavor, the primary network will feel rejection. It is quite normal for them to feel ashamed and betrayed by their family when accepting such foreign religion. Actually, having such a well-developed and contextualized Gospel takes a long time, and it is difficult for many to believe in the early stage. In spite of all this, missionaries must do their best to communicate with a receptor-oriented mind to help the audience understand the Gospel from their perspectives.

---

31. Livingstone, *Planting Churches in Muslim Cities*, 134–35.

Opportunities from the Secondary Network

We need to be aware of the fact that the opportunity for unreached groups to hear the Gospel has increased through more diverse secondary networks. Usually, someone from an unreached people group faces dramatic social pressure and resistance when they first come to the Lord. However, in an urban setting, people give less attention to others' private lives. Even if they do give attention, if an individual chooses not to mention a personal story that does not relate to the whole group, the group members would never know. So even if a person from an urban unreached group does believe in the Gospel, it is difficult for other social groups that he or she is involved in to know or care about it.

In general, the people directly involved in an urbanite's religious activity usually are not the kind of people who would help in the financial or social success of the urbanite. Therefore, the new believer's life and the basic needs would not be threatened. Especially in an urban setting, religion is regarded as a private matter. Thus, social persecuting of a new religious convert becomes difficult.

Secondly, missionaries need to be aware of the fact that the modern city's social atmosphere diversifies the ethnic minorities' secondary networks. The traditional way has been a unilateral decision made by missionaries to move to a mission field by learning their culture. However, now those people casually interact with missionaries and believers in other people groups through the expanded secondary networks. In other words, modern society has brought the locals out to the street where they have to work with many other people. Today, the traditional incarnation-centered way, which is to live among the locals, should be practiced along with welcoming them at the junction strategy, which missionaries can go and meet those who have changed and are coming toward us at the midpoint.

To conduct this welcoming at the junction-type mission, missionaries need to carefully watch the main secondary networks the ethnic minority comfortably joins in. Such effort may include an apprehension of the social group (association or club) that they naturally join, the occupation or economic activities that they easily work with other ethnic groups. Once we find out those places and junctions, the next step is to send workers or organizations to reach the specific people groups. Maybe we can train Christians in the association for reaching unreached people who are in the same association.

Besides these, a strategy that meets the need of urban ethnic minorities is also necessary. They embrace anxiety and fatigue as part of their lives. There are countless opportunities for such ministry that would fulfill these needs and give hope to those who are in need.

In order to carry out the ministry mentioned above, it is necessary to collect overall and specific field data. In order to help the ethnic minorities in the long-term, missionaries who can help the ethnic minorities, local people, and foreign ethnic Christians in the secondary networks, need to have missiological and scientific understanding of their roles and the situation of the mission field and their needs. For this to work, cooperation between experts, field workers, and supporters is important.

City as the Frontier Line of Unreached Ethnicities

Traditionally, missionaries were viewed as people who go out and live in remote areas to reach the unreached ethnic people groups. Of course, such mission work should be continued, and I believe that God acknowledges the patience and efforts contributed by those missionaries. At the same time, we should be able to see the God-given mission opportunities in modern urban cities.

This does not mean that the urbanites are more important for the mission than the people in countries. God is interested in people, and that is why urban cities are important for mission. In other words, cities are the places where people gather; and for this reason, God puts his heart and interest in cities.

Modernization pulls numerous unreached ethnic groups into the city, which turns the city into a museum made by these numerous ethnicities. Like puzzle pieces, the city is formed by many unreached peoples and ethnic minorities. Therefore, in order to reach the unreached people, we must change our old perspective of the typical concept of mission that a view going to rural areas is the only way to meet unreached people, and know that cities are the museums and frontier lines for unreached people groups.

For these reasons, Greenway's vein of gold analogy is valuable. Although it is difficult to find out where and what kind of activities that the unreached people are participating in, once it is found, they become the endless resource to find similar people. In the same way, to find a vein of gold, called the unreached ethnicity, a missionary will be involved with hard work. Some ethnic groups are easily spotted and approached, but some, though they live in the city, are difficult to approach and maintain this relationship for a long time due to different social and political reasons. Therefore, coworkers and supporters who work for such ministry must trust and consistently support missionaries so they can successfully find the vein of gold. Moreover, missionaries also need to continually improve their strategy, and make it more appropriate for finding the gold. Comparing to other types of ministry is not recommended because this type of ministry is fundamentally different in its approach. They should only be comparing and reflecting their attitude and strategy with the model given by Jesus.

Despite the difficulties, finding the vein of gold is worth the investment and much effort. Furthermore, this vein of gold is different from the alluvial that was once found, and one can continuously find the next gold rocks. The price of finding the vein of gold is immensely high. To do this, the missionary for the city's immigrants and minorities must develop a more creative, practical, and empirical manual that fits their situations. It is an urgent matter for the missionaries to find out how to locate the group, how the ethnic class is distributed and how it transforms, and what kind of backgrounds and functions of missionaries are preferentially needed. Even in the case of finding the gold vein, not anybody can excavate it. That is why missionaries with proper gifts and skill sets, who can naturally stay and work in the place where the locals are, should be sent. For this, selecting field-requested missionaries must take place. In selecting the right candidate for the mission work, the required conditions must be sent from the mission field, and the candidate must meet the requirements.

8

Subcultural Groups
New Communication Channels
that Unlock the Gospel (III)

CONTINUING FROM THE NEIGHBOR and friends in chapters six and seven, this chapter will introduce various small groups, which are the third new channel of the gospel. In this chapter, we will understand the characteristics of changes and communication channels of various subcultural groups in city to develop mission strategy. As we conclude the chapter, we will examine which subculture group needs to strategically reach first as missionary's works for ethnicities in the city.

Through this chapter, readers will understand that city creates an environment that connects many subgroups to other subgroups within and outside of the ethnicity. Moreover, at the end of the chapter they can also understand that such new communication channels between ethnicities provides an opportunity for the Gospel to flow into urban ethnicities that are traditionally being neglected of the Gospel. For the outcome, this chapter will deal with the following sociological and mission strategic contents.

- What are the changing processes of subculture groups in an urban environment, and what are the missional opportunities from such change?

- Understanding of how communication channels of urban subculture groups change.

- Understanding of the urban culture that takes individual opinion getting importantly rather than communal opinion.

A CASE—MR. MA'S CHANGING

Mr. Ma, a Chinese Muslim, whom I have known for a long time, moved to Lanzhou, a big city in Gansu province with his wife after the wedding in his hometown, Pinglang. In the beginning, not knowing anyone, he tried to meet neighbors from his hometown and settle down at a place where they introduced him. It was a village where a lot of Muslims from near his hometown lived. Mr. Ma slowly began to learn how to live in a big city by watching what they were doing. With no special skill, he bought mutton every morning, prepared during the day, and roasted and sold them (*yangrouchuar*, lamb meat stick) from a small vehicle at night. As time went by, his family moved to a new place where more of other ethnicities lived. This was his business. He sold lamb meat sticks until the dawn, chatting friendly with customers. I used to be among the customers.

As he lived in a new area, his wife also interacted with a lot of people from morning to night, especially those that have different ethnicities. Within three years of moving into a big city called Lanzhou, the social network of his family expanded.

One day when I visited his house, he was hiding a red lamp in a hurry. Han people in China, who are non-Muslims, hang the lamp under the roof to celebrate a new year. However, Muslims generally do not use such Han Chinese style lamps, because they do not celebrate the Han Chinese holidays. Mr. Ma was desperate to hide the lamp, because he knew that his mother would be angry if she saw it, and she was to visit him soon. When his mother left, he put it back.

Mr. Ma was already interacting with different ethnicities and was in the process of accepting their customs and styles without much repulsion. Every night, he could interact with various customers with different ethnic background, and through it, he formed new networks, which allowed new styles of different ethnicities and trends to enter into Mr. Ma's life, which changed his habits and preferences.

Such phenomenon can easily be found not only in Mr. Ma's life, but also among many other young Muslims in cities. People who move to cities like Mr. Ma's family can be exposed to the change. Their change was possible due to the changes in their own subcultural group. As such, urbanites are exposed to various subculture groups and many communication activities as they are constantly being exposed to new information. One of new information can become the Gospel to them.

INTER-SUBCULTURE GROUP
COMMUNICATION THAT ACTIVATED

Until now, we have examined the city is consisted of many subculture groups, and the citizens are connected with urban networks that are not the same with rural ones. Many subculture groups actively react to the information from both inside and outside, and choose their future and direction each time. At the same time, these subculture groups also continually interact and react with other neighbor subculture groups. Therefore, cities can be called mosaics of subcultural groups. Additionally, understanding city as an organism helps us better understand the characteristics of each subcultural group. Numerous subcultural groups in the city are connected with each other and influence one another. It is as if different small particles within a living animal gather together to make organs and make the entire body.[1]

In a traditional society, subculture groups could not have many interactions with other groups for many reasons. Therefore, under the isolated environment, each subcultural group developed their own subcultures, identities, organization, tradition, and lifestyle. Actually, ethnicities in multi-ethnic cities also traditionally lived with social barriers such as long-held ethnic prejudices and biases, and of course, language and cultural barriers.

Modern cities have made various interactions within subculture groups. Modern people have many opportunities of interactions with the same class, as well as those that are from other classes, and even other ethnicities.

Furthermore, education, occupation, and proximity groups enable urbanites to actively create and be involved in the new subculture groups. Through these activities, the city offers opportunities for new networking and rise of status for the citizens. For example, industrial workers in a developing country are from different ethnicities that surpass ethnic boundaries. Moreover, schools promote ethnic interactions more naturally.

Like so, the fact that urbanites are not limiting themselves just to their ascribed or predestined social group, but rather expanding activities to more diverse subculture groups, brings important meaning to missiology. If a city is a mosaic of subcultural groups, and an organism to actively interact, then we need to bear in mind that the Gospel can flow through diversified channels.

---

1. Greenway and Monsma, *Cities*, 125.

FOUR TYPES OF SUBCULTURE GROUP CHANGE

All of the subcultural groups in the city have varietal ways of reaction to the influences from the outside. These reactions of each subcultural group are the reflection of the reaction of their members. Members continually react to the request of these outside influences. At this point, subcultural group changings come through outside influences and the reactions of the members within it.

Actually, internal issues are not purely promoted from the inside of the subcultural group, but rather from the outside through the members who are connected to the outside network. For example, one group may feel the need for a religious revival or renewal not just because of the internal needs, but also rather from the external criticism from outside or a member who has seen revival in other groups that are similar to them.

Such changes created by a subcultural group may influence others again. In general, the influences are shared to other subcultural groups that are close in proximity, but in some cases, changes may also influence other cultures or ethnicities.

Though there are many kinds of subcultural change, we can summarize the types of change into at least four categories: intensification, extinction, conversion, and continuation.[2] Let us examine these four types with some examples.

Intensification

Intensification refers to the strengthening of the original identity of a subcultural group resulted by outer and inner influences. Sometimes, the city environment may intensify cultural identity of subcultural groups. Traditional identities may also revive or intensify with the help of modern perspectives or new technologies. Religious recurrence to fundamentalism is a good example.

In some cases, the international atmosphere stimulates to increase potential numbers and activates the Islamic movement. For example, Nazih Ayubi explains that among the accused Jihad warriors, "predominance of young militants" are "from the 20–30-year-old age group," and "students

---

2. Burnett introduced four kinds of results after worldview change: demoralization, submersion, conversion, and revitalization. Burnett, *Clash of Worlds*, 33, 122, 25–36.

represent the major category (around 44 percent in both lists)"[3]. As a result of modernization, modern intellectual Muslims can now interpret texts and information more freely and efficiently and have diversified communication channels. Consequently, now they can choose to receive more Muslim ideology or mental armor that they want with diversified and broadened knowledge. Religious groups that actively embrace the modernization intensify their group by bringing outside information and resources.

This kind of intensification of religious conservatism can also be seen in younger generations of Chinese Muslims. I have surveyed a group of educated Muslim young adults in a city about their conservative tendency. The result showed about thirty percent of them with conservative tendencies.[4]

Though they grew up with little Islamic education in the city of China, some of them have more frequent interactions with Middle Eastern or hear news about other Muslims through modern media or through others. As a result, it is estimated that over one-third of young adults have religious and ethnic conservative tendency. Urban environment can intensify some subcultural groups.

Extinction

The second type of change and reaction that happens in subcultural group is extinction. In other words, modernization or outside influences may cause the original group to become extinct. Otherwise, members lose the need and reason for the existence and cause of extinction of the group by their own will. Instances in which minority language zones are absorbed and vanished by a stronger ethnicity or the younger generation moves out to the city while the original culture is not transmitted are considered as Extinction.

In China's case, the dissolution of traditional ethnic enclave due to city developments is a typical example. The government's urbanization policy reorganizes old buildings and roads and builds new residences or new development districts. Due to this, residences in the ethnic enclave that have developed life zones over several hundreds of years are now scattered to the newly allotted modern apartments.

Besides this kind of compulsory decomposition from the external forces, individuals can also disperse out of original groups and into new groups by their own wills. Voluntarily moving for better education, job,

3. Ayubi, *Political Islam.*

4. Kim, "Receptor-Oriented Communication for Hui Muslims in China," 95–102.

or atmosphere could cause extinction of traditional communities and may also create new social groups in other places. If part of a group moves to a different group instead of the whole group, the people's identity changes even more easily because of their small size.

Conversion

The impact of urbanization converses many subculture groups. In this case, the leaders and members of subcultural groups feel the need to change as they face the escalation of internal demands and external influence. As a result, they substitute part of their external image, relationship, and cultural form into an alternative shape or even transformation to a completely different form.

Arabization of Chinese Muslim is an example of conversion. Arabization is a phenomenon, which accepts modern technology yet maintains the image of Arabs in development. Traditionally, Chinese Muslims have worried that Chinese government assimilates the Hui culture. Consequently, the Hui interprets the modernization or westernization of recent Chinese government as another kind of assimilation. Therefore, some Hui subculture groups created Arabization, a third way of neither conforming to the modernization nor only insisting their tradition.[5]

As some Hui groups hesitated between western modernization and cultural insulation, the Arabization introduced a new fresh alternative to the Hui village. Some Hui prefer to follow Arab culture, their emotional root, rather than blindly following the government's modernization policy.[6] They believe that this fits better to their spiritual maturity and purity. As a result, they make effort to absorb or inosculate the Arab's improved technology and modern culture to their own culture in order to create a new Hui culture.

Including this Arabization, urban ethnic minorities change their subculture groups to many different forms as part of the assimilation process and actively choose their own future.

5. Gillette, *Between Mecca and Beijing,* 233.
6. Ibid., 8–14, 53.

Continuation

Some groups may not change despite being deeply impacted by urbanization. This means that some subcultural groups keep their cultural identities, and we can call this continuation. Actually, a great number of the ethnic minorities and migrants would maintain the lifestyles even under the city influence, because they see that change is not necessary. An example of this continual group, the "insulationist," is categorized and introduced by Shirley Achor. Achor researched Mexican-Americans in Dallas barrio.[7] She has categorized Mexicans living in this ethnic village based on the amount of their interactions with those who are on the outside, following four categories: insulationist, accommodationist, and mobilizationist and maladaptive. Among these, the insulationist group is isolated from the external culture, with biases to outside culture, with poor social benefits, and mainly has internal resources and culture. The group forms a defense mechanism against the outside, has pride in their domestic culture, and use their community (barrio) as a refuge. They travel out of town only for specific and selective purposes, and have strong endogamy and preference for religions. A significant number of families send their children to parochial schools, for they believe that the public school has contaminating influences.

Another example of continuation is Islamic sectarianism. Islamic subgroups have been in conflict for more than several hundreds of years. The early Sufi leaders built socioeconomic and religious-political institutions around schools. These institutions became known as the 'menhuan' (門宦: saintly lineage). Today, the Chinese menhuan has four major sects: The Khufiyya, Jahriyya, Qadariyya, and Khubrawiyya menhuan.[8] Although there will be a continuous change, these menhuan systems seem to be maintained for a while.

Earlier in chapter five, we examined urban ethnicities actively choosing their own future as they face the demand of change. Moreover, we saw how urban ethnicities are composed of subculture groups. With this in mind, ethnic change can be understood as diverse changes of many subculture groups within the whole. The demands for change may come from the inside of the subculture group or from other subcultural groups of nearby. Moreover, the demands may also come from the outside of the ethnicities. The actual pattern may be even more diverse as the subculture groups

7. Achor, *Mexican Americans in a Dallas Barrio*, 116–28.
8. Gladney, "Qingzhen."

choose these four cultural types of change that have been introduced. Furthermore, even the direction and speed of change are examined each time as they make decision for the next step. For example, in some cases, groups may change from conversion mode to continuation mode back again.

This is why in cities, an ethnic cultural identity and change phenomenon cannot be explained in a simple way.

There are various and new informational channels that subcultural groups have, and these continually cause them to change. Cities provide an environment for interaction between members of subculture groups with those of other subculture groups. Now we will examine the changes in communication channel.

INTER-ETHNIC VERSUS INTRA-STATUS
COMMUNICATION CHANNELS

The understanding of this communication channels between subculture groups and other subculture groups is crucial for setting mission strategy. Because the communication channels can be used as channels of the Gospel. This session will examine the communication channel that connects urban subculture groups and the outside.

It is important for mission strategy to understand how the unreached ethnicities have various groups within them.[9] Because not only the involvement of an individual's ethnicity, but also the involvement of subculture may influence the receptivity to the Gospel. For example, even within the same Muslim ethnic minority, an English teacher or a worker in a broadcasting system would receive different amounts of new information and have a different capability of change than an employee at a tailor shop or a waiter at a restaurant.[10]

Traditionally, ethnicities exchange information within the ethnicity, called intra-ethnicity communication channels. People in a group usually only have intra-subcultural communication with those in their own subculture group, but if there were a need, they would have an inter-subcultural group within the same ethnicity, intermittently. However, urbanization forces subculture groups to not only use intra-ethnic channels, but also

9. Ferraro, *Cultural Anthropology*, 265–84; Spradley and McCurdy, *Anthropology, the Cultural Perspective*, 117–67; Kraft, *Anthropology for Christian Witness*, 313–42; Hiebert, *Cultural Anthropology*, 275–95; Harris and Johnson, *Cultural Anthropology*, 189–202.

10. Zang, Lipman, and McKeever, "Ethnicity and Urban Life in China."

inter-ethnic channels as well. In other words, there appear groups that actively communicate between ethnicities among subculture groups.

Chart 8–1 is a conceptual diagram that shows the information flow between status and ethnicity. The vertical labels A, B, C, and D are for different ethnicities and the number labels 1, 2, 3, and 4 represent the status in each people group. The picture on the left shows the communication channels that exist in traditional cities or rural societies. Traditionally, the information is limited within ethnic borders (vertically A1-A2-A3-A4). Information flows often within the ethnicities, and especially within the same status. Traditional societies have even clearer social status differences. Therefore, important information does not easily surpass the statuses, especially to the lower ones, even within the same ethnicity.[11] However, ethnicities start emphasizing their own unity and internal profit when there is a conflict or competition with other ethnicities or if there is tension between the majority group and minority group.

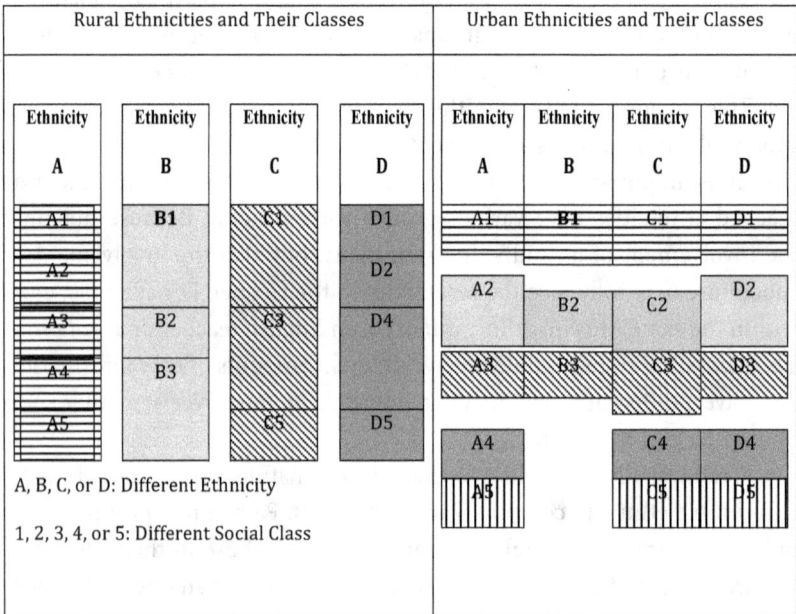

Chart 8–1: Changing Information Flow: Ethnics Versus Social Status[12]

11. Warner and Lunt, *The Status System of a Modern Community*.

12. Developed diagram from Kim, "Receptor-Oriented Communication for Hui Muslims in China," 43.

Traditionally, many classes exist within an ethnicity, but there are more similarities between the classes within the same ethnicity compared to those of other ethnicities. Usually, ethnicities with long shared history have extensive conflicts and oppositions based on prejudice and confrontations rather than interchange. The information channels are limited when the culture and language of an ethnicity is greatly different form surrounding ethnicities. The left side of Chart 8–1 shows this situation. There are 1, 2, 3, 4, and 5 classes within ethnicity A, but the gaps between them are a lot smaller than those between ethnicities B, C, and D.

If the image on the left shows traditional social communication, the image on the right shows communication between urban ethnicities. The characteristic of the right side is the increase of the inter-ethnic communication. As the urban influence increase, traditional ethnicities' relationships or relationships among classes within ethnicities also change. As a result of modernism, gaps among classes even within the same ethnicity have increased, and different classes have different degrees of interaction with other ethnicities.

In the city, people create more commonness between different ethnicities of the same status and class, and this has allowed them to diversify cross-cultural communication channels. In Chart 8–1, the right side shows ethnicities and their classes in a modern urban situation. Unlike the traditional society, the different social classes in the same people group—noted vertically—may not have as much in common with each other. A horizontal information flow increases rapidly between different ethnicities (A1-B1-C1-D1 and A3-B3-C3-D3).[13] For example, I often hear the following from young Korean or Chinese people. They say, "I cannot talk with my dad." This is because different networks have different interests and needs even though they are in the same ethnicity. Distances between intergeneration and social status will grow further apart, and the distance between the same status and generation will grow closer.

In contrast, the city structure itself forces other ethnicities to gather together. For example, many different ethnicities study together in the same classroom. Sometimes, classmates who are from a different ethnicity become closer friends, and Chinese Muslims in cities were no exceptions.

Actually, the city is too complicated to trust others just because they are from the same ethnicity. Moreover, even if they are from the same ethnicity, it does not mean that they will provide all the information one needs. On the other hand, even other ethnicities may provide important information

13. Greenhow and Burton, "Help from My 'Friends.'"

if they share the same interests and are in the same class. However, this does not mean that all classes would be closer with other ethnicities equally. Depending on the class, environment, ability, and need to interact with different ethnicities, outcomes may differ.

For example, a CEO of a company has more interactions with other CEOs from different ethnic groups than with lower class members of the same ethnic group. Teachers, students, and workers also seek likeminded groups or same classes for information and cooperation, rather than have different classes within their own ethnicity. Therefore, the information density increases inter-ethnically, but the inter-group communication, like intergeneration or inter-status, decreases compared to the traditional society. This phenomenon is more vivid among elites and higher positions, and also groups that seek diverse and frequent interactions with the outside.[14]

Generally, the high class or wealthy people group have more opportunities to interact with new culture, thus they comparatively tend to be less resistant and have fewer obstacles to change. Of course, it is dangerous to assume that all high classes are opened or all the aspects of individuals are opened. We should also not be quick to conclude that they are closer to other ethnicities and they disregard their own ethnic spirit. This is because the interethnic relationships of the high-class are more functional, rather than like a community relationship, which interacts in all aspects. Thus, modern ethnic classes neither unconditionally sticks together just because others are the same ethnicity, nor regard same class in other ethnicities as their own. Now, they can use diverse communication paths or capabilities based on their needs. Sometimes they may unite with diverse ethnicities for their needs or show brotherly love toward their own ethnicities when necessary. As a result, individuals themselves decide how much, to whom, and of which direction of their lives and functions to open.

CHAPTER PATHFINDER

In this chapter, we have examined changing processes that various subcultural groups in the city and its missional opportunity, as a third point of the A new Communication Channels that Unlocks the Gospel series. We found that ethnicities in cities do not automatically go through cultural assimilation, but rather make various choices because the subculture groups

14. Xiaowei Zang conducted a field research to understand each class' conservatism and degree of interaction among the Hui Muslims in China. Zang, Lipman, and McKeever, "Ethnicity and Urban Life in China," 21.

within the ethnicity make such choices. Moreover, it is the new communication channels that make the subcultural group possible for active change. In other words, city forces subculture groups to change from intra-class communication (isolated and communicated mostly within their class) to intra-ethnic communication and inter-ethnic communication. As a result, this chapter pays attention to the fact that the channel of Gospel, a flow of information, has become more diverse than ever before. Through these diversified communication channels, city can now be seen as a place where unreached people or classes who were neglected of the Gospel before now interact naturally with those who have the Gospel.

IMPLICATION TO MISSION STRATEGY

Ethnicities in the city are experiencing much change and are developing new communication channels. What do these changes mean in developing mission strategy? Of course, living in the city cannot simply guarantee increased receptivity. Rather, some groups in the city can build stronger barriers to the gospel.[15] We will now reflect on the significance of these newly formed and constantly changing communication channels between ethnicities and classes, from the perspective of mission strategists.

We have classified subcultural group changes as four types: intensification, extinction, transformation, and continuation. Missionaries must understand the strategic meaning of these four types of change and approach each of them appropriately. Furthermore, being able to discern strategically and having a prioritized approach among these four types is necessary.

The intensification type group strengthens the original characteristic, meaning that if the group was originally opposed to the Gospel, this opposition will grow even stronger as time passes. Unreached ethnic minorities usually have strong culture and religion, along with closed communal characters. Consequently, it is easy for them to reject external culture. In this kind of intensification category, the group intensifies its rejection of the Gospel, outside information, and the group diminishes receptivity.

The second type, extinction, may be easily approached at first, but the ethnicity will gradually weaken and eventually may be dispersed into different groups. This is a group that temporarily gathers and scatters again, and the fruits that missionaries finally bear after much effort may become scattered and eventually vanished. University campus ministries that target

15. Conn, *"Urbanization and Its Implications,"* 68.

the urban unreached ethnicities are a good example. After students become new Christians, it is common for them to scatter back to their hometowns or work after finishing school. If the missionary does not have a backup plan for this scattering in his or her ministry, there will be much difficulty in the future. Strategically, this group may work through quick training, commissioning members to different areas.

Next, let us examine the conversion type and its strategic characteristics. Approach to transformational subcultural group is strategically favorable when the ethnicity is traditionally opposed to evangelism or it is difficult for missionaries to approach ethnic members socially, culturally, and politically. This is because generally in the transformation process, the Gospel receptivity rate increases.[16] That is why Christian workers should carefully assess where the transformative subcultural groups are located within the ethnicity.

The continuation type can have a low receptivity for the Gospel due to slow transformation. This is because the group has low sensitivity to external influences.

As I summarize all these analysis, I recommend approaching transformation-type groups when missionaries mainly aim for the unreached ethnic minorities. Because the transformation group is ready to change and there may be mobilizer groups, as Achor characterized.[17] These mobilizer groups have positive attitudes toward external information and have genuine love for their ethnicities. Once they realize what they truly need is the Gospel, they can lead the rest of the group by spreading the Gospel as early adaptors.[18]

In contrast, Christian workers must take caution when approaching intensification groups and continuation groups at the early stage of their mission work. This is because the groups may be slow or even resistant to the change. Instead, missionaries who have been called to serve these groups should deeply examine to find which strategy is best appropriate to the cultural setting, rather than trying to bring change to the external appearance. Assuming that the culture will last long, the Christian workers must draw out the local Christians' features based on the contextualized principles. Also, they must find the appearance of the Gospel that is appropriate to the culture and a missiological roadmap, which locals can follow step by step for changing. Missionaries who are devoted to this approach must have a clear call for this ministry, patience, and well-prepared teamwork.

16. Ibid., 75.
17. Chapter 2 of this book
18. Rogers, *Diffusion of Innovations*, 400.

Bibliography

Abercrombie, Nicholas et al. *The Penguin Dictionary of Sociology.* 5th ed. London: Penguin, 2006.

Achor, Shirley. *Mexican Americans in a Dallas Barrio.* Tucson: University of Arizona Press, 1978.

———. *Mexican Americans in a Dallas Barrio.* Edited by Achor Shirley. Tucson: University of Arizona Press, 1978.

Alba, Richard D., and Victor Nee. *Remaking the American Mainstream Assimilation and Contemporary Immigration.* Cambridge: Harvard University Press, 2003.

Aleksandra, Grzymała-Kazłowska. "The Role of Different Forms of Bridging Capital for Immigrant Adaptation and Upward Mobility. The Case of Ukrainian and Vietnamese Immigrants Settled in Poland." *Ethnicities* 15.3 (2015) 460–90.

Amparo, González-Ferrer, Baizán Pau, and Beauchemin Cris. "Child-Parent Separations among Senegalese Migrants to Europe: Migration Strategies or Cultural Arrangements?" *The Annals of the American Academy of Political and Social Science* 643 (2012) 106–33.

Anderson, A., et al. "Social Network Analysis of Children with Autism Spectrum Disorder: Predictors of Fragmentation and Connectivity in Elementary School Classrooms." *Autism* 20.6 (2015) 9.

Andreas, Wimmer. "Herder's Heritage and the Boundary-Making Approach: Studying Ethnicity in Immigrant Societies." *Sociological Theory* 27.3 (2009) 244–70.

Andrew, K. Jorgenson, Rice James, and Clark Brett. "Cities, Slums, and Energy Consumption in Less Developed Countries, 1990 to 2005." *Organization & Environment* 23.2 (2010) 189–204.

Andrew, W. Bausch. "The Geography of Ethnocentrism." *Journal of Conflict Resolution* 59.3 (2015) 510–27.

Aschenbrenner, Joyce, and Lloyd R. Collins, eds. *The Processes of Urbanism: A Multidisciplinary Approach.* World Anthropology. Hague: Mouton, 1978.

Ayubi, Nazih N. *Political Islam: Religion and Politics in the Arab World.* London: Routledge, 1991.

BIBLIOGRAPHY

Banovetz, James M. *Managing the Modern City* Washington, DC: Published for the Institute for Training in Municipal Administration by International City Management Association, 1971.

Barnes, J. A. "Class and Committees in a Norwegian Island Parish." *Human Relations* 7.1 (1954) 39–58.

———. "Graph Theory and Social Networks: A Technical Comment on Connectedness and Connectivity." *Sociology* 3.2 (1969) 215–32.

Barth, Fredrik, and Universitetet i Bergen. *Ethnic Groups and Boundaries: The Social Organization of Culture Difference.* Scandinavian University Books. Bergen: Universitetsforlaget, 1969.

Basham, Richard. *Urban Anthropology: The Cross-Cultural Study of Complex Societies.* 1st ed. Palo Alto, CA: Mayfield, 1978.

Beauregard, Robert A. "City of Superlatives." *City & Community* 2.3 (2003) 183–99.

Bell, Daniel. "Ethnicity and Social Change." Chap. 5 In *Ethnicity: Theory and Experience*, edited by Nathan Glazer and Daniel Moynihan, 141–74. Cambridge: Harvard University Press, 1975.

Bell, David R., and Mary Douglas. "Natural Symbols: Explorations in Cosmology." *The Philosophical Quarterly* 22.88 (1972) 280.

Bennett, Andy. "Subcultures or Neo-Tribes? Rethinking the Relationship between Youth, Style and Musical Taste." *Sociology* 33.3 (1999) 599–617.

Berry, W. John, Ulchol Kim, and Pawel Boski. "Psychological Acculturation of Immigrants." In *Cross-Cultural Adaptation: Current Approaches*, edited by Young Yun Kim and William B. Gudykunst, 62–89. Newbury Park, CA: Sage, 1988.

Bino, G. D., and M. Krishna. "Does Social Network Matter in Knowledge Output?" *Science Technology & Society* 16.2 (2011) 235–55.

Blackman, Shane. "Youth Subcultural Theory: A Critical Engagement with the Concept, Its Origins and Politics, from the Chicago School to Postmodernism." *Journal of Youth Studies* 8.1 (2005) 1–20.

Bohannan, Paul. *Social Anthropology.* New York: Holt Rinehart & Winston, 1963.

Boissevain, Jeremy. *Friends of Friends; Networks, Manipulators and Coalitions.* Pavilion Series, Social Anthropology. Oxford: Blackwell, 1974.

Bourhis, Richard, Lena Celine Moise, Stephane Perreault, and Sacha Senecal. "Towards an Interactive Acculturation Model: A Social Psychological Approach." *International Journal of Psychology* 32.6 (1997) 369–86.

Brenner, Neil. "Stereotypes, Archetypes, and Prototypes: Three Uses of Superlatives in Contemporary Urban Studies." *City & Community City and Community* 2.3 (2003) 205–16.

Brody, E. B. "Migration and Adaptation: The Nature of the Problem." *American Behavioral Scientist American Behavioral Scientist* 13.1 (1969) 5–13.

Broomhall, Marshall. *Islam in China. A Neglected Problem.* New York: Paragon, 1966.

Brubaker, Rogers. *Ethnicity without Groups.* Cambridge: Harvard University Press, 2004.

Burgess, Ernest W. "The Growth of the City: An Introduction to a Research Project." In *The City*, edited by Robert Ezra Park, E. W. Burgess, and Roderick Duncan McKenzie, 47–62. Chicago: University of Chicago Press, 1967.

Burnett, David. *Clash of Worlds* Eastbourne: Monarch, 1990.

Chaonan, Chen. "A Household-Based Convoy and the Reciprocity of Support Exchange between Adult Children and Noncoresiding Parents." *Journal of Family Issues* 27.8 (2006) 1100–36.

Bibliography

Chen, L., and G. C. Feng. "Host Environment, Host Communication, and Satisfaction with Life: A Study of Hong Kong Ethnic Minority Members." *Communication Research Communication Research* (2015) 1–25.

Claerbaut, David. *Urban Ministry*. Grand Rapids: Zondervan, 1983.

Cohen, Abner. *Two-Dimensional Man; an Essay on the Anthropology of Power and Symbolism in Complex Society*. London: Routledge, 1974.

Conn, Harvie M. "Urbanization and Its Implications." in *Muslim and Christians on the Emmaus Road*. Monrovia, CA: MARC, 1989.

Conn, Harvie M., and Manuel Ortiz. *Urban Ministry: The Kingdom, the City, & the People of God*. Downers Grove, IL: InterVarsity, 2001.

Cooley, Charles Horton. *Human Nature and the Social Order*. New York: Scribner, 1902.

Crandall, C. S., and A. Eshleman. "A Justification-Suppression Model of the Expression and Experience of Prejudice." *Psychological Bulletin* 129.3 (2003) 414–46.

Cross, William E. *The Negro to Black Conversion Experience* Brooklyn: East, 1971.

———. *Shades of Black: Diversity in African-American Identity*. Philadelphia: Temple University Press, 1991.

Davis, Mike. *Planet of Slums* London: Verso, 2007.

Devos, T., and M. R. Banaji. "American = White?" *Journal of Personality and Social Psychology* 88.3 (2005) 447–66.

Dewey, Richard. "The Rural-Urban Continuum." In *Urban Man and Society: A Reader in Urban Sociology*, edited by Albert N. Cousins and Hans Nagpaul, 78–82. New York: Knopf, 1970.

Dillon, Michael. *China's Muslim Hui Community: Migration, Settlement and Sects*. London: Curzon, 1999.

Douglas, Mary. *Cultural Bias*. 2nd ed. Royal Anthropological Institute Occasional Paper 35. Berkeley: University of California Press, 1978.

Du Toit, Brian M., and Helen Icken Safa. *Migration and Urbanization: Models and Adaptive Strategies*. World Anthropology. Chicago: Mouton, 1975.

Durkheim, Émile. *The Division of Labor in Society*. New York: Free, 1964.

Eames, Edwin, and Judith Goode. *Anthropology of the City: An Introduction to Urban Anthropology*. Prentice-Hall Series in Anthropology. Englewood Cliffs, NJ: Prentice-Hall, 1977.

Eames, Edwin, and Judith Granich Goode. *Anthropology of the City: An Introduction to Urban Anthropology*. Englewood Cliffs, NJ: Prentice-Hall, 1977.

Edensor, Tim, and Mark Jayne. *Urban Theory beyond the West*. Abingdon, UK: Routledge, 2011.

Edling, C., and J. Rydgren. "Neighborhood and Friendship Composition in Adolescence." *SAGE Open* 2.4 (2012) 1–10.

Ember, Carol R. *Cultural Anthropology*. Englewood Cliffs, NJ: Prentice-Hall, 1993.

Engel, James F. *Getting Your Message Across*. Manila: OMF Literature, 1989.

Ely, Todd, L., and Paul Teske. "Implications of Public School Choice for Residential Location Decisions." *Urban Affairs Review* 51.2 (2015) 175–204.

Euler, Leonhard. *The Seven Bridges of Königsberg*. N.p.: Benton.

Farley, John E. *Majority-Minority Relations* Englewood Cliffs, NJ: Prentice-Hall, 1995.

Farrell, Chad R. "Immigrant Suburbanisation and the Shifting Geographic Structure of Metropolitan Segregation in the United States." *Urban Studies* 45.4 (2014) 825–43.

Feagin, Joe R., and Clairece Booher Feagin. *Racial and Ethnic Relations*. Englewood Cliffs, NJ: Prentice-Hall, 1993.

Ferraro, Gary P. *Cultural Anthropology: An Applied Perspective*. Minneapolis: West, 1995.

Findlay, G. Andrew. *The Crescent in North-West China*. London: China Inland Mission, 1921.

Fischer, Claude S. *To Dwell among Friends: Personal Networks in Town and City*. Chicago: University of Chicago Press, 1982.

———. *The Urban Experience*. 2nd ed. San Diego: Harcourt Brace Jovanovich, 1984.

Flanagan, William G. *Urban Sociology: Images and Structure*. 2nd ed. Boston: Allyn & Bacon, 2002.

Floro, K. George. Review of *The Sociological Eye: Selected Papers*, by Everett C. Hughes. *Journal of the History of the Behavioral Sciences* 22.1 (1986) 66–72.

Fong, Eric, Emily Anderson, Wenhong Chen, and Chiu Luk. "The Logic of Ethnic Business Distribution in Multiethnic Cities." *Urban Affairs Review* 43.4 (2008) 497–519.

Fong, Eric, and Shen Jing. "Explaining Ethnic Enclave, Ethnic Entrepreneurial and Employment Niches: A Case Study of Chinese in Canadian Immigrant Gateway Cities." *Urban Studies* 48.8 (2011) 1605–33.

Foster, George M., and Robert V. Kemper. *Anthropologists in Cities*. Boston: Little, Brown, 1974.

Gallo, E., and F. Scrinzi. "Outsourcing Elderly Care to Migrant Workers: The Impact of Gender and Class on the Experience of Male Employers." *Sociology* 50.2 (2015) 366–82.

Gans, Herbert J. *The Levittowners: Ways of Life and Politics in a New Suburban Community*. New York: Pantheon, 1967.

———. *The Urban Villagers; Group and Class in the Life of Italian-Americans*. New York: Free, 1962.

———. "Urbanism and Suburbanism as Ways of Life: A Re-Evaluation of Definitions." In *Human Behavior and Social Processes: An Interactionist Approach*, edited by Arnold Marshall Rose, 507–21. Boston: Houghton Mifflin, 1962.

Geertz, Clifford. "The Integrative Revolution: Primordial Sentiments and Civil Politics in the New States." *Old Societies and New States* (1963) 105–57.

Gellner, Ernest. *Thought and Change*. London: Weidenfeld & Nicholson, 1969.

George, Wilson. "Racialized Life-Chance Opportunities across the Class Structure: The Case of African Americans." *The Annals of the American Academy of Political and Social Science* 609.1 (2007) 215–32.

Gibson, N. C. "Introduction: A New Politics of the Poor Emerges from South Africa's Shantytowns." *Journal of Asian and African Studies* 43.1 (2008) 5–17.

Gillette, Maris Boyd. *Between Mecca and Beijing: Modernization and Consumption among Urban Chinese Muslims*. Stanford: Stanford University, 2000.

Giuffre, Katherine. *Communities and Networks: Using Social Network Analysis to Rethink Urban and Community Studies*. New York: Wiley, 2013.

Gladney, Dru C. *Dislocating China Reflections on Muslims, Minorities, and Other Subaltern Subjects*. Chicago: University of Chicago Press, 2004.

———. "Qingzhen: A Study of Ethnoreligious Identity among Hui Muslim Communities in China." Phd diss., University of Washington, Seattle, 1987.

Glaser, Daniel. "Dynamics of Ethnic Identification." *American Sociological Review* 23.1 (1958) 31–40.

Glazer, Nathan, and Daniel P. Moynihan. *Beyond the Melting Pot; the Negroes, Puerto Ricans, Jews, Italians, and Irish of New York City.* Cambridge: MIT Press, 1963.

Gordon, Milton Myron. *Assimilation in American Life: The Role of Race, Religion, and National Origins.* New York: Oxford University Press, 1964.

Gottdiener, Mark, and Leslie Budd. *Key Concepts in Urban Studies.* Sage Key Concepts. London: Sage, 2005.

Gottdiener, Mark, and Ray Hutchison. *The New Urban Sociology.* 3rd ed. Boulder, CO: Westview, 2006.

Greeley, Andrew M. *Ethnicity in the United States: A Preliminary Reconnaissance.* New York: Wiley, 1974.

———. *Why Can't They Be Like Us? America's White Ethnic Groups.* New York: Dutton, 1971.

Greenhow, Christine, and Lisa Burton. "Help from My 'Friends': Social Capital in the Social Network Sites of Low-Income Students." *Journal of Educational Computing Research* 45.2 (2011) 223–45.

Greenway, Roger S., and Timothy M. Monsma. *Cities: Missions' New Frontier.* 2nd ed. Grand Rapids: Baker, 2000.

Gulick, John. *The Humanity of Cities: An Introduction to Urban Societies.* Granby, MA: Bergin & Garvey, 1989.

Gutkind, Peter Claus Wolfgang. *Urban Anthropology: Perspectives on Third World Urbanization and Urbanism.* New York: Barnes & Noble, 1974.

Hanham, H. J., and Michael Hechter. "Internal Colonialism: The Celtic Fringe in British National Development, 1536–1966." *American Historical Review* 83.1 (1978) 876–79.

Hannerz, Ulf. *Exploring the City: Inquiries toward an Urban Anthropology.* New York: Columbia University Press, 1980.

———. *Soulside: Inquiries into Ghetto Culture and Community* New York: Columbia University Press, 1969.

Harris, Marian S., and Ada Skyles. "Kinship Care for African American Children: Disproportionate and Disadvantageous." *Journal of Family Issues* 29.8 (2008) 1013–30.

Harris, Marvin, and Orna Johnson. *Cultural Anthropology.* Boston: Allyn & Bacon, 2003.

Hartmann, Douglas, and Joseph Gerteis. "Dealing with Diversity: Mapping Multiculturalism in Sociological Terms." *Sociological Theory* 23.2 (2005) 218–40.

Hartshorn, Truman A. *Interpreting the City: An Urban Geography.* New York: Wiley, 1980.

Healey, Joseph F. *Race, Ethnicity, Gender, and Class: The Sociology of Group Conflict and Change.* Thousand Oaks, CA: Pine Forge, 2011.

Heberer, Thomas. *China and Its National Minorities: Autonomy or Assimilation?* Armonk, NY: Sharpe, 1989.

Hechter, Michael. "Industrialization and National Development in the British Isles." *The Journal of Development Studies* 8.3 (2007) 155–82.

Hechter, Michael. "The Political Economy of Ethnic Change." *American Journal of Sociology* 79.5 (1974) 27.

Helms, Janet E. *Black and White Racial Identity: Theory, Research, and Practice.* Westport, CT: Praeger, 1993.

Heydari, A., A. Teymoori, E. F. Haghish, and B. Mohamadi. "Influential Factors on Ethnocentrism: The Effect of Socioeconomic Status, Anomie, and Authoritarianism." *Social Science Information* 53.2 (2014) 240–54.

BIBLIOGRAPHY

Hibel, Jacob. "Roots of Assimilation: Generational Status Differentials in Ethnic Minority Children's School Readiness." *Journal of Early Childhood Research* 7.2 (2009) 135–52.

Hiebert, Paul G. *Cultural Anthropology.* 2nd ed. Grand Rapids: Baker, 1983.

Hiebert, Paul G., and Eloise Hiebert Meneses. *Incarnational Ministry: Planting Churches in Band, Tribal, Peasant, and Urban Societies.* Grand Rapids: Baker, 1995.

Hooper, Michael, and Ortolano Leonard. "Motivations for Slum Dweller Social Movement Participation in Urban Africa: A Study of Mobilization in Kurasini, Dar Es Salaam." *Environment & Urbanization* 24.1 (2012) 99–114.

Horowitz, Donald L. "Ethnic Identity." In *Ethnicity: Theory and Experience,* edited by Nathan Glatzer and Daniel P. Moynihan, 111–40. Cambridge: Harvard University Press, 1975

Huq, Rupa. *Beyond Subculture: Pop, Youth and Identity in a Postcolonial World.* London: Routledge, 2006.

Huyssen, Andreas. *Other Cities, Other Worlds: Urban Imaginaries in a Globalizing Age.* Durham: Duke University Press, 2008.

Jindrich, Jason. "The Shantytowns of Central Park West: Fin de Siècle Squatting in American Cities." *Journal of Urban History* 36.5 (2010) 672.

Karinthy, Frigyes. "Chain-Links." In *The Structure and Dynamics of Networks,* edited by Mark Newman, Albert-Laszlo Barabasi, and Duncan J. Watts, 21–26. Princeton: Prineton University Press, 2006.

———. *Minden Másképpen Van (Ötvenkét Vasárnap).* Budapest: Athenaeum, 1929.

Katerndahl, D., et al. "Differences in Social Network Structure and Support among Women in Violent Relationships." *Journal of Interpersonal Violence* 28.9 (2013) 1948–64.

Kher, J., S. Aggarwal, and G. Punhani. "Vulnerability of Poor Urban Women to Climate-Linked Water Insecurities at the Household Level: A Case Study of Slums in Delhi." *Indian Journal of Gender Studies Indian Journal of Gender Studies* 22.1 (2015) 15–40.

Kim, Enoch Jinsik. "Power and Pride: A Critical Contextual Approach to Hui Muslims in China." *International Journal of Frontier Missiology* 30.1 (2013) 189–95.

———. "Receptor-Oriented Communication for Hui Muslims in China: With Special Reference to Church Planting." PhD diss., Fuller Theological Seminary, 2009.

———. "Unpublished Survey in ANC Onnuri Church Highschool Survey." Los Angeles: ANC Onnuri Church, 2013.

———. "'Us' or 'Me'? Modernization and Social Networks among China's Urban Hui." Chap. 10 In *Longing for Community: Church, Ummah, or Somewhere in Between?,* edited by David Greenlee, 86–96. Pasadena, CA: William Carey Library, 2013.

Kim, Moonwook. *Joongang Asia Ui Hangook Moonhua.* Seoul: Jotunddang, 2014.

Korinek, Kim, Barbara Entwisle, and Aree Jampaklay. "Through Thick and Thin: Layers of Social Ties and Urban Settlement among Thai Migrants." *American Sociological Review* 70.5 (2005) 779–800.

Koster, M. "Mediating and Getting 'Burnt' in the Gap: Politics and Brokerage in a Recife Slum, Brazil." *Critique of Anthropology* 32.4 (2012) 479–97.

Kotter, Herbert. "Changes in Urban-Rural Relationship in Industrial Society." In *Urbanism and Urbanization,* edited by Nels Anderson, 273. International Studies in Sociology and Social Anthropology 2. Leiden: Brill, 1964.

BIBLIOGRAPHY

Kraft, Charles H. *Anthropology for Christian Witness*. Maryknoll, NY: Orbis, 1996.

Lawton, John. "Muslim in China: An Introduction." *Aramco World* 36.4 (1985) 20–29.

Leerkes, A., G. Engbersen, and M. Van San. "Shadow Places: Patterns of Spatial Concentration and Incorporation of Irregular Immigrants in the Netherlands." *Urban Studies* 44.8 (2007) 1491–516.

Lefranc, Arnaud. "Unequal Opportunities and Ethnic Origin: The Labor Market Outcomes of Second-Generation Immigrants in France." *The American Behavioral Scientist* 53.12 (2010) 1851–82.

Leslie, Donald. *Islam in Traditional China: A Short History to 1800.* . Belconnen, Australia: Canberra College of Advanced Education, 1986.

Levin, Jack, and William C. Levin. *The Functions of Discrimination and Prejudice*. New York: Harper & Row, 1982.

Lewis, Oscar. "Urbanization without Breakdown a Case Study." *The Scientific Monthly* 75.1 (1952) 31–41.

Li, Shujiang, and Karl W. Luckert. *Mythology and Folklore of the Hui, a Muslim Chinese People*. Translation by Fenglan Yu, Zhilin Hou, and Ganhui Wang. Albany: SUNY Press, 1994.

Lingenfelter, Sherwood. *Transforming Culture: A Challenge for Christian Mission*. 2nd ed. Grand Rapids: Baker, 1998.

Lipman, Jonathan N., and Steven Harrel. "Ethnic Violence in Modern China: Hans and Huis in Gansu, 1781–1929." In *Violence in China*, edited by Jonathan N. Lipman and Steven Harrel, 71–73. Albany: SUNY Press, 1990.

Lipman, Jonathan Neaman. *Familiar Strangers: A History of Muslims in Northwest China*. Studies on Ethnic Groups in China. Seattle: University of Washington Press, 1997.

Lipset, Seymour Martin, and Stein Rokkan. *Party Systems and Voter Alignments: Cross-National Perspectives*. New York: Free, 1967.

Litaker, H. L. "Understanding Dual Rover Communications Using Social Network Analysis." *Proceedings of the Human Factors and Ergonomics Society Annual Meeting* 55.1 (2011) 1351–55.

Liu, Cathy Yang, and Gary Painter. "Immigrant Settlement and Employment Suburbanisation in the Us: Is There a Spatial Mismatch?" *Urban Studies* 49.5 (2012) 979–1002.

Livingstone, Greg. *Planting Churches in Muslim Cities: A Team Approach*. Grand Rapids: Baker, 1993.

MacIver, Robert M., and Leon Bramson. *Robert M. Maciver on Community, Society and Power; Selected Writings* Chicago: University of Chicago Press, 1970.

MacIver, Robert M., and Charles Hunt Page. *Society; an Introductory Analysis*. New York: Rinehart, 1949.

Mackerras, Colin. *China's Minority Cultures: Identities and Integration since 1912*. Melbourne: Oxford University Press, 1995.

Mahler, Sarah J., and Patricia R. Pessar. "Gender Matters: Ethnographers Bring Gender from the Periphery toward the Core of Migration Studies." *International Migration Review* 40.1 (2006) 27–63.

Mangalam, J. J., and Harry K. Schwarzweller. "Some Theoretical Guidelines toward a Sociology of Migration." *International Migration Review* 4.2 (1970) 5–21.

Marshall, T. H. *Class, Citizenship, and Social Development; Essays*. Garden City, NY: Doubleday, 1964.

Bibliography

Martin, Greg. "Subculture, Style, Chavs and Consumer Capitalism: Towards a Critical Cultural Criminology of Youth." *Crime, Media, Culture* 5.2 (2009) 123–45.

Massey, Douglas S., and Nancy A. Denton. *American Apartheid: Segregation and the Making of the Underclass.* Cambridge: Harvard University Press, 1993.

McCann, Eugene, and Kevin Ward. "Relationality/Territoriality: Toward a Conceptualization of Cities in the World." *GEOF Geoforum* 41.2 (2010) 175–84.

McCarty, Christopher. "Structure in Personal Networks." *Journal of Social Structure* 3 (2002). http://www.cmu.joss/.

McKenzie, Roderick Duncan. *The Metropolitan Community.* New York: McGraw-Hill, 1933.

McLuhan, Herbert Marshall. *Understanding Media: The Extensions of Man.* London: MIT Press, 1964.

———. "Towards a Theory of Ethnic Change." *Politics & Society* 2.1 (1971) 21–45.

Michaelson, William M. *Man and His Urban Enviornment: A Sociological Approach.* Rev. ed. Reading, MA: Addison-Wesley, 1976.

Mitchell, J. Clyde, and Institute for Social Research, University of Zambia. *Social Networks in Urban Situations: Analyses of Personal Relationships in Central African Towns.* Manchester: Manchester University Press, 1969.

Moore, Joan W., Robert Garcia, and Chicano Pinto Research Project. *Homeboys: Gangs, Drugs, and Prison in the Barrios of Los Angeles.* Philadelphia: Temple University Press, 1978.

Morgan, Lewis Henry. *Systems of Consanguinity and Affinity of the Human Family.* Oosterhout, Netherlands: Anthropological Publications, 1970.

Muller, Roland. *Honor and Shame: Unlocking the Door.* Philadelphia: Xlibris, 2000.

Mumford, Lewis. *The City in History: Its Origins, Its Transformations, and Its Prospects.* New York: Harcourt, Brace & World, 1961.

Musterd, Sako, et al. "Adaptive Behaviour in Urban Space: Residential Mobility in Response to Social Distance." *Urban Studies* 53.2 (2014) 227–46.

Musterd, Sako, and Rinus Deurloo. "Unstable Immigrant Concentrations in Amsterdam: Spatial Segregation and Integration of Newcomers." *Housing Studies* 17.3 (2002) 487–503.

Myers, Garth Andrew. *African Cities: Alternative Visions of Urban Theory and Practice.* London: Zed, 2011. Ebook Library http://public.eblib.com/choice/publicfullrecord.aspx?p=688559.

Ndofor, Hermann. Achidi., and Richard. L. Priem. "Immigrant Entrepreneurs, the Ethnic Enclave Strategy, and Venture Performance." *Journal of Management* 37.3 (2011) 790–818.

Noh, Choonhee, and Iltae Kim. *Dosihak Gaeron.* Rev. ed. Seoul, Korea: Hyungsul, 2004.

Oishi, Nana. *Women in Motion: Globalization, State Policies, and Labor Migration in Asia.* Stanford, CA: Stanford University Press, 2005. Ebook Library http://public.eblib.com/choice/publicfullrecord.aspx?p=3037518.

Olzak, Susan. "Does Globalization Breed Ethnic Discontent?" *Journal of Conflict Resolution* 55.1 (2011) 3–32.

Palen, J. John. *The Urban World.* New York: McGraw-Hill, 1975.

Parham, Thomas A., and Janet E. Helms. "Relation of Racial Identity Attitudes to Self-Actualization and Affective States of Black Students." *Journal of Counseling Psychology* 32.3 (1985) 431–40.

Park, Robert Ezra. "The City: Suggestions for Investigation of Human Behavior in the Urban Enviornment." *American Journal of Sociology* 20.5 (1915) 577–612.

———. *Race and Culture*. Glencoe, IL: Free, 1950.

Park, Robert Ezra, and E. W. Burgess. *Introduction to the Science of Sociology, Including the Original Index to Basic Sociological Concepts*. Chicago: University of Chicago Press, 1969.

Park, Robert Ezra, et al., eds. *The City: Suggestions for Investigation of Human Behavior in the Urban Enviornment*. University of Chicago Studies in Urban Sociology. Chicago: University of Chicago Press, 1925.

Paul, Sohini. "Creditworthiness of a Borrower and the Selection Process in Micro-Finance: A Case Study from the Urban Slums of India." *Margin: Journal of Applied Economic Research* 8.1 (2014) 59–75.

Peck, Jamie, Nikolas Theodore, and Neil Brenner. "Neoliberal Urbanism: Models, Moments, Mutations." *SAIS Review* 29.1 (2009) 49–66.

Petersen, William. "A General Typology of Migration." *American Sociological Review* 23.3 (1958) 256–66.

Piper, Nicola, and Mina Roces. *Wife or Worker?: Asian Women and Migration* Lanham, MD: Rowman & Littlefield, 2003.

Portes, Alejandro, and Rubén G. Rumbaut. *Legacies: The Story of the Immigrant Second Generation*. Berkeley: University of California Press, 2001. ACLS Humanities E-Book: http://hdl.handle.net/2027/heb.31535.

Qingfang, Wang. "Race/Ethnicity, Gender and Job Earnings across Metropolitan Areas in the United States: A Multilevel Analysis." *Urban Studies* 45.4 (2008) 825–43.

Rebelo, Emília Malcata. "Work and Settlement Locations of Immigrants: How Are They Connected? The Case of the Oporto Metropolitan Area." *European Urban and Regional Studies* 19.3 (2012) 312.

Reiss, Albert J., and Columbia University. *The Analysis of Urban Phenomena*. New York: Columbia University, 1954.

Reminick, Ronald A. *Theory of Ethnicity: An Anthropologist's Perspective*. Lanham, MD: University Press of America, 1983.

Roberts, Bryan R. *Organizing Strangers: Poor Families in Guatemala City*. Texas Pan American. Austin: University of Texas Press, 1973.

Robson, William Alexander. *Great Cities of the World; Their Government, Politics and Planning*. London: Allen & Unwin, 1954.

Rogers, Everett M. *Diffusion of Innovations*. 5th ed. New York: Free, 2003.

Romanucci-Ross, Lola, and George A. De Vos. *Ethnic Identity: Creation, Conflict, and Accommodation*. 3rd ed. Walnut Creek, CA: Altamira, 1995.

Roy, Ananya, and Aihwa Ong. *Worlding Cities: Asian Experiments and the Art of Being Global*. Malden, MA: Wiley-Blackwell, 2011.

Rydgren, Jens. "The Power of the Past: A Contribution to a Cognitive Sociology of Ethnic Conflict." *Sociological Theory* 25.3 (2007) 225–44.

Sander, William. "Educational Attainment and Residential Location." *Education and Urban Society* 38.3 (2006) 307–26.

Saracostti, Mahia. "Social Capital as a Strategy to Overcome Poverty in Latin America." *International Social Work* 50.4 (2007) 515–27.

Schönwälder, Karen, and Janina Söhn. "Immigrant Settlement Structures in Germany: General Patterns and Urban Levels of Concentration of Major Groups." *Urban Studies* 46.7 (2009) 1439–60.

Sennett, Richard. *Classic Essays on the Culture of Cities*. New York: Appleton-Century-Crofts, 1969.

Shaw, R. Daniel. *Transculturation: The Cultural Factor in Translation and Other Communication Tasks*. Pasadena, CA: William Carey Library, 1988.

Shoujie, Wang. *Niu Jie Huimin Shenghuo Tan" (Discussion of the Lifestyle of the Oxen Street Hui)*. Yue Hua, 1930.

Sidanius, Jim, and Felicia Pratto. *Social Dominance: An Intergroup Theory of Social Hierarchy and Oppression*. Cambridge: Cambridge University Press, 1999.

Simmel, Georg. "The Metropolis and Mental Life." In *Classic Essays of the Culture of Cities*, edited by Richard Sennett, 47–60. New York: Appleton-Century-Crofts, 1965.

Sjoberg, Gideon. *The Preindustrial City, Past and Present*. Glencoe, IL: Free, 1960.

Smith, Donald K. *Creating Understanding: A Handbook for Christian Communication across Cultural Landscapes*. Grand Rapids: Zondervan, 1992.

Snyder, G. J. "The City and the Subculture Career: Professional Street Skateboarding in La." *Ethnography* 13.3 (2012) 306–29.

Son, Dongwon. *Sahoe Network Bunsuk*. Seoul, Korea: Kyungmoonsa, 2002.

Spillius, Elizabeth Bott. *Family and Social Network; Roles, Norms, and External Relationships in Ordinary Urban Families*. New York: Free, 1971.

Spradley, James P., and David W. McCurdy. *Anthropology, the Cultural Perspective*. New York: Wiley, 1980.

Suh, Yijong *Internet Community Wa Hangook Sahue (Internet Community and Korean Society)*. Seoul: Hanwool, 2002.

Sunquist, Scott W. *Understanding Christian Mission: Participation in Suffering and Glory*. Grand Rapids: Baker, 2013.

Tess, Kay, and Spaaij Ramón. "The Mediating Effects of Family on Sport in International Development Contexts." *International Review for the Sociology of Sport* 47.1 (2012) 77–94.

Thomas, William Isaac, and Morris Janowitz. *On Social Organization and Social Personality: Selected Papers*. Chicago: University of Chicago Press, 1966.

Timms, Duncan. *The Urban Mosaic: Towards a Theory of Residential Differentiation*. Cambridge Geographical Studies 2. Cambridge: Cambridge University Press, 1971.

Ting-Toomey, Stella, and Leeva C. Chung. *Understanding Intercultural Communication*. Los Angeles: Roxbury, 2005.

Todaro, Michael P. "Urbanization in Developing Nations: Trends, Prospects, and Policies." In *Urban Development in the Third World*, edited by Pradip K. Ghosh, 7–26. International Development Resource Books. Westport, CT: Greenwood, 1984.

Tönnies, Ferdinand. *Community & Society (Gemeinschaft und Gesellschaft)*. Edited and translated by Charles Price Loomis. New York: Harper & Row, 1957.

Travis, J. Grosser, Lopez-Kidwell Virginie, and Labianca Giuseppe. "A Social Network Analysis of Positive and Negative Gossip in Organizational Life." *Group & Organization Management* 35.2 (2010) 177–212.

Truong, Thanh-Dam, and Des Gasper. "Trans-Local Livelihoods and Connections." *Gender, Technology and Development* 12.3 (2008) 285–302.

Tyner, James A. "Global Cities and Circuits of Global Labor: The Case of Manila, Philippines." *Professional Geographer* 52.1 (2000) 61–74.

United Nations Department of Economic and Social Affairs, Pupulation Division. "World Urbanization Perspects: The 2014 Revision, Highlights (St/Esa/Ser.A/352)."

United Nations Department of Economic and Social Affairs, Pupulation Division, 2014.

Uzzell, J. Douglas, and Ronald Provencher. *Urban Anthropology*. Elements of Anthropology. Dubuque, IA: Brown, 1976.

Vecchio, F., et al. "Cortical Brain Connectivity and B-Type Natriuretic Peptide in Patients with Congestive Heart Failure." *Clinical EEG and Neuroscience* 46.3 (2015) 224–29.

Wagner, Philip L. *The Human Use of the Earth*. Glencoe, IL: Free, 1960.

Wagner, Ulrich, et al. "Prejudice and Minority Proportion: Contact Instead of Threat Effects." *Social Psychology Quarterly* 69.4 (2006) 380–90.

Waldinger, R. "Crossing Borders: International Migration in the New Century." *Contemporary Sociology: A Journal of Reviews* 42.3 (2013) 349–63.

Wang, C., H. Lao, and X. Zhou. "The Impact Mechanism of Social Networks on Chinese Rural-Urban Migrant Workers' Behaviour and Wages." *Economic and Labour Relations Review* 25.2 (2014) 353–71.

Warner, W. Lloyd, and Paul S. Lunt. *The Status System of a Modern Community*. New Haven: Yale University Press, 1942.

Warren, Rachelle B., and Donald I. Warren. *The Neighborhood Organizer's Handbook*. Notre Dame: University of Notre Dame, 1977.

Warren, T. C., and K. K. Troy. "Explaining Violent Intra-Ethnic Conflict: Group Fragmentation in the Shadow of State Power." *Journal of Conflict Resolution* 59.3 (2015) 484–509.

Wasserman, Stanley, and Katherine Faust. *Social Network Analysis Methods and Applications*. Structural Analysis in the Social Sciences 8. Reprinted, New York: Cambridge University Press, 1994.

Weber, Max. *The City*. Translated and edited by Don Martindale and Gertrud Neuwirth. Glencoe, IL: Free, 1958.

———. *Economy and Society: An Outline of Interpretive Sociology*. Edited by Guenther Roth and Claus Wittich. Translated by Ephraim Fischoff et al. New York: Bedminster, 1968.

Weidmann, Nils B. "Geography as Motivation and Opportunity: Group Concentration and Ethnic Conflict." *Journal of Conflict Resolution* 53.4 (2009) 526.

Wellman, Barry. "The Community Question: The Intimate Newworks of East Yorkers." *American Journal of Sociology* 84.5 (1978) 1201–31.

———. *Networks in the Global Village: Life in Contemporary Communities*. Boulder, CO: Westview, 1999.

———. "Physical Place and Cyberplace: The Rise of Personalized Networking." *International Journal of Urban and Regional Research* 25.2 (2001) 227–52.

Wellman, Barry, and Milena Gulia. "Virtual Communities as Communities: Net Surfers Don't Ride Alone." In *Communities and Cyberspace*, edited by Peter Kollock and Marc Smith, 167–94. London: Routledge, 1997.

Wen, Jun. "*Ershishijijiushiniandaizhongguominzurenkoudebiandong Jianping* (20世纪90年代中国各民族人口的变动 简评)." *Minzu Yanjiu*(民族研究) 3 (2006) 2.

White, Kenneth R. "Scourge of Racism: Genocide in Rwanda." *Journal of Black Studies* 39.3 (2009) 471.

White, Paul. "The Settlement Patterns of Developed World Migrants in London." *Urban Studies* 35.10 (1998) 1725–44.

Whitten, Norman E., and Alvin W. Wolfe. "Network." *Handbook of Social and Cultural Anthropology* (1973) 717–46.

Whyte, Martin King, and William L. Parish. *Urban Life in Contemporary China*. Chicago: University of Chicago Press, 1984.

Williams, J. P. "Authentic Identities: Straightedge Subculture, Music, and the Internet." *Journal of Contemporary Ethnography* 35.2 (2006) 173–200.

Williams, T. A., and D. A. Shepherd. "Mixed Method Social Network Analysis: Combining Inductive Concept Development, Content Analysis, and Secondary Data for Quantitative Analysis." *Organizational Research Methods* 20.2 (2015) 268–98.

Winders, J. "Seeing Immigrants: Institutional Visibility and Immigrant Incorporation in New Immigrant Destinations." *Annals of the American Academy of Political and Social Science* 641.1 (2012) 58–78.

Wirth, Louis. *The Ghetto*. University of Chicago Sociological Series. Chicago: University of Chicago Press, 1928.

———. "Urbanism as a Way of Life." *American Journal of Sociology* 44.1 (1938) 1–24.

Yang, Philip Q. *Ethnic Studies: Issues and Approaches*. Albany: SUNY Press, 2000.

Young, Michael Dunlop, and Peter Willmott. *Family and Kinship in East London*. Reports of the Institute of Community Studies 1. Glencoe, IL: Free, 1957.

Zang, Xiaowei, Jonathan N. Lipman, and Matthew McKeever. "Ethnicity and Urban Life in China: A Comparative Study of Hui Muslims and Han Chinese." *China Journal = Chung-kuo yen chiu* 60 (2008) 205.

Subject Index

Author Index

Author Index

Scripture Index